Introductory Course

South-Western

College Keyboarding Enhanced

Charles H. Duncan, Ed.D.
Eastern Michigan University

Susie H. VanHuss, Ph.D.
University of South Carolina

S. ElVon Warner, Ed.D.
S. E. Warner Software, Inc.
Salt Lake City, Utah

Contributing Authors:

Connie Forde, Ph.D.
Mississippi State University

Donna L. Woo
Cypress College, California

JOIN US ON THE INTERNET
WWW: http://www.thomson.com
EMAIL: findit@kiosk.thomson.com   A service of I(T)P®

South-Western Educational Publishing
an International Thomson Publishing company I(T)P®

Cincinnati • Albany, NY • Belmont, CA • Bonn • Boston • Detroit • Johannesburg • London • Madrid
Melbourne • Mexico City • New York • Paris • Singapore • Tokyo • Toronto • Washington

Managing Editor: Karen Schmohe

Project Manager—Keyboarding: Jane Phelan

Production Services: CompuText Productions, Inc.

Production Coordinator: Jane Congdon

Manufacturing Coordinator: Carol Chase

Marketing Coordinator: Tim Gleim

Photo Editor: Alix Parson

Design Coordinator: Michelle Kunkler

Photo Credits:

Cover © Walter Wick Photography

Level openers: Location courtesy of Northwestern Mutual Life, 312 Walnut Street, Cincinnati, Ohio

p. xiii: Greg Grosse

pp. 18, 49, 51, 65, 84: © 1995, PhotoDisc Inc.

p. 16: Courtesy of International Business Machines Corporation

p. 105: Herman Miller, Inc.

p. 133: Michael Philip Manheim/Photo Network

I⃝TP®

International Thomson Publishing

South-Western Educational Publishing is a division of International Thomson Publishing Inc. The ITP logo is a registered trademark used herein under license by South-Western Educational Publishing.

ISBN: 0-538-71652-5

1 2 3 4 5 6 7 8 9 H 03 02 01 00 99 98 97

Printed in the United States of America

The names of commercially available software mentioned herein are used for identification purposes only and may be trademarks or registered trademarks of their respective owners. South-Western Educational Publishing disclaims any affiliation, association, connection with, sponsorship, or endorsement by such owners.

◆ Preface

Keyboarding is the foundation skill for today's workers. It is a skill needed for success in virtually every career. The keyboard, once used primarily by secretaries and clerks, is now a tool used extensively by managers, scientists, engineers, and a host of other workers. Attached to a powerful computer, the keyboard provides access to information worldwide.

Keyboarding is a skill. As with any skill, you will be successful if you apply proper techniques and meaningful practice in each session.

COLLEGE KEYBOARDING, Introductory Course, is designed to help you achieve the following goals:

◆ Key the alphabetic and numeric keys by touch using proper techniques.

◆ Format basic letters, memoranda, reports, and tables.

Many subskills—such as the ability to use language effectively and to evaluate the quality of your work— are embodied in these goals. Emphasis is placed on applying these skills so that you will be able to use the keyboard to facilitate communication.

What's New in the Enhanced Version?

Several features have been added to the Introductory Course to address word processing and ensure mastery of formatting skills.

Welcome to Windows. A three-page introduction to *Windows 3.1/Windows 95* has been added to the Appendix to get you up and running.

Word Processing Workshop. A six-page workshop presents a brief overview and activities for learning the basic functions for creating, editing, and formatting documents using the popular *Windows*-based programs. All of these functions can be applied in this text.

Selkirk Communications—Project. This in-depth project gives you a chance to work independently and apply the keyboarding, formatting, and word processing skills you have learned in this course. Options are included for extending your skills using features such as Copy, Paste, and Bullets.

Timed Writings. Extra timed writings (of both easy and average difficulty) are in Appendix D.

New Topics. A special segment called News and Views highlights issues or topics of current interest. Discussion of repetitive stress injury and illustrative exercises that can

prevent the injury have been added to this enhanced version.

Software Support

◆ Alphanumeric keyboarding software will help you learn the keys by touch and build a strong foundation skill. Numeric keypad is included. This software correlates to Lessons 1-30.

◆ MicroPace Pro (for *Windows*) or MicroPace Plus (for DOS) are timed writing and skill-building software. Error diagnostics is an option. Timings available for measurement are labeled with an icon.

◆ Word processing functions that may be applied within various documents are identified with a word processing icon.

Icons

Additional icons appear throughout this textbook; each conveys a specific message:

OS Appearing only in Lessons 19-30, this formatting exercise may be completed in the open screen of Alphanumeric software. You also have the option of using word processing software.

> *Keyboarding is a skill needed for success in virtually every career.*

This icon indicates that a timed writing is available on the diskette labeled Timed Writings Selected from *College Keyboarding*, 13th edition. This disk may be used with either MicroPace Plus or MicroPace Pro (for *Windows*). Your instructor may want to add the new timed writings from the Appendix to the MicroPace template.

LA The letter(s) in the icon indicate the level of difficulty of timed writings: Lessons 1-30 are labeled E (easy); Lessons 31-45, LA (low average); and Lessons 46-60, A (average).

The authors gratefully acknowledge the contributions made by instructors and students who have used prior editions of this textbook.

Table of Contents

Level 1   Learning to Operate the Keyboard,
Lessons 1-30

Level 2   Formatting Basic Business
Documents, Lessons 31-60

Computers consist of these essential parts:

1. **Central processing unit:** The internal operating unit, including the processing unit, memory chips, disk drives, etc.

2. **Disk drive:** A unit that reads and writes onto disks.

3. **Monitor:** A screen that displays information as it is keyed and messages from the computer called *prompts*.

4. **Mouse:** Input device. *Windows* software is designed to be used with a mouse.

5. **Keyboard:** Input device for entering alphabetic and numeric data and symbols as well as special keys for entering commands.

Monitor

The monitor, or screen, displays information as it is keyed and messages from the computer called **prompts**. Most monitors have a separate on/off switch.

Adjustments for brightness and contrast can be made on most monitors. Monitors are either monochrome or color. A monochrome monitor displays in one color and a color monitor displays many colors.

The System Unit (CPU)

The system unit is the box that houses the Central Processing Unit (CPU), memory chips, disk drives, and the on/off switch.

The on/off switch may be located on the right side of the system unit or on the front side, depending on the model of computer you are using. The computer is turned on by moving the switch to the on position.

The CPU, or "brain" of the computer, is a processor chip that controls the keyboard, mouse, monitor, and printer and performs all of the computing instructions.

The CPU also includes memory. Random Access Memory (RAM) stores data while it is being processed. Programs, such as word processing, are loaded or read into RAM. The amount of RAM determines the programs that can be run.

Disk Drives

Disk drives enable the user to save data entered in the computer's memory onto a disk and to read information from the disk drives into the memory of the computer for processing.

A computer must have at least one disk drive. If it has only one drive, it is designated as drive A. If the computer contains two disk drives, the drive on top is designated drive A and the one on the bottom drive B. If the two drives are side by side, the drive on the left is drive A and the one on the right is drive B. Computers today generally contain hard disks, which are completely enclosed in the system unit. Hard disks are referred to as drive C. More elaborate computers contain built-in zip drives, usually designated Drive D.

Printers

A printer provides a paper printout of the copy keyed. A variety of printers are found in schools, such as dot matrix, ink-jet, daisy wheel, and laser. The quality of print that is produced by each of these printers differs considerably. Consult your instructor about the location and operation of the printer you will be using.

Keyboard Arrangement

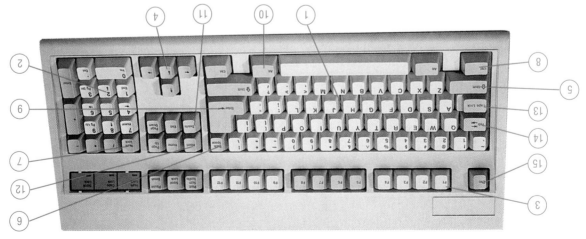

Keyboard

The keyboard is used to enter instructions and text into the CPU. Most keyboards resemble the keyboard shown above.

Alphanumeric keys. The center portion of the keyboard contains the alphanumeric keys. The symbols may vary slightly in location, but the letter and number keys are in the same location as those of a typewriter.

Numeric keypad. The numeric keypad, with keys arranged similar to those of a calculator, is used for entering statistical data or doing arithmetic calculations. To activate the keypad, press the NUM LOCK key.

1. **Alphanumeric keys:** Center portion of the keyboard.

2. **Numeric keypad:** Calculator-type keys used for entering statistical data. To turn on the keypad, press the NUM LOCK key.

3. **Function keys:** Perform a software function; used by themselves.

Function keys. Function keys are located across the top of the keyboard or along the left. They help you perform specific functions depending upon the software. Function keys will not place numbers or letters on the screen.

Cursor movement. The cursor is a symbol on the screen, such as a block or underline, that indicates where the next character will be displayed. The cursor usually flashes so that it can be identified easily. The cursor moves one space to the right as text is entered.

Software

The computer cannot function by itself; it needs a set of instructions to direct it. Such instructions are called soft-

4. **Arrow keys:** Move the insertion point.

5. **SHIFT:** Makes lowercase letters uppercase.

6. **BACKSPACE:** Deletes the character to the left of the insertion point.

7. **NUM LOCK:** Switches the numeric keypad between numeric and editing.

ware. Software comes in two forms: operating systems software and applications software.

Operating systems software. The operating systems software direct the operations of the computer, such as the input, printing, and storing of data.

Applications software. Applications software enables the computer to perform specific functions or applications. Word processing software such as *WordPerfect* and *College Keyboarding Alphanumeric* software are examples of applications software.

Disks

Disks store information entered into the computer. Storage disks are available in

8. **CTRL:** Expands the use of function keys.

9. **ENTER:** Advances the insertion point to the next line. ENTER is often used to execute a command.

10. **ALT (Alternate):** Used with another key to execute a function.

11. **DELETE:** Erases text to the right of the insertion point.

various sizes. The most prevalent sizes are 5.25 inches and 3.5 inches. The 3.5-inch disks hold twice as much data as the 5.25-inch disks.

Disks are coated with a magnetic substance; therefore, they must be handled carefully.

◆ Do not touch exposed areas of the disk.

◆ Keep 5.25" disk in a protective paper jacket when not in use.

◆ Use a felt-tip pen to write on the disk label.

◆ Keep disk away from magnetized objects, heat, and liquids.

12. **INSERT:** Toggles the software between insert mode and typeover/overstrike mode.

13. **CAPS LOCK:** Capitalizes all alphabetic characters.

14. **TAB:** Moves the cursor to a preset position.

15. **ESC (Escape):** Exits a menu or dialog box in word processing software.

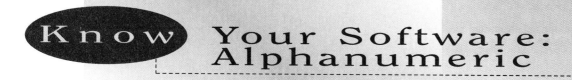

Know Your Software: Alphanumeric

With the full-featured *College Keyboarding Alphanumeric* software, you can use the power of your IBM-compatible computer to learn alphabetic and numeric keyboarding. The 30 software lessons correlate to the first 30 lessons in the *College Keyboarding* textbook.

The lessons contain a variety of activities, including practice drills, textbook keying, and timings. Many lessons introduce new keys—letters, punctuation, numbers, and symbols—while·others review what you have learned. Some lessons include document formatting exercises performed in the Open Screen, a simple word processor. Others contain a challenging keyboarding game.

You will key from the screen and from the textbook, with software prompts to guide you. The software tracks your performance and provides feedback. You can display or print daily your cumulative progress reports.

Loading the Alphanumeric Software

Follow these steps to load the software:
1. To save your data to disk, have a formatted disk ready. If you plan to save on a hard drive, create a directory or subdirectory for data storage. You will enter the name of this directory or subdirectory as the pathname in the configuration options.

2. If the software is installed on a hard drive, change to the directory where the program is stored and key **control** at the C> prompt. If you are running the software from the program disk, key **control** at the A> prompt.

Setting the Configuration Options

Press ENTER to move through the opening screens until you see the Drive and Pathname screen (Figure 1). Fill in drive and path [drive (a); path (\)] and strike F1. Follow instructions until you reach Create New Records File. Fill in appropriate information and strike F1. The first time you use the program, you will set the configuration options. Later, you can press ESC at the opening screen to go directly to the Main menu. Insert your program disk and strike ENTER The next screen is the Main menu.

Main Menu

You can access any feature of the *College Keyboarding Alphanumeric* software from the Main menu through the pull-down menus at the top—File, Lessons, and Open Screen. Choose one of these by using the left and right arrow keys and ENTER to select, or by striking the appropriate character. Striking ESC closes the pull-down menu and returns you to the Main menu.

Helpful instructions on how to use the software appear at the bottom of the screen. Notice that some of the configuration options you set are shown in the *Current* status line.

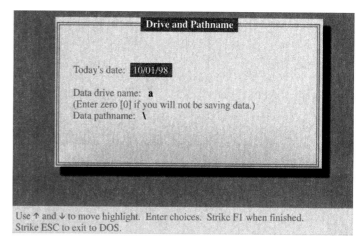

Figure 1: Drive and Pathname Screen

File Menu

The File menu lets you manage information. To save and print data, you must have selected these options on the Configuration Screen. An asterisk (*) beside an option indicates that it is available. Strike ESC to close the File menu.

Save records. Saves records to your data disk, including the exercises you have completed, your speed scores, and the drill lines keyed.

Print lesson report. Prints a report of your performance on a specific lesson and lets you print the drill lines keyed.

Display summary report. Shows which lesson parts you have completed and, for timed writings, your average keying speeds.

Print summary report. Prints the summary report and gives you an option to print the drill lines.

Print open screens. Prints files saved in the Open Screen.

Delete open screens. Deletes files saved in the Open Screen.

Change configuration. Lets you change the configuration options you set.

Quit. Ends the program, performs an automatic save of your records, and takes you to the DOS prompt.

Lesson Menu

All 30 lessons on the software are listed in the Lesson pull-down menu. Scroll down to the bottom of the box to see more lessons. An asterisk (*) beside a lesson indicates that you have completed it. Strike ESC at any time to close the Lesson menu.

When you choose a lesson, the menu for this lesson appears beside the Lessons menu, as shown in Figure 2. After you complete an exercise, the program automatically advances to the next one. You can strike ESC at any time to return to the menu, but if you quit in the middle of an exercise, no score is retained.

The exercises differ from lesson to lesson, providing a variety of activities for skill building. Each type of exercise is explained below.

Figure 2: Lessons Menu

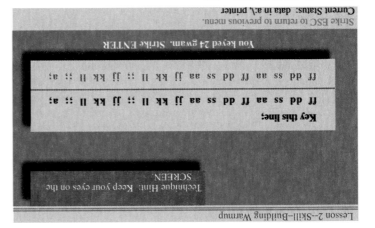

Skill-Building Warmup. The warmup (Figure 3) reinforces the learned keystrokes. Screen cues give instructions, remind you to use good techniques, and tell you how fast you are keying.

Figure 3: Skill-Building Warmup

Learn New Keys. On-screen graphics demonstrate the key reach. Drill lines appear on screen.

All Reaches Learned. On-screen prompts remind you how to make the key reaches, with drill lines for quick review.

Improve Keystroking. Drills emphasize specific keys and good techniques. The software provides technique instructions, and feedback. You will have three opportunities to key a word correctly.

Textbook Keying. The software directs you to key an exercise from the textbook. There is space to key 12 lines. Availability of the backspace key depends on the configuration options. You can print or repeat the exercise.

Build Skill. The software times you and reports results as you key drills from the screen. Technique hints appear along with a speed goal in gross words a minute (gwam).

Game. The game challenges you to meet a speed goal as you key drill lines from the screen. A measurement bar and screen prompts show your progress.

Lesson Report. After the last exercise in a lesson, a lesson report appears showing which exercises were completed and, if applicable, your speed scores. The software then asks if you wish to go on to the next lesson.

The Open Screen [OS]

The Open Screen (Figure 4) is a simple word processor available from the Main menu. An icon (shown above) in the textbook identifies timed writings and formatting exercises to be completed in the Open Screen. The software will tell you when to complete these exercises. Use **Timed keyboarding** for taking timed writings and **Keyboarding practice** for entering any type of document. Documents entered in the Open Screen may be retrieved, edited, and printed. Instructions are available on-screen.

Figure 4: Open Screen

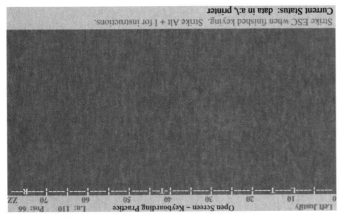

The Open Screen has line and position indicators in the upper right corner to assist you in formatting documents. The editing and formatting features include the following:

Backspace key. Deletes the character to the left of the cursor.

Cursor. Arrow keys and Page Up/Page Down move the cursor.

Word wrap. Text automatically moves to the next line.

Centering. Press Alt + C to change from centered text.

Formatting (margins and tabs). Press Alt + F to use the ruler at the top of the screen to set margins and tabs. Default margins are set at 10 and 75. Position the cursor and strike the letters L and R to set left and right margins. Press the TAB key to set or clear a tab. Default tabs are set at 15 and 42 (center).

Strike ESC when you are finished keying a document, or clear the Open Screen. You may then print or save a document, or clear the screen and start again. Note that you can also print a saved Open Screen document from the File menu.

Quitting the Alphanumeric Software

Use the Quit option under the File pull-down menu to exit to the DOS prompt. If you have been saving data, the Quit option automatically saves your records.

Introduction to MicroAssistant Software

MicroAssistant is production software that will enable you to key and format any exercise in this text. It has features for timing, checking, as well as recording your progress on drills, timed writings, production exercises, and tests. You will receive immediate feedback on your progress while you develop keyboarding and formatting skills.

To use MicroAssistant, you will need the following:

1. A program disk.

2. A template disk.

3. A formatted storage disk for saving activities.

The program disk and template may be loaded on a hard drive or network; additionally, documents may be saved to a hard drive or network—check with your instructor.

Loading MicroAssistant

1. Format a disk for storing your work. If you plan to save your work on the hard drive, your instructor will need to identify the subdirectory that has been set up for this purpose. (You will enter the name of the subdirectory as the *pathname*.)

2. If the software is loaded on a hard drive or network, change to the directory where the program is stored and key **control**. If you are running the program from the program disk, key **control** at the A>.

Configuration Menu

Your instructor will prepare a Class Options File prior to your using MicroAssistant. If the program cannot find this file, it will terminate. The first time you use MicroAssistant, you will need to create a student record. Check with your instructor to determine if an ID code has been assigned to you. Follow these steps to configure your system:

1. Enter a three-digit ID code. Remember your ID code; you will need to enter this code each time you use the program.

2. Enter your name. Once accepted as correct, your name will be permanently written to your student record. All your work will be identified by your name and ID code.

3. Follow the prompts on the screen. You can change the options if your instructor has given you this right (F1).

4. Enter your ID Code when prompted and strike ENTER.

5. Review the preliminary information screens and strike ENTER. You may press F1 to bypass these screens the next time you use the software. The Main menu is now displayed.

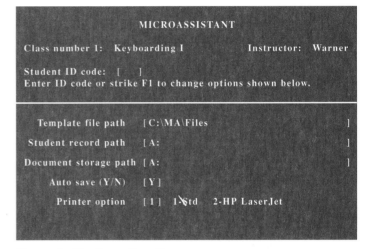

Figure 1: Configuration Menu

Main Menu

From the Main menu you can select a lesson, enter the Open Screen, display or print your performance record, or quit the program. See Figure 2 on p. x.

To select a lesson, key the number of the lesson and strike ENTER. If the activities are found in a workshop, the Laboratory Materials, or an Achievement Test, enter the letter and number of the workshop/activity. Examples are shown below.

S1	Skill-Building Workshop 1
C1	Communication Workshop 1
F1	Formatting Workshop 1
E1	Enrichment Activity 1 (from Laboratory Materials)
A1	Achievement Test 1

Entering a Lesson

Figure 4 displays the work screen. While creating or editing a document, you can use special function keys to format it. These keys are described briefly below.

F1 = Setup — Displays the default options for this exercise. The ability to change these defaults depends upon how your instructor has set the Class Options File.

F2 = Set Tab/Mar — Sets tabs and margins.

F3 = Help — Accesses all commands.

F5 = File — Loads, deletes, prints, or prepares a backup file. Displays or prints performance record (not available while keying an exercise).

F6 = Count-down timer — Sets the length of your timing while keying an exercise (e.g., 3 minutes).

Alt + B = Bold — Turns bold on or off.

Alt + D = Delete line — Deletes a complete line of text.

Alt + I = Temporary left margin (indent) — Sets a temporary left margin 5 spaces from the left margin. Alt turns the function on and off.

Alt + U = Underline — Turns underline on or off.

When you have completed an exercise, MicroAssistant will automatically check and save the document. Both keyboarding and formatting errors may be displayed.

Figure 4: Work Screen

```
F1=Setup  F2=Tab/Mar  F3=Help  F5=File Menu  F7=Exit
Lesson 31    Part C    Page 70                    Insert



L[ ]                                                R
|...1....|....2....|....3....|....4....|....5....|....6....|....7....|....8
Page: 1   Line: 4   Space: 10   Spacing: SS
F6: Set count-down timer option
```

Handling Documents

Once a document is keyed, you can print it and save it to a formatted disk. It can then be retrieved, edited, saved, and printed again. An entire lesson may be printed from the Lesson menu or individual exercises may be printed using the File option (F5).

Documents may be printed with or without error identification. The document is printed with a three-line header, including the following information and more: your name, date, class; the status of various options, such as correction and errors (keying and formatting); the number of times the error checker was run; your GWPM.

Production Tests

Documents can be combined and graded as one production test. This option is available on the Lesson menu of lessons that contain measurement. You will need to set the timer for the appropriate time.

Student Performance Record

While you use MicroAssistant, a record of your work is maintained, including:

◆ Five best straight-copy official timed writings (labeled OFT on the Lesson menu).

◆ Five best rough-draft, script, or statistical timed writings.

◆ The number of attempts at each lesson part.

◆ Results (errors, words, percent complete) for each production job.

Your student performance record may be displayed or printed from the Main menu.

Figure 3: Lesson Menu

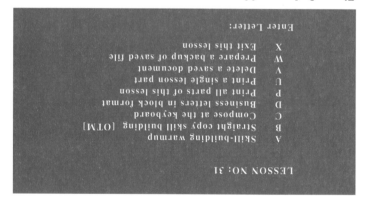

```
LESSON NO: 31

A   Skill-building warmup
B   Straight copy skill building [OTM]
C   Compose at the keyboard
D   Business letters in block format
P   Print all parts of this lesson
U   Print a single lesson part
V   Delete a saved document
W   Prepare a backup of saved file
X   Exit this lesson

Enter Letter:
```

Lesson Menu

After you select a lesson, the Lesson menu will display. The subparts of the menu correspond directly with the lesson exercises in the text. Should an exercise contain more than one drill/document, they will be listed on another submenu. You may return to the Main menu or quit the program from the Lesson menu.

Figure 2: Main Menu

```
MICROASSISTANT

Entry lesson number: 31        (Alt-C=Clean field.)
or enter one of the following codes:
O - Open screen
D - Display student performance record
P - Print student performance record
U - Print a saved document
V - Delete a saved document
W - Prepare a backup file of saved documents
Q - Quit

If the exercise is found in a nonnumbered lesson, enter the letter
and number of the activity (for example, C1=Communication Workshop 1):
A=Achievement      E=Enrichment       S=Skill-building
C=Communication    F=Formatting
```

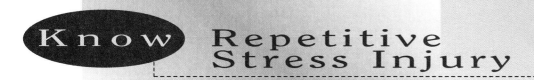

Know Repetitive Stress Injury

Repetitive Stress Injury (RSI)

Repetitive stress injury (RSI) is a result of repeated movement of a particular part of the body. A familiar example is "tennis elbow." Of more concern to keyboard users is the form of RSI called **carpal tunnel syndrome (CTS)**.

CTS is an inflammatory disease that develops gradually and affects the wrist, hands, and forearms. Blood vessels, tendons, and nerves pass into the hand through the carpal tunnel (see illustration below). If any of these structures enlarge or if the walls of the tunnel narrow, the median nerve is pinched, and CTS symptoms may result.

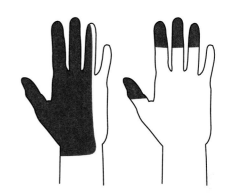

Areas affected by carpal tunnel syndrome

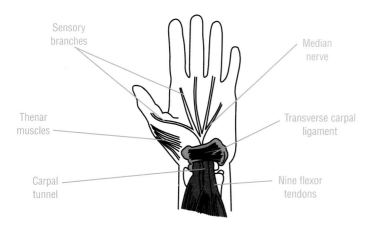

Sensory branches

Median nerve

Thenar muscles

Transverse carpal ligament

Carpal tunnel

Nine flexor tendons

Areas affected by carpal tunnel syndrome

Repetitive Stress Injury (RSI)

CTS symptoms include numbness in the hand; tingling or burning in the hand, wrist, or elbow; severe pain in the forearm, elbow, or shoulder; and difficulty in gripping objects. Symptoms usually appear during sleeping hours, probably because many people sleep with their wrists flexed.

If not properly treated, the pressure on the median nerve, which controls the thumb, forefinger, middle finger, and half the ring finger (see top right), causes severe pain. The pain can radiate into the forearm, elbow, or shoulder and can require surgery or result in permanent damage or paralysis.

Causes of RSI/CTS

RSI/CTS often develops in workers whose physical routine is unvaried. Common occupational factors include: (1) using awkward posture, (2) using poor techniques, (3) performing tasks with wrists bent *(see below)*, (4) using improper equipment, (5) working at a rapid pace, (6) not taking rest breaks, and (7) not doing exercises that promote graceful motion and good techniques.

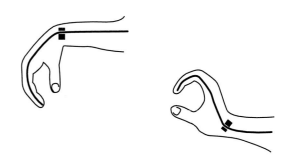

Improper wrist positions for keystroking

Other factors associated with CTS include a person's genetic makeup; the aging process; hormonal influences; obesity; chronic diseases such as rheumatoid arthritis and gout; misaligned fractures; and hobbies such as gardening, knitting, and woodworking that require the same motion over and

Repetitive Stress Injury (RSI)

Carpal tunnel syndrome is frequently a health concern for workers who use a computer keyboard or mouse. The risk of developing CTS is less for computer keyboard operators who use proper furniture or equipment, keyboarding techniques, posture, and/or muscle-stretching exercises than for those who do not.

Keyboard users can reduce the risk of developing RSI/CTS by taking these precautions:

1. Arrange the workstation correctly:
   a. Position the keyboard directly in front of the chair.
   b. Keep the front edge of the keyboard even with the edge of the desk or table so that the wrist movement will not be restricted while you are keying.
   c. Position the keyboard at elbow height.
   d. Position the monitor about 18 to 24 inches from your eyes with the top edge of the display screen at eye level.
   e. Position the mouse next to and at the same height as the computer keyboard and as close to the body as possible.

2. Use a proper chair and sit correctly:
   a. Use a straight-backed chair, or adjust your chair so that it will not yield when you lean back.
   b. Use a seat that allows you to keep your feet flat on the floor while you are keying. Use a footrest if your feet cannot rest flat on the floor.
   c. Sit erect and as far back in the seat as possible.

3. Use correct arm and wrist positions and movement:
   a. Keep your forearms parallel to the floor and level with the keyboard so that your wrists will be in a flat, neutral position rather than flexed upward or downward.
   b. Keep arms near the side of your body in a relaxed position.

4. Use proper keyboarding techniques:
   a. Keep your fingers curved and upright over the home keys.
   b. Keep wrists and forearms from touching or resting on any surface while keying.
   c. Strike each key lightly using the fingertip. Do not use too much pressure or hold the keys down.

over. CTS affects over three times more women than men, with 60 percent of the affected persons between the ages of 30 and 60.

5. When using a keyboard or mouse, take short breaks. A rest of one to two minutes every hour is appropriate. Natural breaks in keyboarding action of several seconds' duration also help.

6. Exercise the neck, shoulder, arm, wrist, and fingers before beginning to key each day and often during the workday (see Precaution 5). Suggested exercises for keyboard users are described below. You can do all the exercises while sitting at your workstation.

Exercises for Keyboard Users

1. **Strengthen finger muscles.** (See Drill 1 on p. xiii.) Open your hands, extend your fingers wide, and hold with muscles tense for two or three seconds; close the fingers into a tight fist with thumb on top, holding for two or three seconds; relax the fingers as you straighten them. Repeat 10 times. Additional finger drills are shown on p. xiii.

2. **Strengthen the muscles in the carpal tunnel area.** While sitting with your arms comfortably at your side and hands in a fist, rotate your hands inward from the wrist. Repeat this motion 10 to 15 times; then rotate outward from the wrist 10 to 15 times. Extend your fingers and repeat the movements for the same number of times.

3. **Loosen forearms.** With both wrists held in a neutral position (not bent) and the upper arm hanging vertically from the shoulder, rotate both forearms in 15 clockwise circles about the elbow. Repeat, making counterclockwise circles.

4. **Stretch the arms.** Interlace the fingers of both hands; with the palms facing forward, stretch your arms in front of you and hold for ten seconds. Repeat at least once. Next, with your fingers still interlaced, stretch your arms over your head and hold for ten seconds. Repeat at least once.

5. **Loosen elbows.** Place your hands on your shoulders with elbows facing forward; slowly move your arms in increasingly larger circles in front of you 10 to 15 times.

6. **Relieve shoulder tension.** Interlace the fingers of both hands behind your head and slowly move the elbows back, pressing the shoulder blades together; hold for ten seconds. Repeat at least once.

Finger gymnastics

Brief daily practice of finger gymnastics will strengthen your finger muscles and increase the ease with which you key. Begin each keying period with this conditioning exercise. Choose two or more drills for this practice.

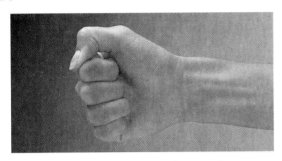

DRILL 1. Hands open, fingers wide, muscles tense. Close the fingers into a tight "fist," with thumb on top. Relax the fingers as you straighten them; repeat 10 times.

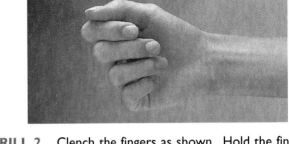

DRILL 2. Clench the fingers as shown. Hold the fingers in this position for a brief time; then extend the fingers, relaxing the muscles of fingers and hand. Repeat the movements slowly several times. Exercise both hands at the same time.

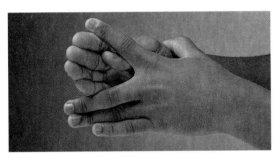

DRILL 3. Place the fingers and the thumb of one hand between two fingers of the other hand, and spread the fingers as much as possible. Spread all fingers of both hands.

DRILL 4. Interlace the fingers of the two hands and wring the hands, rubbing the heel of the palms vigorously.

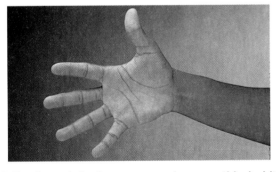

DRILL 5. Spread the fingers as much as possible, holding the position for a moment or two; then relax the fingers and lightly fold them into the palm of the hand. Repeat the movements slowly several times. Exercise both hands at the same time.

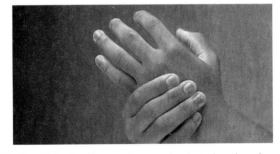

DRILL 6. Rub the hands vigorously. Let the thumb rub the palm of the hand. Rub the fingers, the back of the hand, and the wrist.

DRILL 7. Hold both hands in front of you, fingers together. Hold the last three fingers still and move the first finger as far to the side as possible. Return the first finger; then move the first and second fingers together; finally move the little finger as far to the side as possible.

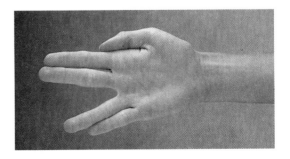

Know Your Electronic Typewriter

The parts of an electronic typewriter are illustrated at the right. Because all typewriters have similar parts, you probably will be able to identify the parts on your equipment from these illustrations; but if you have the manufacturer's booklet for your typewriter, use it to locate each machine part identified.

1. **Left platen knob**—used to turn platen manually (not on some models).

2. **Line-of-writing (margin) scale**—indicates pitch scales (10, 12, and 15); may indicate margin positions and the printing point.

3. **Paper-bail release lever**—used to pull paper bail away from platen.

4. **Paper guide**—used to position paper for insertion.

5. **Paper support**—supports paper when it is in the machine.

6. **Print carrier**—includes ribbon cassette, correction tape, carrier adjust lever, and printing mechanism.

7. **Paper bail and rollers**—used to hold paper against platen.

8. **Platen (cylinder)**—provides a hard surface against which the print mechanism strikes.

9. **Paper release lever**—used to adjust position of paper.

10. **Backspace**—used to move printing point to left one space.

11. **Paper insert**—used to feed paper to specified loading position.

12. **Relocate (RELOC)**—used to return printing point to previous position after corrections are made.

13. **Return**—used to return printing point to left margin and to move paper up.

14. **Right shift**—used with keys controlled by the left hand to key capitals or symbols.

15. **Correction**—used to erase a character.

16. **Space bar**—used to move printing point to the right one space at a time.

17. **Code**—used simultaneously with another key to cause that key to perform a special function.

18. **Left shift**—used with keys controlled by the right hand to key capitals or symbols.

19. **Caps Lock**—used to key text in ALL CAPS (capital letters).

20. **Tab set**—used with set tabulator stops (tabs); tab clear may be same key on some models.

21. **Repeat**—used to repeat a previously struck key or function.

22. **Bold**—used to print bold-face characters.

23. **Underline (UNDLN)**—used to print underlined characters.

24. **Pitch select**—used to set type size (10-, 12-, or 15-pitch) to correspond to the printing device being used.

25. **Line-space selector**—sets machine to advance the paper 1, 1.5, 2, 3 lines when return key is used.

26. **Centering**—used to center text automatically between the left and right margins.

27. **Auto**—set to return the printing point automatically to the left margin, next line when it reaches the right margin.

28. **Margin release**—used to move printing point beyond the margin settings.

29. **Left margin (L MAR)**—used to set left margin.

30. **Right margin (R MAR)**—used to set right margin.

31. **Tabulator (Tab)**—used to move printing point to tab locations.

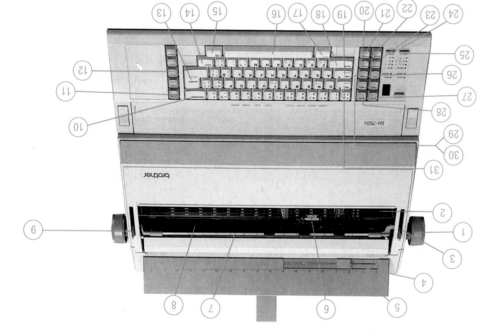

Level One
Learning to Operate
the Keyboard

OBJECTIVES

KEYBOARDING
To key the alphabetic and numeric keys "by touch" using the proper techniques.

FORMATTING SKILLS
To set margins and tabs, and center text horizontally.

COMMUNICATION SKILLS
To apply proofreaders' marks and revise text.

Drill 3

Improve speed/accuracy on statistical copy

1' and 2' writings; figure *gwam*; circle errors

 all letters/figures

.	4	.	8	.	12	

For the period that began January of last year, the revenue   6

for common stock was $197 million, a rise of 23.3% over the same   13

interval last year. With a yield of 8.78% in average shares out-   19

standing, revenues per share rose an extra 10.7%, from $1.61 for   26

the period just over in January this year to $1.84 in an earlier   32

period. The primary reason for an increment this size is due to   39

a 5.21% increment in area quotas, many of which were met on time.   45

gwam 2' | 1 | 2 | 3 | 4 | 5 | 6 | 7 |

Drill 4

Measure skill: statistical copy

3' or 5' writings

 all figures and letters

gwam 3' | 5'

The Barak & Rinezi folio for the end of the year (Memo #98)   4 | 2

says that its last-quarter income was "26% above the historic   8 | 5

revenues of last year." The folio also says that the increase was   13 | 8

due to an upsurge in net sales of "just over 4 1/3%."   16 | 10

The increase is the seventh consecutive quarter in which   20 | 12

Barak & Rinezi have shown a profit; and the chief executive of   24 | 15

this old firm--Paul Rinezi--has told one industrial group that he   29 | 17

is slated to ask his board for an "increase of almost $1.50 a   33 | 20

common share" as its dividend for this financial year.   36 | 22

The company for the past 24 years has had its primary office   41 | 24

at 400 Big Ruby Road; the main plant is in Abilene at 17 Autumn   45 | 27

Avenue. The company employs about 350 area people, and yearly   49 | 29

sales will total about $3.5 million. Paul Rinezi has acted as   53 | 32

company CEO for 11 years; he took over the post after his uncle   57 | 34

had been the head for over 22 years.   60 | 36

gwam 3' | 1 | 2 | 3 | 4 | 5 |
5' | 1 | 2 | 3 |

1
Letter Keyreaches

Learning goals:
1 To master alphabetic reaches.
2 To key "by touch"–without looking at fingers or keyboard.
3 To key easy paragraph copy smoothly and fluently.
4 To key at a rate of 14 or more gross words a minute (*gwam*).

Formatting guides:
1 Default margins or 50-space line.
2 Single-space drills; double-space between groups.

1a

Get ready to key

1 Read "Get ready to key."
2 Prepare equipment for keying.

Get ready to key

Prepare your work station
• Elevate the textbook.
• Clear unneeded books and clothing from work area.

Prepare your equipment

Typewriters
• Set paper guide so that the left edge of your paper will be at 0 on the line-of-writing scale.
• Set left margin for a 50-space line (pica, 17 and 67; elite, 26 and 76; set right margin at end of line-of-writing scale).
• Set line-spacing for single spacing (1).
• Turn on machine; insert paper.

Computers
• Turn power switch to "on."
• Turn monitor on if it has a separate switch.
• Use the default (preset) margins.
• Refer to page xi for directions for using the keyboarding software.

Take proper position
• Sit back in chair, body erect.
• Place both feet on floor to maintain proper position.
• Let your hands hang at your sides. Notice that your fingers relax in a curved position. This relaxed, curved position is the one always used for keying. Repeat this step each day before you begin to key.

Drill 2
Guided writing: improve speed/accuracy

Key as 1' guided writings, working for either speed or control.

Optional: Key as a 3' writing.

To access writings on MicroPace Plus, key **W** and the timing number. For example, key **W14** for Writing 14.

Writing 14

gwam 3'

	.	4	.	8	.	12		
Anyone who expects some day to find an excellent job should | 4 | 34

begin now to learn the value of accuracy. To be worth anything, | 8 | 38

completed work must be correct, without question. Naturally, we | 13 | 43

realize that the human aspect of the work equation always raises | 17 | 47

the prospect of errors; but we should understand that those same | 20 | 51

errors can be found and fixed. Every completed job should carry | 26 | 56

at least one stamp; the stamp of pride in work that is exemplary. | 30 | 60

Writing 15

No question about it: Many personal problems we face today | 4 | 34

arise from the fact that we earthlings have never been very wise | 8 | 38

consumers. We haven't consumed our natural resources well; as a | 13 | 43

result, we have jeopardized much of our environment. We excused | 17 | 47

our behavior because we thought that our stock of most resources | 20 | 51

had no limit. So, finally, we are beginning to realize just how | 26 | 56

indiscreet we were; and we are taking steps to rebuild our world. | 30 | 60

Writing 16

When I see people in top jobs, I know I'm seeing people who | 4 | 34

sell. I'm not just referring to employees who labor in a retail | 8 | 38

outlet; I mean those people who put extra effort into convincing | 13 | 43

others to recognize their best qualities. They, themselves, are | 17 | 47

the commodity they sell; and their optimum tools are appearance, | 20 | 51

language, and personality. They look great, they talk and write | 26 | 56

well; and, with candid self-confidence, they meet you eye to eye. | 30 | 60

gwam 3' | 1 | 2 | 3 | 4 | 5 |

1b

Locate home keys, space bar, and return

Find the keys **a s d f** and **j k l ;** . Practice several times the steps at the right for placing fingers in home row position and for reaching to the Return key and Space bar.

1 Drop hands to side allowing fingers to curve naturally.
2 Lightly place the left fingertips over **a s d f** .
3 Lightly place right fingertips over **j k l ;** .
4 Repeat.

Return: Reach with the 4th (little) finger of the right hand to the **return/ enter** key and tap it. Quickly return the finger to its home position (over **;**).

Space bar: Strike the **space bar** with a down-and-in motion of the right thumb.

1c

Learn home keys

Key each line twice single spaced (SS); strike the return key twice to double-space (DS) between 2-line groups. Do not key the numbers.

Note: Even if your equipment has word wrap, use the Return key here.

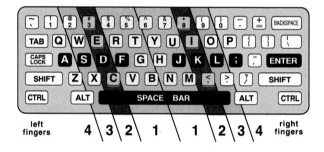

left fingers 4 \ 3 \ 2 \ 1   1 / 2 / 3 / 4 right fingers

```
1 ff jj ff jj fj fj fj dd kk dd kk dk dk dk  Return
2 ff jj ff jj fj fj fj dd kk dd kk dk dk dk
```
Strike Return twice to double-space (DS)

```
3 ss ll ss ll sl sl sl aa ;; aa ;; a; a; a;
4 ss ll ss ll sl sl sl aa ;; aa ;; a; a; a;
```
(DS)

```
5 fj fj dk dk sl sl a; a; fjdksla; jfkdls;a
6 fj fj dk dk sl sl a; a; fjdksla; jfkdls;a
```
(DS)

1d

Practice return

Key each line once; double-space (DS) between lines.

```
7 f j d k s l a ;  Return twice

8 ff jj dd kk ss ll aa ;;

9 fff jjj ddd kkk sss lll aaa ;;;

10 ff jj dd kk ss ll aa ;; fjdksla; fjdksla;
```

Skill-Building Workshop 3

Drill 1
Variable rhythm patterns

each line twice SS; DS
between 2-line groups; rekey
difficult lines

Fluency (key phrases and words, not letter by letter)

1 it is | it is he | to us | am due | by the man | an end | by the body | go with
2 cut the firm | due to the | go to the end | did pay us | form a half firm
3 they wish us to go | kept the man down | held the box down | cut the ox

4 Did the busy men dismantle the shamrock ornament for the visitor?
5 The key to the eighth problem is to spell rogue and theory right.
6 When Jane and I go to the city, we may visit the chapel and mall.

7 The auditor had problems with the theory to make a profit for us.
8 Diane did rush the lapdog to the city when it bit their neighbor.
9 If the altos are on key, they may enrich the chant in the ritual.

| 1 | 2 | 3 | 4 | 5 | 6 | 7 | 8 | 9 | 10 | 11 | 12 | 13 |

Control (key at a steady but not fast pace)

10 we saw | ad in | as my | we are | on him | ate up | we act ill | add gas to oil
11 age was | you are only | jump on art | my faded nylon | red yolk | few were
12 best care | you read | tax base | after we oil | saw data | agreed rate was

13 Water and garbage rates fell after my rebates were added in July.
14 Acres of wet grass and poppy seeds were tested for zebras to eat.
15 Jo ate the lumpy beets and sweet tarts but craved a stewed onion.

16 Jimmy saw a cab in my garage; I was awarded it in an estate case.
17 Dad feared we'd pay extra estate taxes after debts were assessed.
18 Rebates on oil, added to decreases in taxes, affect oil reserves.

| 1 | 2 | 3 | 4 | 5 | 6 | 7 | 8 | 9 | 10 | 11 | 12 | 13 |

Variable-rhythm sentences (vary pace with difficulty of words)

19 Dad attested to the fact that the barbers paid the auditor's tax.
20 Giant oaks and sassafras trees edged the east lane of the street.
21 Holly may join us by the pool to meet the eight big team members.

22 Did you get sufficient green material to make the eight sweaters?
23 All crates of cabbages were saved after I agreed to make payment.
24 Both visitors were totally enchanted as they watched the regatta.

| 1 | 2 | 3 | 4 | 5 | 6 | 7 | 8 | 9 | 10 | 11 | 12 | 13 |

1e

Practice home row

Key each line twice (SS); (DS) between 2-line groups.

Note: Even if your machine has an automatic return or word wrap, use the Return key here.

```
11  a; sl a;sl dk fj dkfj a;sl dkfj a;sldk a;sldkfj a;
12  a; sl a;sl dk fj dkfj a;sl dkfj a;sldk a;sldkfj a;
```
Strike return twice to double-space (DS)
```
13  as as ask ad ad jak lad all fall add lass all fall
14  as as ask ad ad jak lad all fall add lass all fall
```
(DS)
```
15  a lass; ask dad; a lad asks dad; ask all; jak fall
16  a lass; ask dad; a lad asks dad; ask all; jak fall
```

1f

Learn i

1 Find **i** on the illustrated keyboard; then find it on your keyboard.

2 Study "Reach technique for i."

3 Watch your finger make the reach to **i** and back to **k** a few times without striking the keys. Keep fingers curved and wrists low.

4 Key each line twice; DS between groups. Try to keep your eyes on the copy as you key.

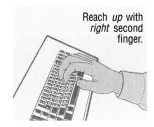

Reach *up* with *right* second finger.

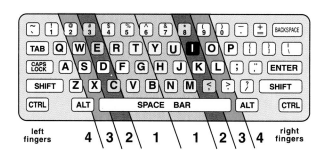

left fingers   4 3 2 1   1 2 3 4   right fingers

```
17  i ik ik ik is is id id if if il il ail did kid lid
18  i ik aid ail did kid lid lids kids ill aid did ilk

19  id aid aids laid said ids lids kids kiss disk dial
20  id aid ail fail sail jail ails slid dill sill fill

21  fill a sail; aid a lad; is silk; if a dial; a jail
22  is a disk; dads said; did fall ill; if a lass did;
```

1g

End the lesson

(standard procedures for all lessons)

Electronic typewriters
1 Press Eject key to remove the paper.
2 Turn off the power.

Computers
1 Exit the software.
2 Remove disk from drive and store it.
3 Turn off power if directed to do so.
4 Turn off monitor if it has a separate switch.

Tabulated reports

Center each document horizontally and vertically.
Reference: pages 114, 116

Document 10
Key title in bold.
Reference: pages 81, 114

words

THE SPRINGARN MEDAL AWARD 5

Selected Winners 9

1974	Henry (Hank) Aaron	13
1978	Rosa L. Parks	17
1982	Lena Horne	20
1984	Bill Cosby	24
1988	Jesse Jackson	27
1989	L. Douglas Wilder	32
1990	Colin L. Powell	36

Document 11

COLUMBUS KIDS BASEBALL LEAGUE 6

Coaches of the Year 10

1987	Mike LaRue	Giants	15
1988	Dan McKee	Bears	19
1989	Millie Day	Cougars	24
1990	Betsy Lahr	Colts	28
1991	Rich O'Hare	Eagles	31
1992	Jane Ruiz	Bears	36
1993	Mike LaRue	Giants	40

Document 12
Reference: pages 119, 123

ANNUAL MUNICIPAL WASTE GENERATION 7

In Millions of Tons 11

Waste	Tons	Percent	
			18
Paper	117.8	39.87	22
Food	13.2	7.85	25
Yard	31.6	17.59	28
Metals	15.3	8.52	31
Glass	12.5	6.96	35
Plastic	14.4	8.02	38
Other	*9.8*	*11.58*	41
DS			45

Source: National Municipal (Assn.) *sp* 51

2 ▶ E and N

2a

each line twice SS;
DS between 2-line
groups
- ✓ **Eyes** on copy
- ✓ **Fingers** curved
- ✓ **Wrists** low
- ✓ **Elbows**
  hanging loose

home row 1	ff dd ss aa ff dd ss aa jj kk ll ;; jj kk ll ;; a;
i 2	i i ill ilk did kid lid aid ail kid kids lids slid
all reaches 3	if a lad; as a jail; is silk; fill a dais; did aid
easy 4	jak aid did flak laid said is id if dial disk jaks

2b

Learn e and n

Read carefully the "Standard
procedure" at the right. Use
it to learn new keyreaches in
this lesson and in lessons
that follow.

Standard procedure for learning new keyreaches

1 Find the new key on the illustrated
keyboard; then find it on your keyboard.
2 Study the illustrated keyreach.
3 Watch your finger make the reach to the
new key a few times. Keep other fingers
curved in home position. For an upward

reach, straighten the finger slightly; for a
downward reach, curve it a bit more.
4 Key each line twice (slowly, then faster);
DS between 2-line groups.
5 Repeat if time permits. Work to eliminate
pauses.

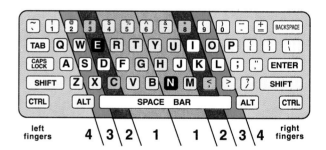

left
fingers 4 3 2 1   1 2 3 4 right
fingers

Reach *up* with
left second finger.

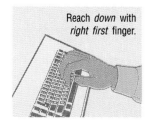

Reach *down* with
right first finger.

e

5 e ed ed led led lea lea ale ale elf elf eke eke ed

6 e el el eel els elk elk lea leak ale kale led jell

7 e ale kale lea leak fee feel lea lead elf self eke

n

8 n nj nj an an and and fan fan and kin din fin land

9 n an fan in fin and land sand din fans sank an sin

10 n in ink sink inn kin skin an and land in din dink

all reaches learned

11 den end fen ken dean dens ales fend fens keen knee

12 if in need; feel ill; as an end; a lad and a lass;

13 and sand; a keen idea; as a sail sank; is in jail;

Two-page unbound report

References: pages 98,100

Document 9

Add the title, **THE GIFT OF LOUIS BRAILLE**, in bold.

Thanks to the dedicated work of special groups, funds, gifts, and the | 19
boundless efforts of the sightless themselves, people without sight can enjoy | 35
the printed word. Actually, they have had this "miracle" gift of reading for | 50
more than 165 years, made possible by braille printing--the wonderful gift of | 66
Louis Braille (1809-1852). "The introduction of the braille system of printing | 82
probably accomplished more for a greater number of people than any | 95
innovation of the early nineteenth century, truly a marvel of ingenuity" | 110
(Sung, 1991, 57). | 114

The Innovator | 119

Louis Braille, who lost his own sight at age three, enrolled in the | 133
National Institute for the Blind in Paris when he was ten. A very good | 147
student, he excelled in music and science; and following graduation, he | 162
stayed on at the Institute as a teacher. In this capacity, "probably by | 176
adapting a dot-dash system then in use by the French military for night | 191
signaling," he developed in 1829 the system of printing that carries his name | 206
(Tippett, 1991, 12). | 211

The Innovation | 216

Young Louis believed that a series of small, raised (embossed) dots on | 231
paper could be interpreted, or "read," by sensitive fingertips. Arranged in a | 246
six-dot configuration called a "cell," 63 possible combinations could form | 261
letters, figures, punctuation marks, etc. With practice, such printing, he | 277
conjectured, could be comprehended rapidly and accurately. He was right, | 291
of course; and braille has since widened personal and professional avenues | 305
for millions of sight-diminished people. | 314

Today, easing its use, a number of shortcuts and abbreviations have | 327
been introduced into the braille system. Still, despite its obvious merits, | 343
braille remains cumbersome; because of its larger "print," braille copy | 357
requires more space than other kinds of copy. | 366

Picture if you will an ordinary set of encyclopedias of, say, 15 | 379
volumes. Such a set printed in braille likely would involve about 150 | 394
volumes, weigh about 700 pounds, and fill about 45 feet of shelf | 407
space (Dunn, 1992, 78). | 412

Braille may be keyed on a special braillewriter, on which the keyboard | 426
consists of six striking keys, each capable of establishing an embossed dot in | 442
a certain location, and three directional keys. With such a keyboard, a writer | 458
is able to communicate in print with braille readers--all in all, a fine gift | 473
indeed from Louis Braille. | 479

REFERENCES | 481

Dunn, Sondra B. Bits and Pieces. Atlanta: Montberry Press, 1992. | 497

Sung, Charles Kye. "Little Steps, Big Strides." American Science and | 515
History, October 1991. | 521

Tippett, Wilson A. "Braille: A Short History." Paragon Monthly, August | 539
1991. | 540

2c

Practice keying techniques

each line twice SS; DS
between 2-line groups

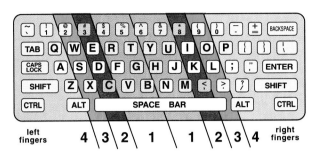

left fingers 4 \ 3 \ 2 \ 1 \ 1 \ 2 \ 3 \ 4 right fingers

home row
14 a fad dad all fall as ad ask lass sad lad fad jaks

e
15 el see ale eke ade eel eld fed fee kea led lea sea

i
16 is id ill dill if aid ail fail did kid ski lid ilk

n
17 an fan and land fans flan sans sand sank flak dank

all reaches
18 ade alas dike else fife ken; jell ink jak inns if;

2d

Practice keying words and phrases

each line at least twice SS;
DS between groups

Use correct technique
✓ Fingers curved and upright
✓ Wrists low but not touching machine
✓ Forearms parallel to keyboard
✓ Eyes on copy
✓ Elbows hanging loosely
✓ Body erect; feet flat on floor

all reaches learned
19 a an ale an and as ask fa fan la lad el elk inn if
20 ad ale an and did end a is elf els fie jak ken lei
21 alas a dial el elan elf kale la lake an lane is if
22 add a line; and safe; asks a lass; sail in a lake;
23 dine in an inn; fake jade; lend fans; as sand sank
24 and nine less; sad lads; adds line nine; dank lane

2e

End the lesson

(use standard procedures)

Turn off power; clear work area.   Exit software.

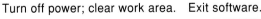

Interoffice memorandums

(plain sheets)
Proofread and correct errors.
Reference: page 82

Document 6

	words
TO: Lonny Ashmyer	**FROM:** Breton S. Vreede	**DATE:** January 11, 19--		13
SUBJECT: Wheelchair Access	19

Recently I explained to you my efforts on a variety of projects to facilitate wheelchair entry into public buildings. I may have found a solution to one problem, Lonny; that is, how does someone open a large public door from a wheelchair.

The answer may lie in the installation of an electrical signal (similar to a garage door opener) that can be activated from the chair. All signals would be identical, of course, permitting universal application.

Can you provide me with a rough estimate of the costs for these items:

1. Conducting the necessary preliminary research.

2. Equipping a wheelchair.

3. Tooling our factory to manufacture this item. | xx

Word counts: 35, 50, 65, 67, 83, 98, 110, 124, 135, 140, 151

Document 7

TO: Katrin Beaster
FROM: J. J. Bouhm
DATE: Current
SUBJECT: May Seminar

I have invited Lynda A. Brewer, Ph.D., Earlham College, Richmond, Indiana, to be our seminar leader on Friday afternoon, May 10.

Dr. Brewer, a well-known psychologist who has spent a lot of time researching and writing in the new field of ergonomics, will address "Stress Management."

Please make arrangements for rooms, speaker accommodations, staff notification, and refreshments. I will send you Dr. Brewer's vita for use in preparing news releases.

Word counts: 25, 34, 41, 50, 61, 73, 82, 93, 102, 107

Document 8

TO: J. Ezra Bayh
FROM: Greta Sangtree
DATE: August 14, 19--
SUBJECT: Letter-Mailing Standards

)DS

chk sp

Recently the post office delivered late a letter that caused us some embarassment. To avoid reoccurrence, please ensure that all administrative assistants and mail personnel follow postal service guidlines.

U.S.

because of the delay,

Perhaps a refresher seminar on correspondence guidelines is in in order. Thanks or you help. for your

Word counts: 4, 8, 13, 20, 36, 48, 60, 67, 79, 85

Remember: Practice should be purposefully done, not just copied. Simply swinging at a golf ball does not create a better golfer; skill growth requires purposeful practice.

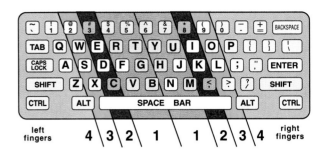

left fingers   4 \ 3 \ 2 \ 1   1 \ 2 \ 3 \ 4   right fingers

3 ◆ Review

Skill-Building Warmup

3a

each line twice SS (slowly, then faster); DS between 2-line groups

home keys 1	a s d f j k l ; as df jk l; asdf jkl; a; sl dk fj;
home row 2	ad ads lad fad dad as ask fa la lass jak jaks alas
i / e / n 3	fan fin an eel el nine in life if kiss is idea did
all reaches 4	a jak and a land and an elf and a dial and a lens;

3b

Practice keying phrases

lines 5-12 once as shown; keep eyes on copy

Strike the space bar with a quick down-and-in motion. Do not pause before or after striking the space bar.

Reach to the Enter key, strike the key, and release it quickly.

Note: Do not key the vertical rules separating phrases.

home row

5 as a jak;|as a lass|ask dad|as a lad;|as a fall ad
6 ask a lass;|as a dad|a fall fad|as all ask;|sad ad

i

7 if as is;|is a disk|aid all kids|did ski|is a silk
8 skis skid|is a kid|aid did fail|if a dial|laid lid

e

9 as kale|sees a lake|elf fled|as a deal|sell a sled
10 sell a lead|seal a deal|feel a leaf|as a jade sale

n

11 in an inn|sank in sand|nine fans|in a land|and end
12 line is in ink | send in a fan | line nine | a fine land

Letters in modified-block format

(plain sheets)

1 Estimate letter length.
2 Supply letter address from the business cards. Use current date; add an appropriate salutation.
3 Correct errors; prepare envelopes.

Reference: pages 70, 77-78

Document 3

Estancia Imports
Ramon Figueroa, Prop.
192 Las Palamas
San Juan, PR 00911-9110
Telephone (809) 555-3546

Document 4

Baxter, Varnum, & Wertz
Patti Baxter, President
2200 Uhle Street, South
Arlington, VA 22206-0662
Telephone (304) 555-7657
Fax (304) 555-9864

Document 5

Miss June Boehm
5450 Signal Hill Road
Springfield, OH 45504-5440

Document 3

This afternoon we marked your statement "PAID IN FULL." We appreci-	35
ate the prompt manner with which you have always handled your	48
account here, and we sincerely hope we will have an opportunity to serve	62
you again soon.	66
We take this opportunity to introduce our new GINO swim wear line to	80
you. The enclosed sketches illustrate the beauty of the line; and I will	95
ask Eri Rigby, coordinator of the line, to send you a catalog as soon as it	100
comes from the press.	114
Please accept our good wishes for a prosperous spring season.	127
Cordially	Alvin Twodeer	Sales Manager	xx	Enclosure	c Eri Rigby	139

Document 4

As a sales associate for Real Estate Enterprises, Inc., I have had many	41
unique opportunities to analyze and interpret the real estate market. Com-	56
mercial and investment properties, including apartment income buildings,	70
commercial realty, office space, and vacant land, are my specialties.	85
You may take advantage of my expertise in corporate real estate marketing,	100
including selling, buying, and leasing commercial and investment realty. A	115
copy of the recent newsletter published by Real Estate Enterprises is	129
enclosed for your review.	134
Please keep the enclosed business card in a convenient place, and call me	149
when I can be of assistance. Real Estate Enterprises stresses professional-	164
ism and adheres to the code of American Realtors.	175
Sincerely	Wilma Lopez	Sales Associate	xx	Enclosures: Newsletter		188
Business card	190

Document 5

Our head teller, Guy Raberger, tells me that you have	30
closed your account with us. You have been a customer valued	42
by us for years, and we are sorry to lose you business.	52
Our business policy *is to* dictates that we provide *our* you*r*	58
customers with prompt, accurate, courteous service at all	69
times. If we in some way failed to follow this policy, we	78
want to know how and why, if not, you have our genuine	96
appreciation for allowing us to care for your account.	
The staff of this bank is commited to serving you however	107
we can. *Moreover, we want you to know we appreciate your business.*	109
Very truly yours	*Ms.* Cicely A. Murgraff	President	xx	119

3c

Practice common reaches

each line twice SS; DS between 2-line groups

Goals:
- ✓ Strike keys quickly.
- ✓ Strike space bar with down-and-in motions.
- ✓ Return with a quick flick of the little finger.

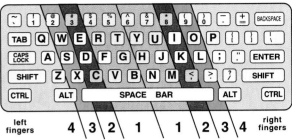

ea
13 ea sea lea seas deal leaf leak lead leas flea keas
as
14 as ask lass ease as asks ask ask sass as alas seas
sa
15 sa sad sane sake sail sale sans safe sad said sand
le
16 le sled lead flee fled ale flea lei dale kale leaf
el
17 el eel eld elf sell self el dell fell elk els jell
ad
18 ad add ads ade jade lad lads fad lead dad fade sad
an
19 an and fan dean elan flan land lane lean sand sane
in
20 in fin inn inks dine sink fine fins kind kine lain

3d

Practice special stroking techniques

each 2-line group twice SS

home row: fingers curved and upright
21 jak lad as lass dad sad lads fad fall la ask ad as
22 asks add jaks dads a alas ads flak adds sad as lad

upward reaches: straighten fingers slightly; return quickly to home position
23 fed die led ail kea lei lea did ale fife silk leak
24 sea lid deal sine desk lie ale like life idea jail

double letters: don't hurry when stroking double letters
25 fee jell less add inn seek fall alee lass keel all
26 dill dell see fell eel less all add kiss seen sell

Formatting Workshop 1

Letters in block format

Use current date; add an appropriate salutation; correct errors; prepare envelopes.
Reference: pages 70-72, 75 (LM pp. S37-S39)

Document 1
Short letter

Miss Vera Grant | 1121 Hunter Avenue | Brooklyn, NY 11214-1124   12

Springtime holds the promise of things to come. That's when the swal-   26
lows come back to Capistrano, the buzzards return to Hinckley, and the   40
ants and spiders set up housekeeping on your back patio.   51

Part of the promise of spring, though, involves telephoning The Garrison   66
and having those little intruders sent scurrying.   76

Make your patio or deck YOUR patio or deck. If it isn't yours now, call   91
The Garrison; and we will take it back for you pronto. Our enclosed   105
brochure has full details.   110

Cordially yours | Ted Estevez | Chief Hunter | xx | Enclosure   121

Document 2
Average-length letter
Use hanging indent for the enumerated items.

Mr. Lance H. Brinks, President | All Grain Shippers, Inc. | 8500 Exeter   14
Street | Duluth, MN 55806-0086   19

This letter serves to notify you of cancellation of the contract between our   35
company and All Grain Shippers to carry our cargo in your ships between   49
Duluth and other ports. Official documents will arrive from our attorneys   64
within a few days.   68

Good and legal cause exists to abnegate this agreement.   80

1. Your ships have delivered late every shipment we have made during the   94
    past four months.   98

2. The cargo bins are unacceptable for carrying grain; damage has   112
    occurred in two shipments.   117

Payment of our balance with your company has been made. Please direct   132
any questions or comments to the attention of our Legal Department.   145

Very truly yours | Grace J. Beebe | President |xx | c Legal Department   158

4 Left Shift, H, T, Period

Skill-Building Warmup

4a

each line twice SS;
DS between 2-line
groups; keep eyes
on copy

home row 1   al as ads lad dad fad jak fall lass asks fads all;
e / i / n 2   ed ik jn in knee end nine line sine lien dies leis
all reaches 3   see a ski; add ink; fed a jak; is an inn; as a lad
easy 4   an dial id is an la lake did el ale fake is land a

4b

Learn left shift and h

each line twice SS; DS
between 2-line groups

Follow the "Standard
procedures for learning new
keyreaches" on page 5 for all
remaining reaches.

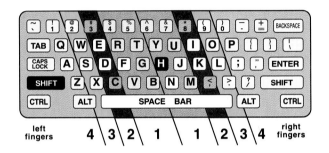

left fingers   4 3 2 1   1 2 3 4   right fingers

Reach *down* with
left little finger;
shift, strike,
release.

Reach to *left* with
right first finger.

left shift

5 J Ja Ja Jan Jan Jane Jana Ken Kass Lee Len Nan Ned
6 and Ken and Lena and Jake and Lida and Nan and Ida
7 Ina Kale; Jill Lask; Nels Insa; Ken Jalk; Lin Nial

h

8 h hj hj he he she she hen aha ash had has hid shed
9 h hj ha hie his half hand hike dash head sash shad
10 aha hi hash heal hill hind lash hash hake dish ash

all reaches learned

11 Nels Kane and Jake Jenn; she asked Hi and Ina Linn
12 Lend Lana and Jed a dish; I fed Lane and Jess Kane
13 I see Jake Kish and Lash Hess; Isla and Helen hike

4c

Practice return

Key the drill once; DS and
repeat. Use fluid, unhurried
movements.

return: return without looking up

14 Nan had a sale;
15 He did see Hal;
16 Lee has a desk;
17 Ina hid a dish;

words

F O R M A T T I N G

Measurement: tables and topic outline

(4 plain sheets)

Time schedule

Assemble materials .... 2'

Timed production .... 25'
(Key problems in order; proofread and correct errors as you work.)

Final check .... 6'
(Proofread and circle any remaining errors. Calculate *g-pram*—total words keyed divided by 25'.)

Document 1
2-column table
Key the table, centering it horizontally and vertically.

Document 2
Topic outline
Key the topic outline; use 3" top margin; add appropriate spacing and capitalization.

Document 3
3-column table
Key the table, centering it horizontally and vertically.

Document 4
If you finish before time is called, repeat Document 1. Alphabetize the entries.

NORTH HOLLYWOOD JUNIOR COLLEGE   6

School Records   9

High Jump	*6 ft. 4.5 in.*	14
Long Jump	*22 ft. 5.0 in.*	19
Triple Jump	*50 ft. 9.1 in.*	24
Discus Throw	*222 ft. 3.7 in.*	30
Javelin Throw	*210 ft. 8.4 in.*	36
Shot-Put	*56 ft. 9.3 in.*	41

THE POWER OF WORDS   4

I.	purpose of words	8
A.	inform	10
B.	convince	13
C.	impress	15
D.	entertain	18
II.	increase word power	23
A.	why	25
1.	to be clearly understood	30
2.	to be specific as required	37
3.	to know/use proper terminology whenever appropriate	48
B.	how	49
1.	listen	52
2.	read	53
III.	learn grammar	57
IV.	learn construction	62
A.	punctuation	65
1.	"read signs"	69
2.	helps with inflection	74
3.	takes the place of facial expression	82
B.	structuring and phrasing	88

NORTH HOLLYWOOD JUNIOR COLLEGE   6

Gifts from Other Countries   12

Country	Coordinator	Total Gifts	
Canada	Wilma E. King	$12,300.35	31
Denmark	H. A. Bjoerma	1,250.68	37
France	Andre V. Tori	150.89	42
Germany	Johann Boehme	700.46	48
Honduras	Hector Garza	1,450.93	54
Italy	Maria A. Toma	5,225.14	60
Japan	Io Maneki	870.90	65
Mexico	Jose H. Ortiz	750.68	70

4d

Learn t and . (period)

each line twice SS; DS
between 2-line groups

Period: Space once after a period that follows an initial or an abbreviation; space twice after a period that ends a sentence. Do not, of course, space after a period at the end of a line.

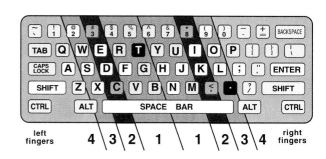

left fingers 4 3 2 1   1 2 3 4 right fingers

Reach *up* with *left first* finger.

Reach *down* with *right third* finger; space twice after . at end of sentence.

t

18 t tf tf aft aft left fit fat fete tiff tie the tin
19 tf at at aft lit hit tide tilt tint sits skit this
20 hat kit let lit ate sit flat tilt thin tale tan at

. (period)

21 .l .l l.l fl. fl. L. L. Neal and J. N. List hiked.
22 Hand J. H. Kass a fan. Jess did. I need an idea.
23 Jane said she has a tan dish; Jae and Lee need it.

all reaches learned

24 I did tell J. K. that Lt. Li had left. He is ill.
25 Lee and Ken left at ten; the jet had left at nine.
26 I see Lila and Ilene at tea. Jae Kane ate at ten.

4e

Key words and phrases

1 Key each line once at an easy, continuous pace, keeping fingers curved and upright as illustrated.
2 Key each line again at a slightly faster pace.

eyes on copy

27 ah an la el ha if is id it aid aha all and did die
28 id end she elf els fit jak ken lei the tie hen sit
29 alas dish disks elan fish flan half halt hand jell
30 kale laid lake land lane leis lend lens than title
31 Ina lies in the sand at ten; she needs a fast tan.
32 Jan asks if I had all the tea that Len said I had.

60a 6'

each line 3 times SS;
DS between 3-line
groups

alphabet 1   Dubuque's next track meet will have prizes given by forty judges.
fig/sym 2   Interest in 1985 climbed $346 (as the rates rose from 7% to 20%).
double letters 3   Ann and Buzz will carry my bookkeeping supplies to Judd's office.
easy 4   The auditor may laugh, but the penalty for chaotic work is rigid.

| 1 | 2 | 3 | 4 | 5 | 6 | 7 | 8 | 9 | 10 | 11 | 12 | 13 |

60b 11'

SKILL BUILDING

Measure skill growth:
rough-draft copy

Key a 3' and a 5'
writing; proofread and
circle errors; determine
gwam on both writings.

A   all letters

	gwam 3'	5'

The Search for Success assumes a more serious aspect when   4 | 2 | 43

we study the factors that measure it. After all, if Success is   8 | 5 | 45

the end of a careful road upon which we have embarked, then we   12 | 7 | 48

certainly should know when we have finally arrived there. How   16 | 10 | 50

can we recognize success? Where will we ultimately find this   20 | 12 | 53

phenomenon we call success?   21 | 13 | 54

How about a fine job and a large apartment for starters? Ad   26 | 15 | 56

a shiny new auto, a lake front home and a boat too. But wait   30 | 18 | 58

a minute. These things show quantity, but not necessarily   34 | 20 | 61

quality. If, for instance a job is truly to identify Success,   38 | 23 | 63

then how much pecking order it should have? How many square   42 | 25 | 66

feet measure a successful office?   45 | 27 | 67

     Success is more readily found when we view our goals in   48 | 29 | 69

terms of personal ideals instead of social achievements.   52 | 31 | 72

Success has no precise measuring stick, so each and everyperson   56 | 34 | 74

has to manufacture one. If we think of success in terms of   60 | 36 | 77

personal satisfaction, term of each of us can recognize and   64 | 39 | 79

enjoy, our search for success can be a success.   67 | 40 | 81

5 ▸ R, Right Shift, C, O

5a

each line twice SS;
DS between 2-line groups; keep eyes on copy

home keys	1	a; ad add al all lad fad jak ask lass fall jak lad
t / h / i / n	2	the hit tin nit then this kith dint tine hint thin
left shift / .	3	I need ink. Li has an idea. Hit it. I see Kate.
all reaches	4	Jeff ate at ten; he left a salad dish in the sink.

5b

Learn r and right shift

each line twice SS; DS between 2-line groups

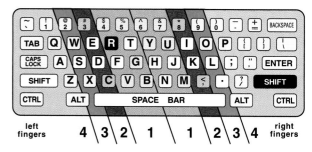

left
fingers 4 3 2 1   1 2 3 4 right
fingers

Reach *up* with *left first* finger.

Reach *down* with *right little* finger; shift, strike, release.

r

5 r rf rf riff riff fir fir rid ire jar air sir lair
6 rf rid ark ran rat are hare art rant tire dirt jar
7 rare dirk ajar lark rain kirk share hart rail tart

right shift

8 D D Dan Dan Dale Ti Sal Ted Ann Ed Alf Ada Sid Fan
9 and Sid and Dina and Allen and Eli and Dean and Ed
10 Ed Dana; Dee Falk; Tina Finn; Sal Alan; Anna Deeds

all reaches learned

11 Jake and Ann hiked in the sand; Asa set the tents.
12 Fred Derr and Rae Tira dined at the Tree Art Fair.
13 Alan asked Dina if Neil and Reed had left at nine.

5c

Practice techniques

each line once, striving for the goals listed below:
Lines 14-15: Smoothly, without pauses.
Lines 16-17: Without looking at hands or keyboard.
Lines 18-20: Without pausing or looking up from the copy.

14 Kent said that half the field is idle in the fall.
15 Lana said she did sail her skiff in the dark lake.

16 All is still as Sarah and I fish here in the rain.
17 I still see a red ash tree that fell in the field.

18 I had a kale salad;
19 Elia ate his steak;
20 and Dina drank tea.

59c 32'

Measurement: reports

(4 plain sheets)

Time schedule

Assemble materials .... 2'
Timed production .... 25'
  (Key problems in order;
  proofread and correct errors
  as you work.)
Final check .... 5'
  (Proofread and circle any
  remaining errors. Calculate
  g-pram—total words divided
  by 25'.)

Document 1
Unbound report

Format and key the unbound
report at the right.

Document 2

Rekey Document 1, omitting
side headings.

THE PROFESSIONAL TOUCH   5

    Although its contents are of ultimate importance, a finished report's   19
looks are of almost equal importance. If it is to achieve the goal for which it   35
was written, every report, whether it serves a business or academic purpose,   50
should be acceptable from every point of view.   60

Citations, for Example   69

    No matter which format is used for citations, a good writer knows   82
they are inserted for the reader's benefit; therefore, anything the writer   97
does to ease their use will be appreciated and will work on the writer's   111
behalf. Standard procedures, such as those stated below, make readers   126
comfortable.   128

    Underline titles of complete publications; use quotation marks   141
with parts of publications. Thus, the name of a magazine is under-   154
lined, but the title of an article within the magazine is placed in   168
quotation marks. Months and certain locational words used in the   181
citations may be abbreviated if necessary (Mayr, 1994, 13).   193

And the Final Report   202

    The final report should have an attractive, easy-to-read look.   214

    The report should meet the criteria for spacing, citations, and binding   223
that have been established for its preparation. "Such criteria are set up by   244
institutional decree, by generally accepted standards, or by subject de-   259
mands" (Chung, 1994, 27). A writer should discover limits within which he   274
or she must write and observe those limits with care.   285

    The final number of copies needed should be determined in advance   297
and made available upon presentation. We are reminded by one author that   313
"preparing too many copies is better than asking readers to double up" (Hull,   328
1994, 93). Also, the report should be presented on time. A lot of good   343
information loses value with age.   350

In Conclusion   355

    Giving the report a professional appearance calls for skill and patience   370
from a writer. First impressions count when preparing reports. Poorly   384
presented materials are not read, or at least not read with an agreeable   399
attitude.   401

REFERENCES   403

Chung, Olin. Reports and Formats. Cedar Rapids: Gar Press, Inc., 1994.   421

Hull, Brenda, and Muriel Myers. Writing Reports and Dissertations. 5th   443
    ed. New York: Benjamin Lakey Press, 1994.   452

Mayr, Polly. "Styles/Formats/Computers." Business Weekly, June 1994.   469

5d

Learn c and o
each line twice SS; DS
between 2-line groups

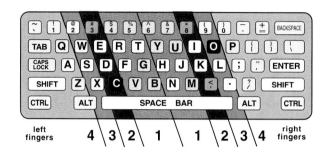

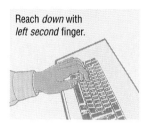

Reach *down* with
left second finger.

Reach *up* with
right third finger.

c
21 c c cd cd cad cad can can tic ice sac cake cat sic
22 clad chic cite cheek clef sick lick kick dice rice
23 call acid hack jack lack lick cask crack clan cane

o
24 o ol ol old old of off odd ode or ore oar soar one
25 ol sol sold told dole do doe lo doll sol solo odor
26 onto door toil lotto soak fort hods foal roan load

all reaches learned
27 Carlo Rand can call Rocco; Cole can call Doc Cost.
28 Trina can ask Dina if Nick Corl has left; Joe did.
29 Case sent Carole a nice skirt; it fits Lorna Rich.

5e

Key words and phrases
each line once DS; maintain
good body position

e / n
30 end need lend lean ken lend fen keen nee dens send
i / t
31 tail lit tiff tilt fit kit lit kits slit silt flit
c / h
32 cash chat chalk hack char hick chic each arch chit
r / o
33 or for lord soar door oar rods roll fork ford oral

all letters learned
34 Jack and Rona did frost nine of the cakes at last.

35 Jo can ice her drink if Tess can find her a flask.

36 Ask Jean to call Fisk at noon; he needs her notes.

59 Report Measurement

59a 6'

each line 3 times SS;
DS between 3-line
groups

Skill-Building Warmup

alphabet 1 Jack Voxall was amazed by the quiet response of the big audience.

fig/sym 2 Our #3865 clocks will cost K & B $12.97 each (less 40% discount).

shift 3 In May, Lynn, Sonia, and Jason left for Italy, Spain, and Turkey.

easy 4 It is the duty of a civic auditor to aid a city to make a profit.

| 1 | 2 | 3 | 4 | 5 | 6 | 7 | 8 | 9 | 10 | 11 | 12 | 13 |

59b 12'

SKILL BUILDING

Measure skill growth:
straight copy

Key a 3' and a 5'
writing; proofread
and circle errors;
determine *gwam*
for both writings.

A all letters

gwam 3' | 5'

At a recent June graduation ceremony, several graduates were | 4 | 2 | 43

heard discussing the fact that they had spent what they thought | 8 | 5 | 46

was a major part of their lives in school classrooms. They esti- | 13 | 8 | 48

mated the amount of time they had been in elementary school, in | 17 | 10 | 51

high school, in college, and in graduate school had to be about | 21 | 13 | 54

nineteen or twenty years. | 23 | 14 | 55

Indeed, two decades is a significant span of time. Even if | 27 | 16 | 57

little additional effort is used seeking education, about a | 31 | 19 | 59

quarter of a person's life will have been spent on learning ac- | 35 | 21 | 62

tivities. Graduation is a time for looking at the past and the | 39 | 24 | 65

present and analyzing how they can be merged to form a future. | 44 | 26 | 67

And thus begins The Search. | 45 | 27 | 68

The Search begins with introspection--attempting to sort out | 50 | 30 | 71

and pinpoint all that has gone before, to identify purpose behind | 54 | 32 | 73

the years of effort and expense, to focus it all on some goal. | 58 | 35 | 76

If encouraged to name the goal, we call it, probably for lack of | 63 | 38 | 78

a more definitive name, Success. We desire to be successful. | 67 | 40 | 81

But what is "success"? | 68 | 41 | 82

gwam 3' | 1 | 2 | 3 | 4 | 5 |
5' | 1 | 2 | 3 |

6 ◆ W, Comma, B, P

6a 8'

each line twice SS;
DS between 2-line
groups; avoid pauses
Note suggested
minutes for practice
shown in heading.

home row 1	a ad as lad las fad sad; jak flask fall jaks salad
n/i/t 2	in tin nit nil its tan din tie ten tine fins stein
c/h/r/o 3	code herd rode cold hock hark roll rock ache chore
all reaches 4	Holt can see Dane at ten; Jill sees Frank at nine.

1 | 2 | 3 | 4 | 5 | 6 | 7 | 8 | 9 | 10

6b 12'

Learn w and , (comma)

each line twice SS; DS
between 2-line groups

Comma: Space once
after a comma.

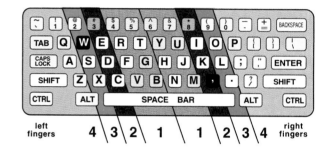

left fingers 4 \ 3 \ 2 \ 1 \ 1 \ 2 \ 3 \ 4 right fingers

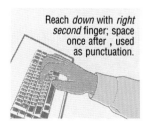

Reach *up* with
left third finger.

Reach *down* with *right
second* finger; space
once after , used
as punctuation.

w

5 w ws ws was was wan wit low win jaw wilt wink wolf

6 ow wow how owl howl owe owed row cow cowl new knew

7 wide sown wild town went jowl wait white down walk

, (comma)

8 k, k, k, irk, ilk, ask, oak, ark, lark, jak, rock,

9 skis, a dock, a fork, a lock, a fee, a tie, a fan,

10 Jan, Lee, Ed, and Dan saw Nan, Kate, Len, and Ted.

all reaches learned

11 Win, Lew, Drew, and Walt will walk to West Willow.

12 Ask Ho, Al, and Jared to read the code; it is new.

13 The window, we think, was closed; we felt no wind.

6c 8'

Improve techniques

each line twice

shift keys: shift; strike key; release both quickly

14 Fiji, Don, Cara, and Ron will see East Creek soon.

15 Kane Losh and Janet Hart will join Nan in Rio Ono.

double letters

16 Renee took a class at noon; call her at Lann Hall.

17 Ed and Anne saw three deer flee across Wood Creek.

FORMATTING

Measurement: letters and memo

Time schedule

Assemble materials .... 2'
Timed production .... 25'
(Key the problems in order; proofread and correct errors as you work.)
Final check .... 6'
(Proofread and circle any remaining errors. Calculate *g-pram*—total words keyed divided by 25'.)

Document 1

Letter in block format

(LM p. S31)

Key this average-length letter in block format; prepare an envelope.

Document 2

Letter in modified block format

(LM p. S33)

Key this average length-letter in modified block format; prepare an envelope.

words

Current date | Mrs. Cluny Baer | 1651 Poplar Street | Erie, PA 16502-5112 | Dear 15
Mrs. Baer 17

Welcome to Erie. I hope that your move from Tulsa has not been overly 31
disruptive and that you are beginning to feel at home here. 43

I apologize for keeping your husband away from home during the past 57
two weeks while he has attended the seminar at our home office. These 71
seminars are very important to us, for we are eager that our representa- 85
tives thoroughly understand our company philosophy, product line, and 99
methods of operation. 104

Enclosed you will find a voucher good for two theater tickets at the Schubert 120
Theater at a time and for a performance of your choice. This is our way of 135
welcoming you to our company family, Mrs. Baer, and of apologizing for 149
spiriting your husband away. 155

Sincerely | J. Dake Hunter | President | xx | Enclosure 164
envelope 178

Current date | Mr. Guy Berger | 544 Duquesne Avenue | Dayton, OH 45431- 13
1334 | Dear Mr. Berger 17

When was the last time you had your roof checked? I don't mean just 31
casting a glance upward at it; I mean really checked. 42

We expect a lot of a roof--protection from heat, wind, and rain in the 56
summer; cold and snow in the winter--and a good roof asks little of us in 71
return. But the elements take a toll on even the best roof, and in time it 86
gives out. 89

That's why we suggest that you have our experts take a look at your roof. 104
For a flat fee of $25, we will come to your home, thoroughly examine your 118
roof to look for potential problems, and prepare a written report for you. 134

Call us today if we can include you on our schedule. 144

Sincerely | Kin-Lo Rigby | Sales Director | xx 152
envelope 166

Document 3
Interoffice memorandum

TO: Eunice A. Bates | **FROM:** Edward Baxter | **DATE:** Current | **SUBJECT:** 13
Car Assignments 17

After the two new representatives in the West Coast District are assigned, we 32
shall need to supply them with automobiles. One vehicle will be assigned to 48
Lynn Brewer, District #3, and the other to Myrle Ortega, District #5. I 62
suggest that we obtain authorizations to buy these two automobiles. 76

Each authorization should cover the purchase price of a light van. The 90
representatives may choose the exact make, color, etc. If a van is not the 106
vehicle of choice, an appropriate substitution may be requested. 119

xx 119

Document 4
Letter in block format

(LM p. S35)

Repeat Document 2, but change "roof" to "chimney" whenever it appears in the letter.

Learn b and p

each line twice; DS between
2-line groups

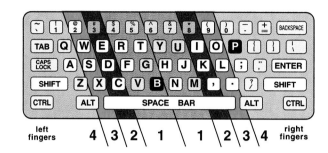

Reach *down* with
left first finger.

Reach *up* with
right little finger.

b

18 b bf bf biff boff bit bid bib bird boa ban bon bow
19 be rib fib sob dob cob bob crib lab slab fobs blob
20 born oboe blab bribe able bode belt bath bide both

p

21 p p; p; pa pa; pal pal pan pad par pen pep pap per
22 pa pa; lap lap; nap nap; hep ape spa asp leap clap
23 span park paper pelt tips soap pane pops rope ripe

all reaches learned

24 Barb and Bob wrapped a pepper in paper and ribbon.
25 Rip, Joann, and Dick were all closer to the flash.
26 Bo will be pleased to see Japan; he works in Oslo.

Determine gross words a minute

1 Key line 27 for 30". Try to finish the line as time is called (12 *gwam*).

2 Key line 28 for 1'. Try to finish the line as time is called (10 *gwam*).

3 Repeat for paired lines 29-34.

all letters learned

27 Dick owns a dock at this lake.
28 Dick owns a dock at this lake; he paid Ken for it.
29 Jane also kept a pair of owls.
30 Jane also kept a pair of owls, a hen, and a snake.
31 I blend the cocoa in the bowl.
32 I blend the cocoa in the bowl when I work for Leo.
33 Blair soaks a bit of the corn.
34 Blair soaks a bit of the corn, as he did in Japan.

| 1 | 2 | 3 | 4 | 5 | 6 | 7 | 8 | 9 | 10 |

To determine gross words a minute:

1 Note the figure beneath your last completed line (6 words for each odd-numbered sentence and 10 words for each even-numbered sentence).

2 For a partial line, note the figure beneath the last word keyed.

3 Add these two figures. The total is gross words a minute (*gwam*) for a 1' writing. (To figure *gwam* for a 30" writing, multiply the total by 2.)

13
Measurement

Measurement goals:
1 To demonstrate basic skill on average difficulty paragraphs in straight, rough-draft, and statistical copy.
2 To demonstrate ability to key letters, tables, reports, and outlines in proper format from semiarranged copy according to directions.

Formatting guides:
1 Default margins or a 65-space line.
2 Single-space drills; double-space paragraphs.
3 Indentions: 5-space ¶ indentions.

58a   6'

Skill-building warmup

each line 3 times SS;
DS between 3-line
groups

alphabet 1 Jayne promised to bring the portable vacuum for next week's quiz.
figures 2 Our main store is at 6304 Grand; others, at 725 Mayo and 198 Rio.
1st fingers 3 After lunch, Brent taught us to try to put the gun by the target.
easy 4 He may make a profit on corn, yams, and hay if he works the land.

| 1 | 2 | 3 | 4 | 5 | 6 | 7 | 8 | 9 | 10 | 11 | 12 | 13 |

58b   11'

SKILL BUILDING

Measure skill growth: statistical copy

Key a 3' and a 5' writing;
circle errors; determine
gwam.

A all letters/figures   *gwam* 3'   5'

Now and then the operation of some company deserves a closer   4   2 41
look by investors. For example, Zerotech Limited, the food, oil,   8   5 44
and chemical company, says in its monthly letter that it will be   13   8 46
raising its second-quarter dividend to 85 cents a share, up from   17 10 49
79 3/4 cents a share, and that a dividend will be paid July 12.   21 13 51

This fine old area firm is erecting an enviable history of   25 15 54
dividend payment, but its last hike in outlays came back in 1987,   30 18 56
when it said a share could go above 65 cents. Zerotech has, how-   34 21 59
ever, never failed to pay a dividend since it was founded in   38 23 61
1937. The recent increase extends the annual amount paid to   42 25 64
$5.40 a share.   43 26 65

In this monthly letter, the firm also cited its earnings for   47 28 67
the second quarter and for the first half of this year. The net   52 31 70
revenue for the second quarter was a record $1.9 billion, up 24.2   56 34 72
percent from a typical period just a year ago. Zerotech has its   61 36 75
main company offices at 9987 Nicholas Drive in Albany.   64 38 77

gwam 3' | 1 | 2 | 3 | 4 | 5 |
5' | 1 | 2 | 3 |

7 Review

7a 8'

each line twice SS;
DS between 2-line
groups; begin new
lines promptly

home row 1   fa la la; a sad lad; jaks fall; a lass had a salad
1st row 2   Ann Bascan and Cabal Naban nabbed a cab in Canada.
3d row 3   Rip went to a water show with either Pippa or Pia.
all letters 4   Dick will see Job at nine if Rach sees Pat at one.

◄   1 | 2 | 3 | 4 | 5 | 6 | 7 | 8 | 9 | 10   ►

7b 14'

Check keyreach technique

lines 5-13 SS as shown; DS
between 3-line groups

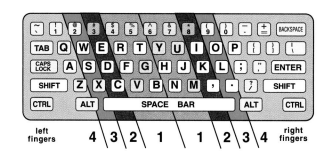

left fingers   4 3 2 1   1 2 3 4   right fingers

concentrate on words

5   a an pan so sot la lap ah aha do doe el elf to tot
6   bow bowl pin pint for fork forks hen hens jak jaks
7   chap chaps flak flake flakes prow prowl work works

concentrate on phrases

8   is in a|as it is|or if|as a|is on a|to do it|is so
9   is for|did it|is the|we did a|and so|to see|or not
10   as for the|as for the|and to the|to see it|and did

concentrate on words and phrases

11   Jess ate all of the peas in the salad in the bowl.
12   I hid the ace in a jar as a joke; I do not see it.
13   As far as I know, he did not read all of the book.

| 1 | 2 | 3 | 4 | 5 | 6 | 7 | 8 | 9 | 10 |

How to set a goal: Use this formula to determine writing time to reach a goal:

$$\frac{\text{words in line being keyed}}{\text{your } gwam \text{ goal}} \times 60" = \text{seconds to key writing}$$

Example: $\frac{10 \text{ words}}{15 \ gwam} \times 60" = 40"$

DALE E. BROWN
404 San Andres Avenue, NW
Albuquerque, New Mexico 97110-1170
(505) 555-0550

Career Objective

Eager to bring education and sales training experience in advertising/retailing to a management trainee position with potential for advancement.

Education

Santa Fe Community College, Santa Fe, New Mexico.
A.S. Degree in Business Management June 19--. Major area of study in advertising with a specialty in art; 3.25 GPA.

Courses relevant to an advertising/retailing position include Retail Marketing I and II, Work Study I and II, behavioral psychology, Marketing Art I and II, economics, information systems.

Albuquerque Senior High School graduate, 1990.

Honors and Activities

President of Marketing Careers Club, current year.
Phi Beta Lambda business organization, 1991-1993.
Summer study (6 weeks) with economic seminar group, sponsored by
   Albuquerque Junior Chamber of Commerce.
National Honor Society in high school.

Experience

Advertising artist. Rendall's, Santa Fe, New Mexico. Assisted in
   advertising layout and design for two major campaigns. January
   1993 to present.

Work-study.
   La Paloma Travel Guides, Santa Fe; advertising campaign; winter
      1992.

   Simmons Sporting Goods, Albuquerque; sales; fall 1992.

   El Senor Men's Shop, Albuquerque; assisted in buying, display,
      and sales; winter 1991.

   Yordi's Appliances, Albuquerque; customer service; fall 1991.

References

Will be furnished upon request.

7c 12'

Check spacing/shifting technique

each set of lines twice SS; DS between 3-line groups

▼ Space once after a period following an abbreviation.

spacing

14 ad la as in if it lo no of oh he or so ok pi be we
15 an ace ads ale aha a fit oil a jak nor a bit a pew
16 ice ades born is fake to jail than it and the cows

spacing/shifting   ▼   ▼

17 Ask Jed. Dr. Han left at ten; Dr. Crowe, at nine.
18 I asked Jin if she had ice in a bowl; it can help.
19 Freda, not Jack, went to Spain. Joan likes Spain.

| 1 | 2 | 3 | 4 | 5 | 6 | 7 | 8 | 9 | 10 |

7d 16'

Build staying power

1 Key line 20.
2 DS; key lines 20 and 21 SS; do not pause at the end of line 20.
3 DS; key lines 20, 21, and 22 SS. Key fluidly; eyes on copy.
4 Key all 4 lines SS. Work for steady, unhurried key flow.
5 Take two 1' writings on all 4 lines. Calculate *gwam*.
Goal: at least 10 *gwam*

20 Jake held a bit of cocoa and an apricot for Diane.
21 Jan is to chant in the still air in an idle field.
22 Dick and I fish for cod on the docks at Fish Lake.
23 Kent still held the dish and the cork in his hand.

| 1 | 2 | 3 | 4 | 5 | 6 | 7 | 8 | 9 | 10 |

*on...*Netiquette

NEWS

With the growth of the Internet, it is becoming increasingly important for people to be aware of good online etiquette. Netiquette (Net etiquette) is the unwritten code of behavior for the Net, news groups, chat rooms, the World Wide Web, e-mail, and other networks. The basic premise of netiquette is to treat people with courtesy and consideration. Apply these basic rules of netiquette:

Stick to the subject, whether chatting in a theme room, posting to a news group or answering e-mail. Posting an irrelevant message is considered rude and exposes you to being "flamed" or electronically abused by others. Also, don't send irrelevant e-mail messages; people don't have time for frivolous mail.

Use shortcuts with care. Emoticons such as :- (sad, :-) happy, ;-) a wink for a joke or sarcasm are sometimes fun to use. Some people believe, however, emoticons are becoming obsolete. Acronyms such as IMO (in my opinion) are effective only if both parties know the meaning.

Write clearly and concisely. State exactly what you mean to reduce time and need for clarification. And, remember to use proper grammar. Avoid using ALL CAPS for emphasis, particularly in a chat room or news group; it is considered SHOUTING.

As the Internet evolves so will its protocols, including netiquette. So stay "plugged in."

57 ▸ Resume

57a 6'

each line 3 times SS;
DS between
3-line groups

alphabet 1 Our unexpected freezing weather quickly killed Jo's mauve shrubs.

figures 2 Paul has moved from 195 East 26th Street to 730 West 48th Street.

double letters 3 Betty fooled Annabell by hitting a ball across the narrow valley.

easy 4 I fish for a quantity of smelt and may wish for aid to land them.

◄ | 1 | 2 | 3 | 4 | 5 | 6 | 7 | 8 | 9 | 10 | 11 | 12 | 13 | ►

57b 14'

COMMUNICATION

Compose at the keyboard

2" top margin
The questions at the right are similar to those sometimes asked in job interviews. Select ten of the questions and answer each of them in a brief SS paragraph. Use complete sentences in answering, as you might if you were being interviewed.

1. Why do you want this particular job?

2. What is the hardest work you have ever done?

3. Why did you leave your last position?

4. How would you feel about an employee who was late or absent once or twice a month?

5. Do you think you would rather work alone or with a group?

6. How do you think group leadership is established?

7. What is the one hobby you enjoy most?

8. What salary do you expect to earn?

9. Describe the "perfect boss."

10. Professionally, where do you plan to be ten years from now?

11. What are your future academic plans?

12. What nonacademic book have you recently read?

57c 30'

FORMATTING

A resume

1" top and side margins
1 Read "Preparing a resume" at the right.
2 Study and key the resume on page 130.

Preparing a resume

A resume is used by a job applicant to present her or his qualifications to a prospective employer. The purpose of sending a resume is to obtain a job interview. Note the following guidelines:

1 Use top, side, and bottom margins that are nearly equal; confine the resume to one page—two at most.

2 Provide headings (centered or flush left) for the information listed.

3 Emphasize important information with capitals, bold type, underlines, etc.

4 Use specific action words (such as *coordinated, increased, organized, prepared*); maintain parallel construction (use phrases or complete sentences, not both).

5 Space evenly within and between sections of the resume.

8 ▸ G, Question Mark, X, U

8a   8'

each line twice SS;
DS between 2-line
groups; eyes on copy

all letters 1 We often can take the older jet to Paris and back.
w/b 2 As the wind blew, Bob Webber saw the window break.
p/, 3 Pat, Pippa, or Cap has prepared the proper papers.
all reaches 4 Bo, Jose, and Will fed Lin; Jack had not paid her.

◀ 1 | 2 | 3 | 4 | 5 | 6 | 7 | 8 | 9 | 10 ▶

8b   6'

Reach for new goals

two 30" writings on each line
Goal: complete each line—
12 *gwam*

5 Blake owns a pen for the foal.
6 Jan lent the bowl to the pros.
7 He fit the panel to the shelf.
8 This rock is half of the pair.
9 I held the title for the land.

| 1 | 2 | 3 | 4 | 5 | 6 |

8c   12'

Learn g and ?

each line twice SS; DS
between 2-line groups; eyes
on copy

Question mark: The
question mark is usually
followed by two spaces.

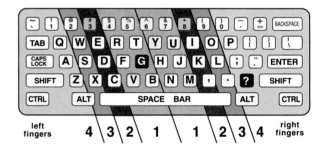

left
fingers   4 \ 3 \ 2 \ 1 \   / 1 / 2 / 3 / 4   right
fingers

Reach to *right* with
left first finger.

Left shift; reach *down*
with *right little* finger;
space twice
after **?** at end
of sentence.

g
10 g g gf gaff gag grog fog frog drag cog dig fig gig
11 gf go gall flag gels slag gala gale glad glee gals
12 golf flog gorge glen high logs gore ogle page grow

?
13 ? ?; ?; ? ? Who? When? Where? Who is? Who was?
14 Who is here? Was it he? Was it she? Did she go?
15 Did Geena? Did he? What is that? Was Jose here?

all reaches learned
16 Has Ginger lost her job? Was her April bill here?
17 Phil did not want the boats to get here this soon.
18 Loris Shin has been ill; Frank, a doctor, saw her.

Return address 404 San Andres Avenue, NW
Albuquerque, NM 97110-1170
April 13, 19--
QS

Mr. Michael S. Brewer
Personnel Manager
Hunter's Department Store
3500 Santa Clara Avenue, SE
Albuquerque, NM 97196-1769
DS

Dear Mr. Brewer
DS

Are you looking for a creative and enthusiastic new employee to join the staff of Hunter's Department Store? If so, please consider my application for employment with you.

I will graduate in June from Santa Fe Community College with an associate of science degree in business management. My goal is to obtain a position as a marketing trainee in a progressive and forward-looking company such as yours. Dr. Ken Davis, professor of marketing, suggested that I contact you.

As you will see from my enclosed resume, advertising is my major area of academic study, with a specialty in art. You will be interested, I know, in noting that my involvement with a work-study program allowed me to gain marketing experience with four diverse retail stores. Also, part of one year was spent studying with an economic seminar group in Albuquerque.

After you have had a chance to read my resume, may I have an opportunity to discuss my qualifications? You may reach me at 555-0550 or at the address shown above.
DS

Sincerely yours
QS

Dale E. Brown
DS

Enclosure

8d 12'

Learn x and u
each line twice SS; DS
between 2-line groups

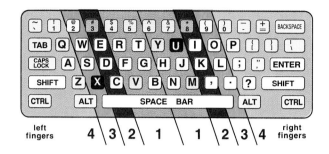

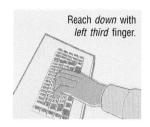

Reach *down* with
left third finger.

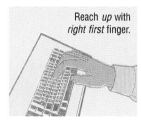

Reach *up* with
right first finger.

x

19 x x xs xs ox ox lox sox fox box ex hex lax hex fax
20 sx six sax sox ax fix cox wax hex box pox sex text
21 flax next flex axel pixel exit oxen taxi axis next

u

22 u uj uj jug jut just dust dud due sue use due duel
23 uj us cud but bun out sun nut gun hut hue put fuel
24 dual laud dusk suds fuss full tuna tutus duds full

all reaches learned

25 Paige Power liked the book; Josh can read it next.
26 Next we picked a bag for Jan; then she, Jan, left.
27 Is her June account due? Has Lou ruined her unit?

8e 12'

Build staying power
1 Key Paragraph 1 (¶1)
twice.
2 DS and key ¶2 twice.
3 Work to avoid pauses, not
for speed.

Optional
1 Take a 1' writing on each ¶.
2 Find *gwam* using the dots
and figures above the lines (a
dot equals 2 words).
Goal: 12 *gwam*

If you are using the
Alphanumeric software,
complete this exercise in the
open screen using the timing
option.

E all letters learned

```
                     .            4              .              8            .
How a finished job will look often depends on how
          12              .              16                    .                20
we feel about our work as we do it.  Attitude has
                     .            24              .              28            .
a definite effect on the end result of work we do.

                     .            4              .              8            .
When we are eager to begin a job, we relax and do
          12              .              16                    .                20
better work than if we start the job with an idea
                     .            24              .              28            .
that there is just nothing we can do to escape it.
```

56c 10'

F O R M A T T I N G

Topical outline

1.5" top margin; key the topical outline.

FINDING THE JOB   4

I.   ANALYZE THE JOB MARKET   9
    A. *Locate Employment Opportunities*   16
    1. A. Read Newspapers and Professional Journals   26
      a. 1. Check help wanted ads   31
      b. 2. Watch for news items   36
    2. B. Ask Knowledgeable Friends and Associates   45
    3. C. Use School Placement Services   52
    4. D. Consider Commercial Placement Services   60
    B. *Research Specific Companies*   67
II. MAKE APPLICATION   71

                              Human Resources
    A. Acquire Information from ~~Personnel Office~~, if Necessary   83
    B. Send Letter and Resume to Appropriate Supervisor   93

III. INTERVIEW FOR THE POSITION   100

    A. Prepare for Interview *Investigate the*   105
      1. ~~Learn about~~ position and company *. the*   114
      2. Know job requirements; have salary range in mind   125
      3. Anticipate questions/prepare answers   133
    B. Dress Appropriately   138
      1. Wear conservative clothing   144
      2. Use accessories sparingly; groom neatly   153
    C. Participate Intelligently   159
      1. Arrive early   162
      2. Have pen, small note pad, extra resume available   173
      3. Answer questions briefly but fully   180
      Listen actively; 4. Ask questions that show your interest and potential   195
      5. Observe interviewer's body language   203

56d 22'

F O R M A T T I N G

Personal/business letters

Document 1

1 Read "Personal/business letters" and "Letter of application" at the right.
2 Key the personal/business letter on page 128 in modified block format; use plain sheet.

Document 2

1 Compose a letter of application that might work well for you. Use as many actual facts as you can. Key in format of your choosing.
2 Edit the first draft; revise as necessary.

Personal/business letters

Personal letters of a business nature may be keyed on plain stationery or personal letterhead. If plain stationery is used, the letter must include the sender's return address. Personal business letters should never be prepared on a company's letterhead stationery.

Personal business letters also contain the other regular parts of a business letter. Either block or modified block format may be used.

Letter of application

A letter of application must accompany a resume. It is formatted as a personal/business letter. The purposes of the letter are to attract attention to the resume and to obtain an interview. Follow these guides:

1 Keep the letter error free. It should appear to have been written especially for the recipient.
2 Address the letter to a specific person.
3 Avoid overuse of *I* and *me*.
4 Keep it brief.
5 Stimulate the reader's interest in your resume; refer indirectly to it in the letter.
6 Indicate the position for which you are applying if you are pursuing a specific job.
7 Mention how you learned of the opening. Mentioning a name always helps, but first have permission to do so.
8 Ask for an interview.

9 ◆ Q, M, V, Apostrophe

9a 8'

lines 1 and 2 twice SS; DS between 2-line groups; try to key lines 3 and 4 in 40" (15 *gwam*), or set your own goal

Skill-Building Warmup

all letters 1 Lex gripes about cold weather; Fred is not joking.
space bar 2 Is it Di, Jo, or Al? Ask Lt. Coe, Bill; he knows.
easy 3 I did rush a bushel of cut corn to the sick ducks.
easy 4 He is to go to the Tudor Isle of England on a bus.

| 1 | 2 | 3 | 4 | 5 | 6 | 7 | 8 | 9 | 10 |

9b 12'

Learn q and m

each line twice SS; DS between 2-line groups

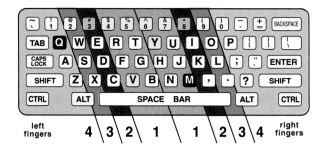

left fingers 4 3 2 1 1 2 3 4 right fingers

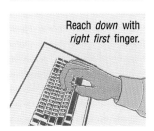

Reach *up* with *left little* finger.

Reach *down* with *right first* finger.

q
5 q qa qa quad quad quaff quant queen quo quit quick
6 qa qu qa quo quit quod quid quip quads quote quiet
7 quite quilts quart quill quakes quail quack quaint

m
8 m mj mj jam man malt mar mar maw me mew men hem me
9 m mj ma am make male mane melt meat mist amen lame
10 malt meld hemp mimic tomb foam rams mama mire mind

all reaches learned
11 Quin had some quiet qualms about taming a macaque.
12 Jake Coxe had questions about a new floor program.
13 Max was quick to join the big reception for Lidia.

9c 8'

Practice downward reaches

each line twice; repeat lines where you sensed a loss of continuity

x
14 Max Exan, their expert, next exposed six wax oxen.
c
15 Chuck can check their inaccurate accident account.
b
16 Robb won; he lobbed the basketball behind Barbara.
m
17 Emma hummed as she aimed her small camera at Mame.
n
18 Ann is not running in the Ninth Annual Nantes Run.

12
Employment Documents

Learning goals:
1 To format a transmittal letter.
2 To format a personal resume.
3 To review topical outlines.
4 To review modified block letter format.

Formatting guides:
1 Default margins or a 65-space line.
2 Single-space drills; double-space paragraphs.
3 Indentions: 5-space ¶ indent.

56a 6'

Skill-building warmup

each line 3 times SS;
DS between 3-line
groups; work for error-free lines

alphabet 1 Pam Beck recognized the excellent quality of this silver jewelry.

figures 2 On May 28, 15 men and 30 women drove 476 miles to Ohio in 9 vans.

3d row 3 We were there when Terrie tried on her pretty new oyster sweater.

easy 4 Due to the rigor of the quake, the city may dismantle the chapel.

| 1 | 2 | 3 | 4 | 5 | 6 | 7 | 8 | 9 | 10 | 11 | 12 | 13 |

56b 12'

SKILL BUILDING

Check straight copy

Take three 3' writings;
compute *gwam* and
number of errors.

  all letters

gwam 3'

Many of us are always in a hurry. We scramble about, trying	4 / 51
quickly and desperately to do dozens of things, but we never have	8 / 56
an adequate amount of time, it seems, to finish any one of them.	13 / 60
As a result, emergencies, not reason, directly affect many of our	17 / 65
decisions; and too many tasks, not done correctly the first time,	22 / 69
keep reappearing in our schedules. On the other hand, though, we	26 / 74
can always look as examples to those capable people who somehow	30 / 78
manage to get jobs done in the same amount of time available to	35 / 82
us. They pace themselves, budget time, and set priorities. They	39 / 86
rarely put off until tomorrow what they can do today, and when	43 / 91
they are done, they are, believe it or not, done. Remarkable!	47 / 95

gwam 3' | 1 | 2 | 3 | 4 | 5 |

9d 12'

Learn v and ' (apostrophe)

each line twice SS (slowly, then faster); DS between 2-line groups

Apostrophe: The apostrophe shows (1) omission (as Rob't for Robert or it's for it is) or (2) possession when used with nouns (as Joe's hat).

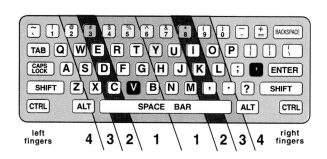

Reach *down* with *left first* finger.

Reach to ' with *right little* finger.

v
19 v vf vf vie vie via via vim vat vow vile vale vote
20 vf vf ave vet ova eve vie dive five live have lave
21 cove dove over aver vivas hive volt five java jive

' (apostrophe)
22 '; '; it's it's Rod's; it's Bo's hat; we'll do it.
23 We don't know if it's Lee's pen or Norma's pencil.
24 It's ten o'clock; I won't tell him that he's late.

all reaches learned
25 It's Viv's turn to drive Iva's van to Ava's house.
26 Qua, not Vi, took the jet; so did Cal. Didn't he?
27 Wasn't Fae Baxter a judge at the post garden show?

9e 10'

Practice returning and spacing

each group once as shown; DS and repeat as time permits

return: reach for the enter key without pausing or looking up
28 Keep fingers in home position;
29 reach little finger to return;
30 flick; return to home position
31 at once. Do not glance up; do
32 not break the flow of the work.

space bar: do not pause before or after striking the space bar
33 we or be up ah go ox it an la ok if ad is he as no
34 When did R. J. Coe go? Lt. Bem ordered her to go.

| 1 | 2 | 3 | 4 | 5 | 6 | 7 | 8 | 9 | 10 |

55c 34'

F O R M A T T I N G

Measurement: tables

(3 plain sheets)

Time schedule:

Assembling materials .... 3'
Timed production .... 25'
Final check; proofread;
   compute *g-pram* .... 6'

$g\text{-}pram = \dfrac{\text{total words keyed}}{\text{time (25')}}$

Directions:

Center each table horizontally and vertically; determine intercolumn spacing.

Document 1

SINGLE-FAMILY DWELLINGS		5
1990 Median Prices		9

		words
Baltimore	$105,900	13
Cleveland	80,600	16
Detroit	76,700	19
Honolulu	325,000	22
Las Vegas	93,000	26
Los Angeles	212,000	30
Milwaukee	84,400	33
Phoenix	84,000	36
Seattle	142,000	39
_____		42
Source: U. S. Realty Group		48

Document 2

AVON SCHOOL OF CULINARY ARTS 6

Metric Conversions 10

Metric Measure	Liquid Measure	words
1 milliliter	.2 teaspoon	26
5 milliliters	1.0 teaspoon	32
34 milliliters	1.0 tablespoon	38
100 milliliters	3.4 fluid ounces	44
240 milliliters	1.0 cup	49
1 liter	34.0 fluid ounces	54
1 liter	4.2 cups	58
1 liter	2.1 pints	61

Document 3

COUNTRIES SELDOM IN THE NEWS 6

World's Smallest Nations 11

Country	Capital	Location	words
Andorra	Andorra la Vella	Europe	27
Djibouti	Djibouti	Africa	32
Kiribati	Tarawa	Mid Pacific	38
Nauru	Yaren	W Pacific	42
San Marino	San Marino	Europe	49
Tonga	Nuku'alofa	S Pacific	53
Tuvalu	Funafuti	SW Pacific	59

10 ▸ Z, Y, Quotation Mark

10a   8'

each line twice SS;
DS between 2-line
groups; line 4 as 40"
writings (15 *gwam*)
Goal: 15 *gwam*

all letters 1	Quill owed those back taxes after moving to Japan.
spacing 2	Didn't Vi, Sue, and Paul go? Someone did; I know.
q/v/m 3	Marv was quite quick to remove that mauve lacquer.
easy 4	Lana is a neighbor; she owns a lake and an island.

1 | 2 | 3 | 4 | 5 | 6 | 7 | 8 | 9 | 10

10b   12'

Learn z and y

each line twice SS; DS
between 2-line groups

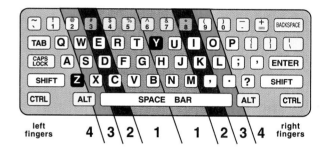

left fingers 4 3 2 1   1 2 3 4 right fingers

Reach *down* with
left little finger.

z
5 za za zap zap zing zig zag zoo zed zip zap zig zed
6 doze zeal zero haze jazz zone zinc zing size ozone
7 ooze maze doze zoom zarf zebus daze gaze faze adze

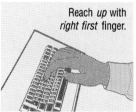

Reach *up* with
right first finger.

y
8 y yj yj jay jay hay hay lay nay say days eyes ayes
9 yj ye yet yen yes cry dry you rye sty your fry wry
10 ye yen bye yea coy yew dye yaw lye yap yak yon any

all reaches learned
11 Did you say Liz saw any yaks or zebus at your zoo?
12 Relax; Jake wouldn't acquire any favorable rights.
13 Has Mazie departed? Tex, Lu, and I will go alone.

10c   10'

Practice specific
keyreaches

each line twice SS; DS
between 2-line groups;
repeat troublesome lines

g
14 Is Gregg urging Gage to ship eggs to Ragged Gorge?
x
15 Dixi expects Bix to fix her tax bill on the sixth.
u
16 It is unusual to house unused units in the bunker.
b
17 Barb Robbes is the barber who bobbed her own hair.
p
18 Pepe prepared a pepper salad for a special supper.

55 ◆ Measurement

55a   6'

each line 2 times
SS; DS between 2-
line groups; 1'
writings
on line 4 (work
for accuracy)

alphabet 1 Jimmy Bond quickly realized we could fix the poor girl's vehicle.

figures 2 On April 12, send me Files 34 and 76; my official number is 5890.

adjacent reaches 3 Last autumn, Guy and Isadore loitered here as they walked to Rio.

easy 4 Eight neighbor girls and I wish to work in the cornfield by dusk.

| 1 | 2 | 3 | 4 | 5 | 6 | 7 | 8 | 9 | 10 | 11 | 12 | 13 |

55b   10'

SKILL BUILDING

Measure straight-copy skill

Take one 3' and
one 5' writing;
determine *gwam*;
proofread and
circle errors.

 A all letters

| | gwam 3' | 5' |

Whether any company can succeed depends on how well it fits `4 | 2 | 44`
into the economic system. Success rests on certain key factors `8 | 5 | 47`
that are put in line by a management team that has set goals for `13 | 8 | 49`
the company and has enough good judgment to recognize how best to `17 | 10 | 52`
reach those goals. Because of competition, only the best orga- `21 | 13 | 55`
nized companies get to the top. `23 | 14 | 56`

A commercial enterprise is formed for a specific purpose; `27 | 16 | 58`
that purpose is usually to equip others, or consumers, with `31 | 19 | 61`
whatever they cannot equip themselves. Unless there is only one `36 | 21 | 63`
provider, a consumer will search for a company that returns the `40 | 24 | 66`
most value in terms of price; and a relationship with such a com- `44 | 27 | 68`
pany, once set up, can endure for many years. `47 | 28 | 70`

Thus our system assures that the businesses that manage to `51 | 31 | 73`
survive are those that have been able to combine successfully an `56 | 33 | 75`
excellent product with a low price and the best service--all in a `60 | 36 | 78`
place that is convenient for the buyers. With no intrusion from `64 | 39 | 80`
outside forces, the buyer and the seller benefit both themselves `69 | 41 | 83`
and each other. `70 | 42 | 84`

| gwam 3' | | 1 | | 2 | | 3 | | 4 | | 5 | |
| 5' | | | 1 | | | 2 | | | 3 | | |

10d   8'

Learn " (quotation mark)

each line once; repeat lines 21-24

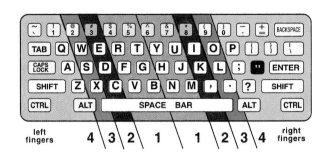

left fingers 4 \ 3 \ 2 \ 1 \ 1 \ 2 \ 3 \ 4 right fingers

Shift; then reach to " with *right little* finger.

" (quotation mark)

19 "; "; " " "lingo" "bugs" "tennies" I like "malts."

20 "I am not," she said, "going." I just said, "Oh?"

all letters learned

21 The expression, "I give you my word," or as it is

22 put quite often, "Take my word for it," is just a

23 way I say, "I prize my name; it clearly stands in

24 back of my words." I offer "honor" as collateral.

10e   12'

Build staying power

1 Key both ¶s once SS line for line; DS between ¶s. Work for smooth, continuous stroking (not speed) without looking up, especially at the ends of lines.

2 Take two 1' writings on each ¶; determine *gwam*.

Suggested goal: 15 *gwam*

OS

Users of Alphanumeric software should complete this exercise in the open screen using the timing option.

E   all letters

           .   4   .   8
All of us work for progress, but it is not always
      12   .   16   .   20
easy to analyze "progress." We work hard for it;
       .   24   .   28
but, in spite of some really good efforts, we may
     32   .   36   .   40
fail to receive just exactly the response we want.

       .   4   .   8
When this happens, as it does to all of us, it is
     12   .   16   .   20
time to cease whatever we are doing, have a quiet
       .   24   .   28
talk with ourselves, and face up to the questions
     32   .   36   .   40
about our limited progress. How can we do better?

F O R M A T T I N G

Tables

Document 1
Long table
Calculate appropriate horizontal and vertical placement and key this wide, long table. Margins will need adjustment.
Reference: page 114.

words

OFFICIAL BIRDS AND FLOWERS			5
For Selected States			9
State	Official Bird	Official Flower	24
Alaska	willow ptarmigan	forget-me-not	31
Arkansas	mockingbird	apple blossom	38
California	California valley quail	golden poppy	48
Connecticut	American robin	mountain laurel	56
Delaware	blue hen chicken	peach blossom	64
Georgia	brown thrasher	Cherokee rose	72
Idaho	mountain bluebird	syringa	78
Illinois	cardinal	native violet	84
Louisiana	eastern brown pelican	magnolia	93
Maryland	Baltimore oriole	black-eyed Susan	101
Massachusetts	chickadee	mayflower	108
Nebraska	western meadowlark	goldenrod	116
New Jersey	eastern goldfinch	purple violet	124
New Mexico	roadrunner	yucca	130
North Carolina	cardinal	dogwood	136
Pennsylvania	ruffed grouse	mountain laurel	145
Rhode Island	Rhode Island red chicken	violet	154
South Dakota	ringnecked pheasant	pasque flower	163
Tennessee	mockingbird	iris	168
Texas	mockingbird	bluebonnet	174
Washington	goldfinch	western rhododendron	183
Wyoming	meadowlark	Indian paintbrush	190

Document 2
Table with source note
1 Format and key the table. Align the colons in Column 3.
2 To place the source note, DS after the last line of the table, key an underline of about 1.5"; then DS and key the source note.

SQUARE ISLAND MARINA RACE RESULTS			7
Official Placements and Times			13
Contestant Boat	Place	Off. Time	25
Challenger A	Fourth	7:18:02	31
Dayswift	Sixth	8:22:32	36
Furious	First	5:31:56	40
Harlen's Dream	Ninth	15:20:25	46
Justabote	Fifth	7:19:03	51
Red Menace	Tenth	15:34:09	56
Rollin' Stone	Second	7:56:44	62
Stalwart	Eighth	9:26:01	67
Swingalong	Third	7:33:48	72

DS
_____   75
DS
Source: New York Maritime Association   82

2
Keyboarding Mastery

Learning goals:
1 To acheive smoother stroking.
2 To improve use of service keys.
3 To develop a relaxed, confident attitude.
4 To increase stroking speed to at least 15 *gwam*.

Formatting guides:
1 Default margins or 50-space line.
2 Single-space drills; double-space between exercises.

11a   8'

Skill-building warmup

each line twice SS (slowly, then faster); DS between 2-line groups

alphabet	1	Max Jewel picked up five history quizzes to begin.
" (quote)	2	Can you spell "chaos," "bias," "bye," and "their"?
y	3	Ty Clay may envy you for any zany plays you write.
easy	4	She kept the fox, owls, and fowl down by the lake.

| 1 | 2 | 3 | 4 | 5 | 6 | 7 | 8 | 9 | 10 |

11b   8'

Improve keying techniques

each line once

first row: keep hand movement to a minimum; pull fingers under

5 Can my cook, Mrs. Zackman, carve the big ox roast?
6 Did Cam, the cabby, have extra puzzles? Yes, one.

home row: use fingertips; keep fingers curved

7 Jack was sad; he had just lost his gold golf ball.
8 Sal was glad she had a flashlight; Al was as glad.

third row: straighten fingers slightly; do not move hands forward

9 Did Troy write to Terry Reppe? Did he quote Ruth?
10 Powers quit their outfit to try out for our troop.

| 1 | 2 | 3 | 4 | 5 | 6 | 7 | 8 | 9 | 10 |

11c   8'

Practice newer keyreaches

1 Key each line once; checkmark any line that you do not key fluently.
2 Repeat each checked line. Work for smoothness, not for speed.

y
11 Why did you not play any really happy songs today?
'
12 I'll see if Lenny can't use Ray's book; it's here.
z
13 Liz Zahl saw Zoe feed the zebra in an Arizona zoo.
m
14 A drummer drummed for a moment, and Mimi came out.
v
15 Have Vivian, Eva, or Vi visited Vista Valley Farm?
q
16 Did Enrique quietly but quickly quell the quarrel?

Document 2

Center the table vertically and horizontally. Block and underline column heads. Remember to set the decimal tab after keying columnar heads.

Document 3

Rekey 51c, Document 3, page 118, aligning the names in Column 2 at the right edge of the column.

			words
BANCHESTER STATE UNIVERSITY			6
Departmental Growth			10
Department/College	Number	Rate	22
Arts and Sciences	218	2.5%	27
Business	1,405	11.3%	31
Education	906	3.9%	35
Engineering	315	10.4%	40
Health/Human Services	85	5.6%	46
Technology	927	8.7%	49

54 ◆ Tables with Source Notes

54a 6'

each line 3 times SS; DS between 3-line groups

Skill-Building Warmup

alphabet 1   Frank expected to solve a jigsaw puzzle more quickly than before.
figures 2   Of 290 pens, Ito stored 9 in Bin 13, 5 in Bin 46, and 7 in Bin 8.
colon 3   Key this: To: Earl Jorin; From: Kay Pohn; Subject: Tax Rates.
easy 4   When did the city auditor pay the proficient firm for a big sign?

| 1 | 2 | 3 | 4 | 5 | 6 | 7 | 8 | 9 | 10 | 11 | 12 | 13 |

54b 14'

SKILL BUILDING

Improve tab control

1 Set five tabs 10 spaces apart with Column 2 beginning 10 spaces from the left margin.

2 Key three 1' writings on lines 5-7. Work to eliminate pauses.

3 Key three 1' writings on lines 8-10. Emphasize smooth, continuous movements.

4 Key two 3' writings on all lines.

Goal: 18 *gwam* on 3' writings (each line = 6 words)

							gwam 1'	3'
5	Kent	Nels	Clem	Glen	Maya	Lana	6	2	14
6	Dick	Iris	Ruby	Tory	Jane	Ivie	12	4	16
7	Buck	Lark	Yale	Jaye	Quan	Tico	18	6	18
8	1828	2039	3758	4920	5718	6304	6	8	20
9	8191	9465	6307	2016	7395	2048	12	10	22
10	2630	8195	2637	8405	1947	6263	18	12	24

11d 12'

Control service keys
each line once

return: key smoothly without looking at fingers

17 Make the return snappily
18 and with assurance; keep
19 your eyes on your source
20 data; maintain a smooth,
21 constant pace as you key.

space bar: use down-and-in motion
22 us me it of he an by do go to us if or so am ah el
23 Have you a pen? If so, print "Free to any guest."

shift keys: use smooth shift-key-release motions
24 Juan Colon will see Lyle Branch in Oak Creek Park.
25 Mo, Lucy, and Sky left for New Orleans, Louisiana.

11e 14'

Reach for new goals

1 Key ¶1 line for line; then take two 1' writings on the ¶. DS between ¶s.
2 Repeat Step 1 for ¶s 2 and 3. Key all ¶s. DS between ¶s. Goal: **16 gwam**

 If using the Alphanumeric software, complete this exercise in the open screen using the timer. This instruction will not be repeated.

 all letters

```
                          .        4         .        8
Have we thought of communication as a kind of war
             12        .        16
that we wage through each day?

                          .        4         .        8         .
When we think of it that way, good language would
             12        .        16            .
seem to become our major line of attack.

                          .        4         .        8         .
Words become muscle; in a normal exchange or in a
             12        .        16            .       20
quarrel, we do well to realize the power of words.
```

on... One Space or Two?

Traditionally, two spaces follow end-of-sentence punctuation in documents. In desktop publishing, one space generally follows end-of-sentence punctuation. As a result of desktop publishing and the proportional fonts of today's word processing programs, some users have suggested change.

With professional fonts, characters use a varied amount of space depending upon their width. Monospace fonts such as Courier (also used by typewriters) use the same amount of space for each character; thus two spaces are required after end-of-sentence punctuation for readability.

We believe the crucial factors are readability and ease of retention, and not all fonts provide a distinct end-of-sentence look. End-of-sentence punctuation decisions will continue to be reevaluated with changing technologies. In this textbook, you will use two spaces after end-of-sentence punctuation for typical document production. In the Word Processing Workshop, however, you may use one.

Improve accuracy

Key a 2' writing; count errors. Key three more 2' writings. Try to reduce errors with each writing.

A all letters used   *gwam 2'*

Little things do contribute a lot to success in keying.   6
Take our work attitude, for example. It's a little thing; yet,   12
it can make quite a lot of difference. Demonstrating patience   18
with a job or a problem, rather than pressing much too hard for a   25
desired payoff, often brings better results than we expected.   31
Other "little things," such as wrist and finger position, how we   38
sit, size and location of copy, and lights, have meaning for   44
any person who wants to key well.   47

gwam 2' | 1 | 2 | 3 | 4 | 5 | 6 | 7 |

53c 30'

FORMATTING

Right align columns

Read "Aligning numbers in columns" at right; then key the drill and Documents 1, 2, and 3.

wp Word processors use a **right align tab** to align numbers or words at the right edge of a column.

Aligning numbers in columns: Numbers within columns align at the first position at the right of the column. Set a tab to accommodate the most frequently appearing number of digits in a column, then space forward or backward for the others.

A decimal tab may also be used to align a column without decimals. Note the position of the decimal tabs below.

Decimal tab	Decimal tab	Decimal tab
$110,000.75	1,423	Rob
760.10	690	Sarah

Drill

Lemon Valley		MO	25
Halford		LA	217
Balsley		MA	1,423
Lake Juno		NV	528
Edelton		RI	690
Lemon Valley	10	MO 10	1,423

Document 1

Center the table vertically and horizontally.

			words
SCHUMANN MANUFACTURING CO.			5
Prize-Winning Suggestions for 19--			12
Prize Winner	Department	Prize	24
Helen Grose	Sales	$1,200	29
John Holtz	Maintenance	200	35
Pedro Lopez	Advertising	550	40
Ernesto Mye	Accounting	75	45
Nyna Paige	Purchasing	550	51
Erica Ortiz	Art	525	55
Rose Ervine	Security	1,200	60
Albert Suoka	Marketing	550	65
Dino Litti	Research	75	70

12 ▸ Review

12a   8'

each line twice SS
(slowly, then faster); DS
between 2-line groups

alphabet 1 Which big market for quality jazz has Vi expanded?
       q 2 Quin Racq quickly and quietly quelled the quarrel.
       z 3 Zaret zipped along sizzling, zigzag Arizona roads.
    easy 4 Can they handle the auditory problems of the city?

◄ 1 ｜ 2 ｜ 3 ｜ 4 ｜ 5 ｜ 6 ｜ 7 ｜ 8 ｜ 9 ｜ 10 ►

12b   9'

Practice newer keyreaches

1 Key each line once; work
for smoothness, not for
speed.
2 Repeat lines you do not
key fluently.

m / b
5 Bob may remember he was a member of my brass band.

z / '
6 Inez isn't fazed by Zeno's use of Al's jazz music.

w / ,
7 I asked Wendy, Lew, and Walt to walk my dog, Paws.

p / "
8 "Oh," gasped Pan, "someone put pepper in my soup."

q / ?
9 Where is Quito? Qatar? Boqueirao? Quebec? Birqash?

h / .
10 Mr. H. H. Hannah asked Dr. Heath to help him push.

12c   10'

Control service keys

each line once

return: do not pause or look up to return
11 Successful keying is not just
12 a matter of speed; rather, it
13 is a combination of rapid and
14 slow, but constant, movements.

space bar: use correct spacing after each punctuation mark
15 Was it here? I saw it; Jan saw it, too. We did.

shift keys: depress shift key firmly; avoid pauses
16 Pam was in Spain in May; Bo Roy met her in Madrid.

｜ 1 ｜ 2 ｜ 3 ｜ 4 ｜ 5 ｜ 6 ｜ 7 ｜ 8 ｜ 9 ｜ 10 ｜

Document 2

Center the table vertically and horizontally. Align numbers at the decimal points. Indent *Total* 5 spaces from the left margin.

Dollar sign: Consider a $ as part of the column. Place a $ before the first amount to accommodate the number with the most digits and before the total if one is included. Indicate a total with a line under the columnn. DS above the total figure.

SCHUMANN MANUFACTURING CO.

Group B Hourly Salaries

John E. Sheard	$ 9.12
Laurel D. Bedore	10.47
Betsy A. Yorke	8.03
Esther Ferrier	9.12
Alan M. Woods	10.47
Louise Ybarra	9.12
Rita A. Montgomery	8.03
Roger E. Osuma	8.03
Orin Swauger	9.12
Total	$81.51

Document 3

Three-column tables:

Determine vertical placement as with any other table. For horizontal placement, include all three columns and two intercolumns in key line.

words

SHERWOOD SCHOOL   ⟧ *Center*   3

Computer Lab   6

Code	Description	Unit Cost	
E4-TC152	Workstation	$189.95	16
S2-90097	3 1/2" Diskettes	16.30	22
S2-90098	5 1/4" Diskettes	8.80	29
T1-0642A	Computer data tabs	.69	35
TA-8R023	Locking disk tray *(5 1/4")*	26.95	41
Total		$244.85	51
			53

53 ▷ Three-Column Tables

Skill-Building Warmup

53a   6'

each line 3 times SS; DS between 3-line groups

alphabet 1	Dixie Vaughn acquired that prize job with a firm just like yours.
figures 2	My May 15 note read: Call Ext. 390; order 472 clips and 68 pens.
easy/figures 3	The 29 girls kept 38 bushels of corn and 59 bushels of rich yams.
easy 4	The men paid half of the aid endowment, and their firm paid half.

◀ | 1 | 2 | 3 | 4 | 5 | 6 | 7 | 8 | 9 | 10 | 11 | 12 | 13 ▶

120

12d 9'

Improve keying technique

1 Key each line once; work for smooth, unhurried keying.
2 Repeat lines you did not key fluently.

adjacent reaches
17 Bert read where she could stop to buy gas and oil.
18 We three are a trio to join the Yun Oil operation.

direct reaches
19 Grace Nurva hunted my canyon for unique specimens.
20 My uncle and my brother have run many great races.

double reaches
21 Jeanne took a day off to see a book show in Hobbs.
22 Will Anne and Betty take three books to the troop?

| 1 | 2 | 3 | 4 | 5 | 6 | 7 | 8 | 9 | 10 |

12e 14'

Build staying power

1 Key each ¶ SS; DS between ¶s.
2 Key each ¶ for two 1' writings.
3 Key both ¶s for 2'.
Goal: 16 gwam

> **To determine gross words-a-minute rate for 2':**
> **1** Note the figure at the end of the last line completed.
> **2** For a partial line, note the figure on the scale directly below the point at which you stopped keying.
> **3** Add these two figures to determine the total gross words a minute (*gwam*) you keyed.

 all letters   *gwam* 2'

```
                    .           4           .           8           .
There  should  be  no  questions,  no  doubt,  about  the   5
              12          .           16          .           20
value  of  being  able  to  key;  it's  just  a  matter  of   10
              .           24          .           28          .
common  sense  that  today  a  pencil  is  much  too  slow.   15

                    .           4           .           8           .
Let  me  explain.   Work  is  done  on  a  keyboard  three   5
              12          .           16          .           20
to  six  times  faster  than  other  writing  and  with  a   10
              .           24          .           28          .
product  that  is  a  prize  to  read.   Don't  you  agree?   15
```

gwam 2' | 1 | 2 | 3 | 4 | 5 |

52 ▸ Tables with Decimals

52a 6'

each line 3 times SS;
DS between 3-line
groups

alphabet 1 Jimmy Favorita realized that we must quit playing by six o'clock.

figures 2 Joell, in her 1987 truck, put 25 boxes in an annex at 3460 Marks.

double letters 3 Merriann was puzzled by a letter that followed a free book offer.

easy 4 Ana's sorority works with vigor for the goals of the civic corps.

| 1 | 2 | 3 | 4 | 5 | 6 | 7 | 8 | 9 | 10 | 11 | 12 | 13 |

52b 14'

FORMATTING

Align decimals

Read "Aligning decimals";
then follow the directions to
key the drill.

Aligning decimals

Numbers with decimals must align at the
decimal point. Electronic typewriters and
word processing software use a **decimal
tab** to align numbers with decimals.

To set a decimal tab, move the carrier
or cursor to the decimal point position and
set the tab. (See equipment manual for
more specific directions.)

On equipment without a decimal tab
feature (electric typewriters and Micro-
Assistant), set a tab to accommodate the
most frequently appearing number of digits
in a column; then space forward or
backward to align the other digits.

Beef	3.29
Cheese	1.07
Chicken	.99
Franks	.68
Pork	2.45
Key line Chicken 10	3.29

Set decimal tab here

52c 30'

FORMATTING

Tables with decimals

Document 1

Center the table horizontally
and vertically. Align numbers at the decimal points.

		words
SCHUMANN MANUFACTURING CO.		5
Group A Salary Factors		10
William Talbot	.87	14
Beatrice Guided	.86	18
Natalie Dress	1.02	21
Otto E. Forrest	.79	26
Melanie Dougherty	1.01	30
Patricia Armstrong	1.10	35
Christine Lorenz	.98	39
Charles Chang	.90	43

13 ⬥ Review

each line twice SS
(slowly, then faster);
DS between 2-line
groups; use line 4 as
1' writings as time
permits

Skill-Building Warmup

alphabet	1	Bev quickly hid two Japanese frogs in Mitzi's box.
shift	2	Jay Nadler, a Rotary Club member, wrote Mr. Coles.
comma	3	Jay, Ed, and I paid for plates, knives, and forks.
easy	4	Did the amendment name a city auditor to the firm?

◄ 1 | 2 | 3 | 4 | 5 | 6 | 7 | 8 | 9 | 10 ►

13b   12'

Practice response patterns

each line once as shown
SS; DS between 3-line
groups

word level response : key short, familiar words as units

5 is to for do an may work so it but an with them am

6 Did they mend the torn right half of their ensign?

7 Hand me the ivory tusk on the mantle by the bugle.

letter level response: key more difficult words letter by letter

8 only state jolly zest oil verve join rate mop card

9 After defeat, look up; gaze in joy at a few stars.

10 We gazed at a plump beaver as it waded in my pool.

combination response : use variable speed; your fingers will let you feel the difference

11 it up so at for you may was but him work were they

12 It is up to you to get the best rate; do it right.

13 This is Lyn's only date to visit their great city.

| 1 | 2 | 3 | 4 | 5 | 6 | 7 | 8 | 9 | 10 |

13c   5'

Practice keyreaches

each line once; fingers
well curved, wrists low;
avoid punching keys with
3d and 4th fingers

left 1st

14 Trevor forgot to drive through the covered bridge.

right 1st

15 Johnny says you jammed your knuckle on this trunk.

left 3d/4th

16 A sad Sam Essex was assessed a tax on his savings.

right 3d/4th

17 Polly L. Apollo polled the populace on Proposal L.

| 1 | 2 | 3 | 4 | 5 | 6 | 7 | 8 | 9 | 10 |

FORMATTING

Tables with special headings

Document 1

Read "Special headings." Then, center the table horizontally and vertically (the longest line in each column is shaded). Decide all spacing.

Special headings
Secondary headings follow the main heading; they are centered and all important words are capitalized.

Column headings identify the information within the column. Blocked column headings begin at the tab. Important words are capitalized, and the heading is underlined.

If a column heading is the longest item in the column, use it for determining the key line. Leave one blank line (DS) above and below all headings, regardless of table spacing.

words

		words
WORD POWER		2
Secondary heading Commonly Used Foreign Terms		8
Blocked column heads Term	Literal Translation	18
ad infinitum	to infinity	23
bona fide	in good faith	27
bon mot	clever saying	32
de facto	in reality	36
fait accompli	deed accomplished	42
faux pas	social blunder	47
flagrante delicto	caught in the act	54
hoi polloi	general populace	60
non sequitur	does not follow logically	68

Document 2

Center the table horizontally and vertically. Decide all spacing.

		words
DELEMORE CLINIC		3
Staff		4
Physician	Specialty	12
Johnny J. Bowers	Cardiovascular Disease	20
H. Myles Bynum	Dermatology	25
Violet A. Geddes	Gastroenterology	32
Julio S. Diaz	Geriatrics	37
Walter T. McWerther	Heart	42

Document 3

Use 1" top and side margins. Make all changes marked.

		words
DS { FROM:	T. Richard Wynn	4 / 9
TO:	Martha L. Trent	13
DATE:	March 15, 19--	21
SUBJECT:	Dinner Program (Order #577-A)	34

Please include the following as the only information on page 3 of the March 30 program you are printing (Order #577-A). 42 / 49

stet DS {
Preliminary remarks	Drew Bargas	55 / 61
Introductions	Herbert Blackmun	66
Address	Viola Mannes Garrett	71
Commentary	Myrle Ortega	
Closing remarks	Drew Bargas	84

We espect the programs will be finished by Friday of this week. 84

XX

13d 13'

Practice stroking techniques

1 Key each line once.
2 Check each line that you could not key smoothly.

✓ fingers curved and upright

p
18 Pat appears happy to pay for any supper I prepare.

x
19 Knox can relax; Alex gets a box of flax next week.

v
20 Vi, Ava, and Viv move ivy vines, leaves, or stems.

'
21 It's a question of whether they can't or won't go.

?
22 Did Jan go? Did she see Ray? Who paid? Did she?

.
23 Ms. E. K. Nu and Lt. B. A. Walz had the a.m. duty.

"
24 "Who are you?" he asked. "I am," I said, "Marie."

;
25 Find a car; try it; like it; work a price; buy it.

| 1 | 2 | 3 | 4 | 5 | 6 | 7 | 8 | 9 | 10 |

13e 12'

OS

Build staying power

1 Key each ¶ for two 1' writings.
2 Key both ¶s for two 2' writings.
Goal: 17 *gwam*

E all letters

gwam 2'

              .   4   .   8
The questions of time use are vital ones; we miss   5
           12   .   16
so much just because we don't plan.   9

              .   4   .   8
When we organize our days, we save time for those   14
           12   .   16
extra premium things we long to do.   17

gwam 2' | 1 | 2 | 3 | 4 | 5 |

Document 2

Calculate horizontal and vertical placement of the table, then key it.

For intercolumn: Is the table wide, average, or narrow?

For single- or double-spacing: Does the table contain more or fewer than 20 lines?

FAMOUS COMPOSERS AND THEIR NATIONS		7
Bela Bartok	Hungary	11
Alban Berg	Austria	15
Leonard Bernstein	United States	21
Benjamin Britten	Great Britain	27
Dietrich Buxtehude	Denmark	33
Frederic Chopin	Poland	37
Aaron Copland	United States	43
Antonin Dvorak	Czechoslovakia	49
Manuel de Falla	Spain	53
George Gershwin	United States	59
Christoph W. Gluck	Germany	65
Arthur Honegger	Switzerland	70
Aram Khachaturian	Armenia	76
Franz Liszt	Hungary	80
Maurice Ravel	France	84
Dimitri Shostakovich	Russia	90
Jan Sibelius	Finland	94
Ralph Vaughan Williams	Great Britain	101
Giuseppe Verdi	Italy	105
Heitor Villa-Lobos	Brazil	111
Richard Wagner	Germany	115

51 ▸ Tables with Column Headings

51a   6'

each line 3 times SS;
DS between 3-line groups

Skill-Building Warmup

alphabet 1	Loquacious, breezy Hank forgot to jump over the waxed hall floor.
figures 2	Invoices 675 and 348, dated June 29 and August 10, were not paid.
one hand 3	Polk traded Case #789--24 sets of rare carved beads--as rare art.
easy 4	They may dismantle the eight authentic antique autos in the town.

| 1 | 2 | 3 | 4 | 5 | 6 | 7 | 8 | 9 | 10 | 11 | 12 | 13 |

51b   14'

SKILL BUILDING

Build speed

Take two 1' writings, two 2' writings, and two 3' writings.

Begin the first writing slowly and allow speed to develop with each subsequent writing.

A all letters

	gwam 2'	3'
A functional vocabulary can be difficult to establish; thus	6	4	30
everybody should realize how very important it is that we choose	13	8	34
with care words we include even in our daily conversations. Not	19	13	38
only will such a routine expedite building a larger and possibly	26	17	43
more stimulating stock of words, it will also require us to stop	32	21	47
and think just a bit before we speak, not a bad habit to develop.	38	26	51

gwam 2' | 1 | 2 | 3 | 4 | 5 | 6 | 7 |
3' | 1 | 2 | 3 | 4 | 5 |

Skill-Building Workshop 1

OS Use the open screen of Alphanumeric software for Workshop 1.

Default margins or 50-space line

Drill 1
Goal: reinforce key locations

Key each line at a comfortable, constant rate; check lines that need more practice; repeat those lines.

Keep
- your eyes on source copy
- your fingers curved, upright
- your wrists low, but not touching
- your elbows hanging loosely
- your feet flat on the floor

A	We saw that Alan had an alabaster vase in Alabama.
B	My rubber boat bobbed about in the bubbling brook.
C	Ceci gave cups of cold cocoa to Rebecca and Rocco.
D	Don's dad added a second deck to his old building.
E	Even as Ellen edited her document, she ate dinner.
F	Our firm in Buffalo has a staff of forty or fifty.
G	Ginger is giving Greg the eggs she got from Helga.
H	Hugh has eighty high, harsh lights he might flash.
I	Irik's lack of initiative is irritating his coach.
J	Judge J. J. Jore rejected Jeane and Jack's jargon.
K	As a lark, Kirk kicked back a rock at Kim's kayak.
L	Lucille is silly; she still likes lemon lollipops.
M	Milt Mumm hammered a homer in the Miami home game.
N	Ken Linn has gone hunting; Stan can begin canning.
O	Jon Soto rode off to Otsego in an old Morgan auto.
P	Philip helped pay the prize as my puppy hopped up.
Q	Quade quit squirting Quarla after quite a quarrel.
R	As Mrs. Kerr's motor roared, her red horse reared.
S	Sissie lives in Mississippi; Lissa lives in Tulsa.
T	Nat told Betty not to tattle on her little sister.
U	It is unusual to have an unused unit in the union.
V	Eva visited every vivid event for twelve evenings.
W	We walked to the window to watch as the wind blew.
X	Tex Cox waxed the next box for Xenia and Rex Knox.
Y	Ty says you may stay with Fay for only sixty days.
Z	Hazel is puzzled about the azure haze; Zack dozes.
alphabet	Jacky and Max quickly fought over a sizable prawn.
alphabet	Just by maximizing liquids, Chick Prew avoids flu.

| 1 | 2 | 3 | 4 | 5 | 6 | 7 | 8 | 9 | 10 |

COMMUNIC...

Compose at the keyboard

1 Read the ¶ at the right.

2 Compose a second 5- or 6-line ¶ to express your ideas about success. Begin with the words shown.

3 Proofread and correct your ¶; then key both ¶s. Center a title (ALL CAPS) over the ¶s.

50c 30'

F O R M A T T I N G

Center tables vertically

Document 1

1 Read "Centering vertically" at right.

2 Calculate vertical placement of the table. Check your calculations as follows:

Lines available	66
Less lines in table	-25
Lines remaining	41
First line (41 ÷ 2 + 1)	=21

3 Calculate horizontal placement: For intercolumn space, decide if the table is wide (4 spaces); average (6-8 spaces); or narrow (10 spaces).

Document 2 is on page 117.

Four philosophers sat in a semicircle around a small, fragrant fire. A stranger, Pilgrim by name, stood at one end of the circle. The philosophers had granted him one question, and he posed it: When could one know that she or he had achieved success? One by one the philosophers spoke. "When one has achieved power," said the first. "When one has found wealth," claimed the second. The third added, "One must find many friends."

The fourth, seemingly wiser than the others, said (compose the remainder of the second paragraph).

Centering vertically

Text that is centered vertically has equal, or near equal, top and bottom margins. To center text vertically, follow these steps:

1 Count the lines within the table, including the title and blank lines.

2 Subtract the lines in the table from the total lines available on paper (full sheet, 66 lines).

3 Divide the remaining lines by 2 to determine the top margin. Ignore fractions.

4 Add 1 line; this is the line on which to begin.

WP The **center page** feature automatically centers copy vertically between the top and bottom margins.

1	SELECTED STATE NICKNAMES	
2		
3	Arizona	Grand Canyon State
4		
5	Florida	Sunshine State
6		
7	Indiana	Hoosier State
8		
9	Kansas	Sunflower State
10		
11	Mississippi	Magnolia State
12		
13	Montana	Treasure State
14		
15	New Hampshire	Granite State
16		
17	New York	Empire State
18		
19	Oklahoma	Sooner State
20		
21	South Carolina	Palmetto State
22		
23	Vermont	Green Mountain State
24		
25	Wisconsin	Badger State

Drill 2
Goal: strengthen up and down reaches

Keep hands and wrists quiet; fingers well curved in home position; stretch fingers up from home or pull them palmward as needed.

home position

1 Hall left for Dallas; he is glad Jake fed his dog.
2 Gladys had a flask of milk; Hal had a jello salad.
3 Jack Hask had a sale; Gala shall add half a glass.

down reaches

4 Did my banker, Mr. Mavann, analyze my tax account?
5 Do they, Mr. Zack, expect a number of brave women?
6 Zach, check the menu; next, beckon the lazy valet.

up reaches

7 Prue truly lost the quote we wrote for our report.
8 Teresa quietly put her whole heart into her words.
9 There were two hilarious jokes in your quiet talk.

Drill 3
Goal: strengthen individual finger reaches

Rekey troublesome lines.

first finger

1 Bob Mugho hunted for five minutes for your number.
2 Juan hit the bright green turf with his five iron.
3 The frigates and gunboats fought mightily in Java.

second finger

4 Dick said the ice on the creek had surely cracked.
5 Even as we picnicked, I decided we needed to diet.
6 Kim, not Mickey, had rice with chicken for dinner.

third/fourth finger

7 Pam saw Roz wax an aqua auto as Lex sipped a cola.
8 Wally will quickly spell Zeus, Apollo, and Xerxes.
9 Who saw Polly? Zoe Pax saw her; she is quiet now.

Drill 4
Goal: strengthen special reaches

Emphasize smooth stroking. Avoid pauses, but do not reach for speed.

adjacent reaches

1 Falk knew well that her opinions of art were good.
2 Theresa answered her question; order was restored.
3 We join there and walk north to the western point.

direct reaches

4 Barb Nunn must hunt for my checks; she is in debt.
5 In June and December, Irvin hunts in Bryce Canyon.
6 We decided to carve a number of funny human faces.

double letters

7 Anne stopped off at school to see Bill Wiggs cook.
8 Edd has planned a small cookout for all the troop.
9 Keep adding to my assets all fees that will apply.

| 1 | 2 | 3 | 4 | 5 | 6 | 7 | 8 | 9 | 10 |

Document 2

2" top margin

Center the narrow table horizontally. Use 10 intercolumn spaces as shown in the key line.

COMMITTEE LEADERS		
		4
Marilee Blazer	Food	8
Braun Stevens	Site	11
Louise Treweser	Games	16
Spike Wing	Programs	20
Chico Alvarez	Tickets	24
Toni Osuka	Parking	28
Key line Louise Treweser	10 Programs	

Document 3

2" top margin

Determine the longest line and intercolumn spaces for this narrow table to construct a key line; center the table horizontally; DS.

TEAMS/STADIUMS VISITED IN JULY		
		6
California Angels	Anaheim Stadium	13
Chicago Cubs	Wrigley Field	18
Cincinnati Reds	Riverfront Stadium	25
Detroit Tigers	Tiger Stadium	31
New York Yankees	Yankee Stadium	38
Houston Astros	Astrodome	43
Philadelphia Phillies	Veterans Stadium	50
San Diego Padres	Jack Murphy Stadium	58

50 ◆ Vertical Centering

Skill-Building Warmup

50a   6'

each line 3 times
SS; DS between 3-line groups

alphabet 1	Zak Jurex worked to improve the basic quality of his paging jobs.	
figures 2	I live at 149 East 56th Street; Ben, at 270 Hier; Li, at 38 Lark.	
direct reaches 3	My brother served as an umpire on that bright June day, no doubt.	
easy 4	If they sign an entitlement, the town land is to go to the girls.	

◄ | 1 | 2 | 3 | 4 | 5 | 6 | 7 | 8 | 9 | 10 | 11 | 12 | 13 | ►

Drill 5
Goal: improve trouble-some pairs

Use a controlled rate without pauses.

d / k
1 Dirk asked Dick to kid Drake about the baked duck.

e / i
2 Abie had neither ice cream nor fried rice in Erie.

b / v
3 Did Harv key jibe or jive, TV or TB, robe or rove?

t / r
4 In Toronto, Ruth told the truth about her artwork.

u / y
5 Judye usually does not buy your Yukon art in July.

Drill 6
Goal: build speed

Key each sentence for 1'. Try to complete each sentence twice (20 *gwam* or more). Ignore errors for now.

1 Dian may make cocoa for the girls when they visit.

2 Focus the lens for the right angle; fix the prism.

3 She may suspend work when she signs the torn form.

4 Augment their auto fuel in the keg by the autobus.

5 As usual, their robot did half turns to the right.

6 Pamela laughs as she signals to the big hairy dog.

7 Pay Vivian to fix the island for the eighty ducks.

| 1 | 2 | 3 | 4 | 5 | 6 | 7 | 8 | 9 | 10 |

Drill 7
Goal: build speed

Take 30" writings on selected sentences. From the columns at the right, choose a *gwam* goal that is 2-3 words higher than your best rate. Try to reach your goal.

words 1' 30" 20"

1 Did she make this turkey dish?   6 12 18

2 Blake and Laurie may go to Dubuque.   7 14 21

3 Signal for the oak sleigh to turn right.   8 16 24

4 I blame Susie; did she quench the only flame?   9 18 27

5 She turns the panel dials to make this robot work. 10 20 30

| 1 | 2 | 3 | 4 | 5 | 6 | 7 | 8 | 9 | 10 |

FORMATTING

Center tables horizontally

1 Study "Tables" carefully at the right.

2 Format and key Documents 1, 2, and 3; correct errors.

Tables

Main heading: Center and key in ALL CAPS; DS below heading. Bold also may be used.

Columns: Vertical lists of information. Center horizontally. Generally, double-space; single-space long tables of 20 or more lines. When a table appears within a document, use the same spacing as the document.

Intercolumn space: Space between columns will vary, depending on the number of columns and their width. Use an even number of spaces:

Narrow	10 spaces
Average	6-8 spaces
Wide	4 spaces

Key line: Used for centering columns horizontally on page, a key line consists of the longest item in each column and the spaces between columns (intercolumn space).

wp The key line is centered using the **automatic centering feature**. A **left tab** (the default) is used to align columns at the left.

To format a table

1 Move margins to the left and right edges of the scale; clear all tabs.

2 Determine the **key line** (longest item in each column and the intercolumn spaces).

3 Center the key line. (Note specific directions for various equipment below.)

4 Set the left margin at Column 1 and a tab for Column 2.

5 Center the heading and key the table.

To center the key line

Electronic typewriters and **MicroAssistant:**

1 Press the center key (MicroAssistant **Alt + C**).

2 Type the key line; strike return. Set the left margin and tab according to the printout or display.

3 Delete the key line.

Electric typewriters

1 From the center of the page, backspace once for every two characters in the key line. Ignore a leftover stroke. Set left margin.

2 Space forward once for each character in Column 1 and the intercolumn spaces. Set tab for Column 2.

Document 1
2" top margin

Main heading FARLEIGH SCHOOL BOARD OF REGENTS
                                               DS

Kathryn Brece McCall	President
V. Brett Badger	Vice President
Gregory E. Becker	Secretary
D. L. Merriwether	Treasurer
Julio A. Esposito	Member
John Y. Baer	Member
B. A. Beebe	Member

Key line Kathryn Brece McCall   10   Vice President

          Column   Intercolumn
                           space

Drill 8
Goal: build staying power

each ¶ SS line for line for a 1'
timing; then a 2' timing on
both ¶s; DS between ¶s

E   all letters

Writing 1: **18** *gwam*

```
              .          4          .          8          .
Why spend weeks with some problem when just a few      5
              12         .          16         .
quiet minutes can help us to resolve it.               9

              .          4          .          8          .
If we don't take time to think through a problem,      15
              12         .          16         .
it will swiftly begin to expand in size.               18
```

Writing 2: **20** *gwam*

```
              .          4          .          8          .
We push very hard in our quest for growth, and we      5
              12         .          16         .          20
all think that only excellent growth will pay off.     10

              .          4          .          8          .
Believe it or not, one can actually work much too      15
              12         .          16         .          20
hard, be much too zealous, and just miss the mark.     20
```

Writing 3: **22** *gwam*

```
              .          4          .          8          .
A business friend once explained to me why he was      5
              12         .          16         .          20
often quite eager to be given some new project to      10
              .
work with.                                             11

              .          4          .          8          .
My friend said that each new project means he has      16
              12         .          16         .          20
to organize and use the best of his knowledge and      21
              .
his skill.                                             22
```

Writing 4: **24** *gwam*

```
              .          4          .          8          .
Don't let new words get away from you.  Learn how      5
              12         .          16         .          20
to spell and pronounce new words and when and how      10
              .          24
finally to use them.                                   12

              .          4          .          8          .
A new word is a friend, but frequently more.  New      17
              12         .          16         .          20
words must be used lavishly to extend the size of      22
              .          24
your own word power.                                   24
```

gwam 2' | 1 | 2 | 3 | 4 | 5 |

11
Tabulated
Documents

Learning goals:
1 To format tables with main and secondary headings and blocked column headings.
2 To recall horizontal centering.
3 To center data vertically.
4 To arrange data in columns.

Formatting guides:
1 Default margins or a 65-space line.
2 Single-space drills; double-space paragraphs.
3 Indentions: 5-space ¶ indent.

49a 6'

Skill-building warmup

each line 3 times
SS; DS between
3-line groups

alphabet 1	Jim Ryan was able to liquify frozen oxygen; he kept it very cold.
figures 2	Flight 259 left here at 8:36 p.m., arriving in Reno at 10:47 p.m.
adjacent reaches 3	We condemn her notion that we can buy safe behavior with rewards.
easy 4	If I burn the signs, the odor of enamel may make a toxic problem.

| 1 | 2 | 3 | 4 | 5 | 6 | 7 | 8 | 9 | 10 | 11 | 12 | 13 |

49b 10'

SKILL BUILDING

Improve control

Key two 1' writings on each ¶ at a steady, but unhurried pace; then key two 3' writings on all ¶s.
Goal: Fewer than 3 errors a minute.

A all letters
gwam 1' | 3'

Chuck is a supervisor in a large department of an eastern   12 | 4 | 63
company. His department recently won a coveted company award for   25 | 8 | 67
excellence. Ask him what is so special about his department, and   38 | 13 | 72
he will tell you the credit goes to an excellent crew that works   51 | 17 | 76
together and gets things done.   57 | 19 | 78

Zadine was recently voted the outstanding employee in the   12 | 23 | 82
home office by the people with whom she works. Ask her why she   24 | 27 | 86
was chosen, and she will say that she was puzzled by the award;   37 | 32 | 91
she just likes her work and her co-workers and quietly does her   50 | 36 | 95
daily assignment without attracting much attention.   61 | 39 | 98

Success is frequently intertwined with one's ability to get   12 | 43 | 102
along with people, to lead them without offending their dignity,   25 | 48 | 107
to work beside them in a team spirit, and to support them fully   38 | 52 | 111
when assistance is needed. Cooperation is just another way of   50 | 56 | 115
saying, "I need you as much as you need me."   59 | 59 | 118

gwam 1' | 1 | 2 | 3 | 4 | 5 | 6 | 7 | 8 | 9 | 10 | 11 | 12 | 13 |
3' | 1 | 2 | 3 | 4 | 5 |

Writing 5: **26** *gwam*

```
         .              4                .              8              .
We usually get best results when we know where we   5
    12               .              16               .              20
are going.  Just setting a few goals will help us   10
          .              24               .
quietly see what we are doing.                      13


         .              4                .              8              .
Goals can help measure whether we are moving at a   18
    12               .              16               .              20
good rate or dozing along.  You can expect a goal   23
         .              24               .
to help you find good results.                      26
```

Writing 6: **28** *gwam*

```
         .              4                .              8              .
To win whatever prizes we want from life, we must   5
    12               .              16               .              20
plan to move carefully from this goal to the next   10
          .              24               .              28
to get the maximum result from our work.            14


         .              4                .              8              .
If we really want to become skilled in keying, we   19
    12               .              16               .              20
must come to see that this desire will require of   14
          .              24               .              28
us just a little patience and hard work.            28
```

Writing 7: **30** *gwam*

```
         .              4                .              8              .
Am I an individual person?  I'm sure I am; still,   5
    12               .              16               .              20
in a much, much bigger sense, other people have a   10
          .              24               .              28               .
major voice in thoughts I think and action I take.  15


         .              4                .              8              .
Although we are each a unique person, we all work   20
    12               .              16               .              20
and play in organized groups of people who do not   25
          .              24               .              28               .
expect us to dismiss their rules of law and order.  30
```

Drill 3
Review confusing words
1 Use 1' top margin; 1" side or default margins.
2 Indent example lines 5 spaces.
3 Use bold for the confusing words and the title.

CONFUSING WORDS

accept (v) to take or receive willingly.
except (v) to exclude, omit.
        They all can **accept** the invitation **except** Bjorn, who is ill.

addition (n) the result of adding.
edition (n) a version in which a text is published.
        This fifth **edition** is an excellent **addition** to our texts.

advice (n) opinion as to what to do; helpful counsel.
advise (v) to recommend; to give information.
        I **advise** you never to listen to bad **advice**.

already (adv) previously; prior to a specified time.
all ready (adj) completely ready.
        It was **already** too late by the time dinner was **all ready**.

any one (n) any singular person in a group.
anyone (pron) any person at all.
        Anyone could tell the hat did not belong to **any one** of us.

assistance (n) the act of helping; help supplied.
assistants (n) those who help.
        We hired the **assistants** to give us **assistance** at five o'clock.

further (adv) to a greater degree (time or quantity).
farther (adv) at a greater distance (space).
        Look **further** into the future; rockets will travel **farther**.

it's contraction of "it is" or "it has."
its (adj) possessive form for the pronoun "it."
        It's a long time since the lion had **its** last meal.

lay (v) to put down; to place.
lie (v) to rest; to be situated.
        Lay a blanket on the bed; I want to **lie** down for awhile.

passed (v) moved along; transferred.
past (adj, adv, prep) gone by; (n) time gone by.
        It was **past** five o'clock when the parade **passed** by.

sale (n) act of exchanging something for money.
sell (v) to exchange property for money.
        We must **sell** these lamps; plan a **sale** for next week.

setting (v) to place.
sitting (v) to rest in place.
        I am **setting** this fruit here; it was **sitting** in the sun.

your (adj) belonging to you.
you're contraction of "you are."
        If **you're** not careful, you will be late for **your** meeting.

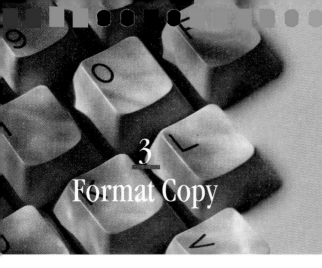

3
Format Copy

Learning goals:
1 To set side and top margins.
2 To clear and set tabs.
3 To center copy horizontally.
4 To change line spacing.

Formatting guides:
1 Default margins or 50-space line.
2 Single-space drills; double-space paragraphs.

14a 7'

Skill-building warmup

each line twice SS; DS between 2-line groups

alphabet 1 Fave Maxwelt quickly jeopardized his buying power.
q 2 Quenched in quandary, he quickly acquitted Quincy.
shift/? 3 Did you ask Paul? Would Ivan, Jon, or Carol know?
easy 4 Ken may wish to pay big bucks for the giant rifle.

| 1 | 2 | 3 | 4 | 5 | 6 | 7 | 8 | 9 | 10 |

14b 7'

SKILL BUILDING

Improve keystroking

Key each line once SS; DS between 2-line groups.

de / ed
5 ed fed led deed dell dead deal sled desk need seed
6 Dell dealt with the deed before the dire deadline.

lo / ol
7 old tolls doll solo look sole lost love cold stole
8 Old Ole looked for the long lost olive oil lotion.

as / sa
9 as say sad ask pass lass case said vase past salsa
10 Ask the lass to pass the glass, saucers, and vase.

op / po
11 pop top post rope pout port stop opal opera report
12 Stop to read the top opera opinion report to Opal.

| 1 | 2 | 3 | 4 | 5 | 6 | 7 | 8 | 9 | 10 |

14c 6'

FORMATTING

Pitch/typeface

1 Read the copy at the right.
2 Determine the pitch of your machine by comparing your type to the copy at the right.

Pitch / typeface

Most keyboarding systems have at least two type sizes or pitches: 10-pitch (pica) and 12-pitch (elite). Pitch refers to the number of keystrokes in one horizontal inch.

```
10 pitch  1234567890
12 pitch  123456789012
```

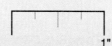

1"

A standard sheet of paper, 8.5 inches wide, has 85 ten-pitch keystrokes (8.5" x 10) or 102 twelve-pitch keystrokes (8.5" x 12).

wp The default *typeface* for many word processing programs (and typewriters) is 10-pitch Courier. Prestige elite is also common. Size is measured in width or *characters per inch (cpi)*.

Courier 10 cpi
Prestige elite 12 cpi

Alternate typefaces, such as Helvetica and Times Roman, may be available and in different point sizes. Point size refers to the height of a letter. The larger the point size, the larger the print.

Times Roman 12 pt. Helvetica 8 pt.

Communication Workshop 2

Drill 1
Review use of the apostrophe

1.5" top margin; 1" or default side margins; use bold and hanging indent format as shown; center the title

USING AN APOSTROPHE TO SHOW POSSESSION

1. Add **'s** to a singular noun not ending in **s**.

2. Add **'s** to a singular noun ending in **s** or **z** sound if the ending **s** is pronounced as a syllable; as, Sis's lunch, Russ's car, Buzz's average.

3. Add **'** only if the ending **s** or **z** is awkward to pronounce; as, series' outcome, ladies' shoes, Delibes' music, Cortez' quest.

4. Add **'s** to a plural noun that does not end in **s**; as, men's notions, children's toys, mice's tracks.

5. Add only **'** after a plural noun ending in **s**; as, horses' hoofs, lamps' shades.

6. Add **'s** after the last noun in a series to show joint possession of two or more people; as, Jack and Judy's house; Peter, Paul, and Mary's song.

7. Add **'s** to each noun to show individual possession of two or more persons; as, Li's and Ted's tools, Jill's and Ed's races.

Drill 2
Review use of quotation marks

1.5" top margin; 1" or default side margins; indent examples 5 spaces

SPACING WITH QUOTATION MARKS

Use quotation marks:

after a comma or a period; as,
     "I bought," she said, "more paper."

before a semicolon; as,
     She said, "I have little money"; she had, in fact, none.

before a colon; as,
     He called these items "fresh": beans, peas, and carrots.

after a question mark if the quotation itself is a question; as,
     "Why did you do that?" he asked.

before a question mark if the quotation is not a question; as,
     Why did he say, "I will not run"?

14d   30'

Margins

Read the information at the right; then do Drills 1 and 2 below.

Determining margin settings

Side margins are the distance between the edge of the paper and the print. Up to this point, you have been using preset or **default** margins.

To achieve an attractive page layout, set the margins an equal distance from both edges of the paper. Documents are often formatted with 1", 1.5", or 2" side margins. The *line of writing* is the space available for keying. It is determined by subtracting the side margins from the width of the paper, 8.5".

Side margins may be expressed in spaces. When spaces are used, the settings will differ depending upon the pitch (pica or elite) used.

In this course, margins will be expressed in inches; it is assumed that the defaults will be 10 pitch (pica) and 1" margins (65-space line).

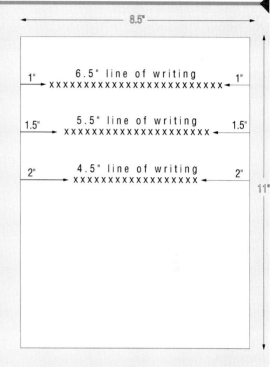

Inches	1"	1.5"	2"
Line of writing	6.5"	5.5"	4.5"
10 pitch (pica)			
Left	10	15	20
Right	75	70	65
12 pitch (elite)			
Left	12	18	24
Right	90	84	78

Setting side margins

Typewriters: Be sure the paper has been inserted with the edge at 0. Move the desired number of spaces from the left and right edge of the paper and set margins.

Keyboarding software: Set margins in the open screen by accessing the format line (**Alt + F**). Then position the cursor and press either **L** or **R**. Exit the format line (**Alt + F**).

Drill 1

Set 1.5" left and right margins. You should be able to key the copy line for line as printed.

Note: A warning may sound as you approach the end of each line; listen for it.

Drill 2

Format the ¶s using 2" side margins.

Copy that is arranged attractively on the page appeals to the reader. An attractive document shows respect for the reader.

Documents are more attractive when the margins are set an equal distance from the left and right edges of the paper. This gives the document the appearance of being balanced. How the copy looks is just as important as what you key.

48c 10'

Key from edited copy

1 Key the ¶ as if it were the beginning of the first page of an unbound report.
2 Compose a title.
3 Make all marked changes and correct errors.

48d 10'

Improve control of manipulative parts

Key each group three times.
Goal:
Lines 10-14: Eyes on copy.
Lines 15-16: Easy, fluid stroking and correct capitalization.
Lines 17-18: Proper spacing between words and punctuation.

48e 13'

Reach for new goals

1 Key four 1' guided writings; determine *gwam*.
2 Take two 2' writings; try to maintain your best 1' rate.
3 Take a 3' writing. Use your *gwam* in Step 1 as your goal.

words

There is no question about it. many of the problems we face 12

now stem from the fact that over the years we have been not very 25

wise consumers. We have not used our natural resources well, 38

and we have jeopardized much of our environment. We have excused these 52

actions often in the belief that our supply of most resources has 65

no limits. Now we are beginning to realize how wrong we were and 79

we are taking steps to re-build our world. 87

10 When eyes are on the copy,
11 body straight, wrists low,
12 fingers curved, elbows in,
13 maybe just a slight smile,
14 then success can be yours.

15 Do Dr. and Mrs. J. D. Mumm take the DENVER POST or the NEWS MAIL?
16 Both Jose and Joy have read MY AFRICA; Tryna Zahn has read UHURU.

17 If you and I can do all of the jobs now, then we all can go home.
18 Watch out; the lamp is lit. See it? I do. I, too, may be seen.

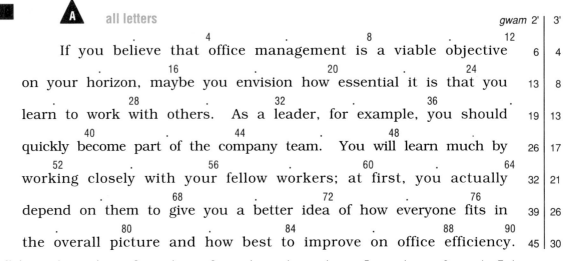

A all letters

	gwam 2'	3'
If you believe that office management is a viable objective	6	4
on your horizon, maybe you envision how essential it is that you	13	8
learn to work with others. As a leader, for example, you should	19	13
quickly become part of the company team. You will learn much by	26	17
working closely with your fellow workers; at first, you actually	32	21
depend on them to give you a better idea of how everyone fits in	39	26
the overall picture and how best to improve on office efficiency.	45	30

gwam 2' | 1 | 2 | 3 | 4 | 5 | 6 | 7 |
3' | 1 | 2 | 3 | 4 | 5 |

15 ◆ Tabs

15a   7'

Note: Line 3 has two ALL-CAP items. To key them, depress the Caps Lock (21) with the left little finger; key the item; release the lock by striking Caps Lock again.

alphabet 1	My fine axe just zipped through the black wood quite evenly.
' / " 2	I said, "Yes, Jan, I know. It's like stepping into a book."
shift/lock 3	ADIEU ANGELINA is a song on the NANA MOUSKOURI French album.
easy 4	Sit here; she may fix a big dish of papaya and mango for us.

1 | 2 | 3 | 4 | 5 | 6 | 7 | 8 | 9 | 10 | 11 | 12

15b   12'

SKILL BUILDING

Improve techniques

1 Key the lines once SS; DS between 3-line groups. Key each phrase (marked by a vertical line) without pauses between words.
2 Repeat drill at a faster pace.

easy words

5 am it go bus dye jam irk six sod tic yam ugh spa vow aid dug
6 he or by air big elf dog end fit and lay sue toe wit own got
7 six foe pen firm also body auto form down city kept make fog

easy phrases

8 it is | if the | and also | to me | the end | to us | if it | it is | to the
9 if it is | to the end | do you wish | to go to | for the end | to make
10 lay down | he or she | make me | by air | end of | by me | kept it | of me

15c   8'

FORMATTING

Tab key

Learn to set tabs on your equipment; then complete the drill below.

Typewriters
1 Clear all tabs: Press the Tab Clear and repeat keys.
2 Clear single tabs: Press the Tab key to move carrier to the tab that is to be cleared. Press Tab Clear key.
3 Set tabs: Strike the space bar to move the carrier to desired tab position. Press Tab Set key.
4 Tabulate (tab): Press Tab with the closest little finger; release it quickly and return to home row position.

Default tabs. Tabs are preset by the word processing software. Default tabs are usually set every 5 spaces.

Keyboarding software: Tabs can be set or cleared in the open screen by pressing **Alt + F**, positioning the cursor and pressing **Tab**.

Drill

1 Set 1" left and right margins. On typewriters, clear all preset tabs.
2 Set tabs 5, 10, and 15 spaces from the left margin.
3 Key each line once. Begin the first line at left margin; tab once for line 2; twice for line 3; three times for line 4.

Format the text by determining the position of tab settings.

tab once → Erase all preexisting tabs using the tab clear feature.

tab twice → Set the tab to move quickly to the various points.

tab three times → Use your fourth finger to strike the tab key.

47c 13'

Strengthen finger reaches

Keep wrists low, fingers curved, elbows in. Key the lines; practice troublesome lines until you can key them fluently.

1st finger

5 My group says that a huge gray monster lunged at the five braves.
6 They truly thought that the tugboat might brave the foul weather.
7 I trust none of you hunt tigers in the jungle of northern Africa.

2d finger

8 Kerrie says these kind, decent acts decidedly reduced skepticism.
9 Di conceded that kicking a cedar stick at Ike was a bad decision.
10 His reed kite descended quickly; lack of wind killed its chances.

3d/4th fingers

11 Was it Polly or was it Sam who saw Sally swallow a sour lollipop?
12 Wallis was appalled at the low slope of that excavation at Aswan.
13 Who applies wax to old autos? It wastes a load of costly polish.

47d 15'

Statistical copy

1 Key ¶ for orientation.
2 Take four 2' writings. Try for a higher *gwam* with each successive writing. Ignore errors temporarily.

A all letters/figures

gwam 2'

Fully inspired only 11 weeks before, I decided to start on | 6 | 44
this project; now I kept telling myself that my residence at 569 | 12 | 50
Azalea Avenue would be done well before the 30th. My contractor | 19 | 57
and a swarm of 48 "quality experts" had promised it would be. I | 25 | 63
needed this house quickly--in precisely 17 days, to be exact. My | 32 | 70
24-month lease was expiring, and I needed a place to live. | 38 | 76

gwam 2' | 1 | 2 | 3 | 4 | 5 | 6 | 7 |

---

48 ▸ Skill Building

48a 7'

each line 3 times; DS between 3-line groups

Skill-Building Warmup

alphabet 1 Jayne Cox puzzled over workbooks that were required for geometry.
figures 2 Edit pages 308 and 415 in Book A; pages 17, 29, and 60 in Book B.
one hand 3 Plum trees on a hilly acre, in my opinion, create no vast estate.
easy 4 Did the foal buck? and did it cut the right elbow of the cowhand?

| 1 | 2 | 3 | 4 | 5 | 6 | 7 | 8 | 9 | 10 | 11 | 12 | 13 |

48b 10'

Build accuracy

Key each line twice at a slow but steady pace. DS between 2-line groups. Rekey twice lines having more than one error.

5 A plump, aged monk served a few million beggars a milky beverage.

6 Few beavers, as far as I'm aware, feast on cedar trees in Kokomo.

7 Johnny, after a few stewed eggs, ate a plump, pink onion at noon.

8 In regard to desert oil wastes, Jill referred only minimum cases.

9 Link agrees you'll get a reward only as you join nonunion racers.

15d   8'

FORMATTING

Indented paragraphs

Set 1.5" side margins and set a tab for a 5-space ¶ indention. SS ¶s; DS between ¶s. Repeat.

Ending lines

    The **word wrap** feature automatically returns the cursor to the next line as you key. Copy too long to fit on one line moves automatically to the next line.

Electronic typewriters (ET): Most ETs have an automatic return option. The carrier returns automatically if the operator strikes the space bar or hyphen within the "Line-ending zone" (about 5 spaces).

Typewriters: A warning sounds from 6 to 10 spaces before the margin stops. When the warning sounds, 1) finish keying the word, 2) key the next word if it is short or strike Return if the next word is long. (In Lesson 25, you will learn to divide words.)

The topic of stress has received considerable attention over the past few years. Everyone has experienced some form of stress during his or her lifetime.

People are affected by stress in many different ways. A situation that causes stress may upset some people but may not have an effect on others. Coping with stress and knowing the difference between productive and nonproductive stress will help you to live a full and happy life style.

15e   15'

FORMATTING

Top margin

Read "Top margin"; key the ¶s below following the instructions for Drills 1 and 2.

Top margin

One vertical inch contains 6 lines. A standard sheet of paper is 11" long; therefore, it contains 66 vertical lines (11 x 6).

Top margins are usually specified as 1", 1.5", or 2". The default top margin in word processing software is often 1", with the first line printing on line 7.

Top Margin	Begin Keying
1"	line 7
1.5"	line 10
2"	line 13

Drill 1

Set 1" side margins, 2" top margin, and a tab for a 5-space ¶ indention.

Drill 2

Set 1.5" side margins, 1.5" top margin, and a tab for a 5-space ¶ indention.

Drill 3 (optional)

Rekey 14d, Drill 1, page 35. Set 1.5" side margins, 1" top margin, and a tab for a 5-space ¶ indention.

Keyboarding is an important skill that everyone needs to survive. Regardless of whether you learn to key on a typewriter or on a computer, the alphanumeric keys are in the same location.

Computer keyboards have additional keys that are not found on typewriters. These keys are function keys, cursor movement keys, and a numeric keypad.

10
Skill Building

Learning goals:
1 To improve keying techniques.
2 To improve concentration.
3 To improve ability to key straight, statistical, and rough-draft copy.

Formatting guides:
1 Default margins or 65-space line.
2 Single-space drills; double-space paragraphs.

47a   7'

Skill-building warmup

each line 3 times
(work for fewer than 3 errors per group)

alphabet 1 Jacky Few's strange, quiet behavior amazed and perplexed even us.
figures 2 Dial Extension 148 or 276 for a copy of the 30-page 95-cent book.
double letters 3 Ann will see that Edd accepts an assignment in the school office.
easy 4 Did a cow, six foals, six turkeys, and a duck amble to the field?

| 1 | 2 | 3 | 4 | 5 | 6 | 7 | 8 | 9 | 10 | 11 | 12 | 13 |

47b   15'

SKILL BUILDING

Improve concentration

1 Key a copy of the ¶ DS. Where a blank occurs, insert either the word **that** or **and**.

2 Proofread and make a final corrected copy.

3 Use your final copy for 3' writings as time permits.

A   all letters   *gwam* 3'

It has been said _____ human intelligence is the ability to   4 | 42

acquire and retain knowledge _____ will permit a person, based on   8 | 46

her or his past experience, to respond quickly _____ with success   13 | 50

to new _____ different occasions and situations. And that's right. 17 | 55

But intelligence is also the ability to use mental power _____ good 21 | 59

judgment--what some people call plain common sense--to recognize   26 | 64

problems and work to find proper solutions for them. It is, in   30 | 68

other words, the exciting force _____ moves our minds and bodies   34 | 72

from place to place, sometimes like game-board pieces.   38 | 76

gwam 3' | 1 | 2 | 3 | 4 | 5 |

---

16 ▸ Spacing and Horizontal Centering

16a   7'

each line twice SS;
DS between 2-line groups
Line 4: Set first tab 5 spaces from left margin. Then set 5 more tabs 10 spaces apart.

alphabet 1   The five proposed jurors were quickly examined by Eliza Wig.

' apostrophe2   It's time to clean Luke's and Coral's rooms; they're a mess.

shift/lock 3   The IRS cooperated with the CIA and the FBI at their behest.

tab review 4   tab right tab ivory tab laugh tab fight tab chaos tab blame

| 1 | 2 | 3 | 4 | 5 | 6 | 7 | 8 | 9 | 10 | 11 | 12 |

16b   18'

FORMATTING

Set line spacing

Read "Line spacing."

Line spacing
Single-spaced text is keyed on each line. Double-spaced text has one blank line between lines of type.

this is
single spacing

this is

double spacing

Typewriters: Double spacing can be achieved by striking return twice at the end of each line or by changing the line space selector to **2.**

Line spacing: The default for line spacing is single spacing.

16c   10'

SKILL BUILDING

Build staying power

DS ¶s; 5-space ¶ indention
1 Key the ¶s as shown once for orientation.
2 Take two 1' timings on each ¶.
3 Take a 3' timing on all ¶s. Determine *gwam.*

Goal: 17 *gwam*

gwam 3'

.   4   .   8   .

Most people will agree that we owe it to our children   4

12   .   16   .   20   .

to pass the planet on to them in better condition than we   7

24   .   28   .   32   .

found it. We must take extra steps just to make the quality   12

36   .

of living better.   13

.   4   .   8   .

If we do not change our ways quickly and stop damaging   16

12   .   16   .   20   .

our world, it will not be a good place to live. We can save   21

24   .   28   .   32   .

the ozone and wildlife and stop polluting the air and water.   25

gwam 3' | 1 | 2 | 3 | 4 |

16d   15'

FORMATTING

Center horizontally

Read the information at the right and the information at the top of page 39 appropriate for your equipment. Then key Drills 1-3 on page 39.

Center point
The horizontal center point of a line of writing is determined by adding the numbers on the line-of-writing scale at the left and right edges of the paper and dividing by 2. If the paper guide (left edge) is at 0, the center point for 10-pitch is 42; for 12-pitch, 51.

Center. This feature centers text horizontally between the left and right margins. Generally, the center command is entered before text is keyed.

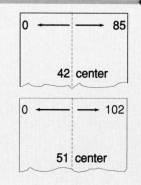

0 ◂——— ———▸ 85

42 center

0 ◂——— ———▸ 102

51 center

words

TIME, TECHNOLOGY, AND TEMPERAMENT 7

"Time marches on." These words were once used to conclude a popular 21
movie series that highlighted current events. The words were meant to 35
indicate to the viewing audience that changes were taking place constantly. 50
The thoughtful listeners, however, sometimes pictured Time as not only 65
marching on, but marching very rapidly--maybe too rapidly. 77

Every human generation is a segment of history unto itself. It 89
has its own customs; dances; taboos; technologies; fashions; and, 103
yes, even its own language. While generational changes are subtle 116
and occur slowly, they are definite. Each generation has always 129
insisted upon its own identification (Ruiz, 1993, 90). 140

Technological changes tend to enhance differences between 152
generations, sometimes very sharply. The First Bank of Rockford, for 166
example, reporting on the popularity of its automated banking facilities, 180
found that users of this service were primarily members of the "younger 195
generation" and that older bank customers much preferred the tradi- 209
tional teller service. "We know that we will not be employing tellers in the 225
forseeable future; but we know, too, that such changes will not happen in 239
just a week's time" (Carver, 1994, 3). 247

Much of the movement for technological change today centers on 260
efficiency, saving time and energy. "Precious metals have tended to 274
fluctuate in value over the years--sometimes up, sometimes down; time, 288
viewed as a commodity, has only become more valuable" (Nyles, 1994, 301
72). 302

Sociologists say that society does not adopt new technology until 316
conditions, always changing, make it ready to do so; then it assimilates 330
change very rapidly. The automobile, for example, was invented years 344
before its acceptance as a popular method of transportation. Society 358
seems to need pioneers with foresight who will continue to "create tech- 373
nological changes with no assurance of immediate, or even ultimate, 386
acceptance" (Su, 1994, 38). 392

Certain "agents of change," often not identifiable, work to prepare 405
developing generations to accept change; to support it financially; and, 420
above all, to use it. Maybe the greatest challenge involving technology is 435
not to create change but to learn how to live with it. 446

REFERENCES 448

Carver, Myrnah L. "'First' to Go Hi-Tech." <u>The Rockford Ledger</u>, January 466
    11, 1993. 469

Nyles, Carolyn Lee. <u>The Magic Time Machine</u>. Montgomery: Brevard 487
    Publishing Company, 1994. 492

Ruiz, Jorge A. "History, Technology, and the Fortune Teller." <u>Computer</u> 508
    <u>News</u>, April 1993. 513

Su, Debra M. <u>Time as a Lineal</u>. Savannah: Amyte Press, Inc., 1994. 529

Drill 1

3" top margin (begin on line 19); center each line; space as shown; the highlighted letter *i* in each line will align when the text is centered properly

AUTOMATIC CENTERING FEATURE
DS
Eliminates Tedious Counting and Backspacing
Expedites Centering Duties
Featured on Electronic Typewriters

Drill 2

2" top margin (begin on line 13); center each line; space as shown

TENTH ANNUAL OFFICE AUTOMATION CONVENTION
DS
Demonstrating the Latest Technologies
Telecommunications
Voice Activated Systems
Laser Optical Discs
FREE ADMISSION

Drill 3

1 Set 2" top margin, 1.5" side margins, DS, 5-space ¶ indention.

2 Center heading. Indent ¶ and end lines properly.

3 Center each of the last 4 lines; change line spacing to SS after keying **MUTUAL FUNDS**.

MAKE THE MOST OF YOUR MONEY

Robert Gronin, a leading Texas economist and financial adviser, will be the guest speaker at the September meeting of the Business Club. The following topics will be included in his speech:

MUTUAL FUNDS
LIMITED PARTNERSHIPS
REAL ESTATE
STOCKS AND BONDS

46   Measurement

46a   7'

each line 3 times SS;
DS between
3-line groups

Skill-Building Warmup

alphabet 1   Dave Cagney alphabetized items for next week's quarterly journal.
figures 2   Close Rooms 4, 18, and 20 from 3 until 9 on July 7; open Room 56.
upward reaches 3   Toy & Wurt's note for $635 (see our page 78) was paid October 29.
easy 4   The auditor is due by eight, and he may lend a hand to the panel.

| 1 | 2 | 3 | 4 | 5 | 6 | 7 | 8 | 9 | 10 | 11 | 12 | 13 |

46b   12'

SKILL BUILDING

Measure straight-copy skill

Key three 3' writings; proofread and circle errors; determine *gwam*.

LA   all letters used   gwam 1'   3'

	gwam 1'	3'
In a recent show, a young skater gave a great performance.	12	4	69
Her leaps were beautiful, her spins were impossible to believe,	25	8	74
and she was a study in grace itself. But she had slipped during	38	13	78
a jump and had gone down briefly on the ice. Because of the high	51	17	82
quality of her act, however, she was given a third-place medal.	64	21	87
Her coach, talking later to a reporter, stated his pleasure	12	25	91
with her part of the show. When asked about the fall, he said	25	30	95
that emphasis should be placed on the good qualities of the per-	37	34	99
formance and not on one single blemish. He ended by saying that	50	38	104
as long as his students did the best they could, he would be	63	42	108
satisfied.	65	43	108
What is "best"? When asked, the young skater explained she	12	47	112
was pleased to have won the bronze medal. In fact, this perfor-	25	51	117
mance was a personal best for her; she was confident the gold	37	55	121
would come later if she worked hard enough. It appears she knew	50	60	125
the way to a better medal lay in beating not other people, but her	64	64	130
own personal best.	67	65	131

gwam 1' | 1 | 2 | 3 | 4 | 5 | 6 | 7 | 8 | 9 | 10 | 11 | 12 | 13 |
     3' | 1 | 2 | 3 | 4 | 5 |

46c   31'

FORMATTING

Measurement: two-page unbound report with references

Time schedule

Assemble materials .... 1'
Timed production .... 25'
Final check; compute
   g-pram .... 5'

Format the report on page 107 as an unbound report DS. Begin again if you have finished and time has not been called. Proofread; circle errors, calculate *g-pram*.

$$g\text{-}pram = \frac{\text{total words keyed}}{\text{time (25')}}$$

17 > Review

17a 6'

each line twice
SS (slowly, then
faster); DS
between 2-line
groups

alphabet 1 Mandif expects to solve my big jigsaw puzzle rather quickly.
" (quotation) 2 She sang the songs "Life Is Eternal" and "Fisherman's Song."
space bar 3 Fill the box with dirt and moss to keep the ivy plant moist.
easy 4 Jane Burien may wish to work downtown for a giant auto firm.

| 1 | 2 | 3 | 4 | 5 | 6 | 7 | 8 | 9 | 10 | 11 | 12 |

17b 7'

SKILL BUILDING

Finger reaches

Key each set of lines SS; DS
between each group; fingers
curved, hands quiet.

first finger
5 by bar get fun van for inn art from gray hymn July true verb
6 brag human bring unfold hominy mighty report verify puny joy
7 You are brave to try bringing home the van in the bad storm.

second finger
8 ace ink did kid cad keyed deep seed kind Dick died kink like
9 cease decease decades kick secret check decide kidney evaded
10 Dedre likes the idea of ending dinner with cake for dessert.

third finger
11 oil sow six vex wax axe low old lox pool west loss wool slow
12 swallow swamp saw sew wood sax sexes loom stew excess school
13 Wes waxes floors and washes windows at low costs to schools.

fourth finger
14 zap zip craze pop pup pan daze quote queen quiz pizza puzzle
15 zoo graze zipper panzer zebra quip partizan patronize appear
16 Czar Zane appears to be dazzled by the apple pizza and jazz.

17c 7'

SKILL BUILDING

Response patterns

Key lines SS; DS between
groups.

words: think and key words
17 may big end pay and bid six fit own bus sit air due map lays
18 also firm they work make lend disk when rush held name spend
19 city busy visit both town title usual half fight blame audit

phrases: think and key phrases
20 is the|to do|it is|but so|she did|own me|may go|by the|or me
21 it may|he did|but if|to end|she may|do so|it is|to do|is the
22 the firm|all six|they paid|held tight|bid with|and for|do it

easy sentences
23 Did the chap work to mend the torn right half of the ensign?
24 Blame me for their penchant for the antique chair and panel.
25 She bid by proxy for eighty bushels of a corn and rye blend.

| 1 | 2 | 3 | 4 | 5 | 6 | 7 | 8 | 9 | 10 | 11 | 12 |

Document 2
Unbound 2-page report
Reference: pages 98, 100, 102.

Document 3
Composition (Optional)
1 Prepare a rough-draft 4- or 5-line ¶ summarizing the content of the report. Use a title.
2 Key a final copy of the ¶ with errors corrected.

UNTAPPED RESOURCES   4

We directors of company personnel have important responsibilities,   17
among the most important being the acquisition of dedicated, conscien-   31
tious workers to carry out the daily functions of our businesses.   44

Staff Resources   51

Generally, we each have developed our own sources, which range   62
from local educational institutions, through employment offices, news-   76
papers, and on down to walk-ins, from which we find new employees.   90
But we always welcome new sources.   97

One supply often overlooked--though not by the more ingenious of   110
us--is the pool of available workers who have one or more noticeable or   124
definable "disabilities" or "handicaps." Occasionally, a supply of these 139
potential workers will go untapped in an area for a long period of time;   154
when discovered, they become a genuine treasure trove for a wide variety   168
of jobs.   170

Performance Level   177

Studies have shown that disabled workers, while perhaps   189
restricted to the exact jobs they can do, perform well above the minimum   203
requirements on jobs not beyond their capabilities. Limitations vary   217
with individuals; but once reasonable accommodations are made, these   231
workers become uniquely qualified employees.   240

Abrahms, writing of the reluctance of some employers to hire   252
handicapped workers, says that "workers with handicaps have high   265
rates of production, often higher than those achieved by other workers"   280
(Abrahms, 1994, 61). Munoz goes one step further by reminding us that   294
disabled workers "have high work-safety histories with low job-changing   308
and absentee records" (Munoz, 1994, 37).   317

From a practical as well as a personal point of view, then, hiring   330
workers who are physically or mentally handicapped can provide a   343
positive occupational impact for a company as well as a very rewarding   357
experience for its personnel director. One such director says: 370

Recently, I told a potential employee who was sitting in my   382
office in her wheelchair of our success with handicapped workers.   396
"That's great," she said. "You know, most of us rarely think about   409
things we can't do. There are too many things we can do and can   422
do well." I hired her (Moky, 1994, 78).   431

And so say all of us who sit in the employer's chair.   442

REFERENCES   444

Abrahms, Hollin C. "Searching for Employees." The Human Services   461
  Monthly, January 1994.   467

Moky, Latanya R. An Investment in Social Action: The Caseville Study.   491
  Macon: Meadowbrook Press, 1994.   498

Munoz, Hector. "Changing Aspects of the American Workforce at the Close   512
  of the Twentieth Century." National Vo-Tech News, May 1994.   529

17d 10'

Measure skill growth

DS ¶s; 5-space ¶ indention

1 Key the ¶s once.

2 Take 1' timings on each ¶ and a 3' writing on all ¶s. Determine *gwam*.

Goal: 18 *gwam*

all letters   *gwam* 3'

A wise man once said that we have two ears and one   3
tongue so that we may hear more and talk less. Therefore,   7
we should be prepared to talk less quickly and exert more   11
effort to listen carefully to what others have to offer.   15

Most people do not realize that when we listen, we use   19
not just our ears, but our eyes and mind as well. To form   23
the art of listening well, show interest in what is said,   27
pay attention, ask questions, and keep an open mind.   30

gwam 3' | 1 | 2 | 3 | 4 |

17e 20'

FORMATTING

Review formatting

Drill 1

1 Set 1.5" top margin, 1.5" side margins, and DS. Center heading and key first ¶. Line endings will be different than shown here.

2 Center the longest line in the listing; set a tab at that point. Begin all other lines at the tab; SS list.

Drill 2 (optional)

1 Set 1.5" top margin and 1.5" side margins; DS; 5-space ¶ indention.

2 Center heading. Do not add extra space between ¶s.

THRIVING IN A MULTICULTURAL WORK PLACE

To avoid conflict and misunderstanding in the work place, we must be aware of the cultural differences that exist among peoples from other cultures. Become more sophisticated in your relationships by knowing some American customs that often prove confusing to persons from other countries.

Love of individualism
Informality of workers
longest line ►Hierarchy and protocol
Directness

THE VALUE OF AN EDUCATION

Who are happier, people with much education or those who have little? Education is no magic elixir.

Education is only a tool that can help us to know how to win out over problems. The answer lies in how we use our education.

We can use what we learn, through experience as well as through school, to recognize those values that have great significance to us. We can use those values to help us find the satisfaction in life we all seek.

45 Enumerations and Review

45a 7'

each line 3 times SS;
DS between 3-line groups

alphabet 1 Max Biqua watched jet planes flying in the azure sky over a cove.
figures 2 Send 105 No. 4 nails and 67 No. 8 brads for my home at 329 Annet.
3d row 3 We two were ready to type a report for our quiet trio of workers.
easy 4 Pamela owns a big bicycle; and, with it, she may visit the docks.

| 1 | 2 | 3 | 4 | 5 | 6 | 7 | 8 | 9 | 10 | 11 | 12 | 13 |

45b 43'

FORMATTING

Review document formats

Document 1
Memorandum
Use bold for the headings.
Correct errors.
Reference: pages 81-82.

words

TO: Andrew Anhut   4

FROM: Marge Oxward   8

DATE: October 5, 19--   12

SUBJECT: Enumerated Items   18

This memo illustrates both the hanging indent format and the block   31
format for numbered items in documents. The hanging indent format   44
provides maximum emphasis, but the block format is more efficient. The 59
purpose of the document should guide the writer in choosing the appro- 73
priate format. Unless specified otherwise, use hanging indent format.   87

Hanging Indent Format   96

1. The numbered items are single-spaced with a double space between   110
    items.   112

2. Indent second and succeeding lines four spaces (or to the position of 126
    the first tab, depending on the software used).   136

Blocked Enumerations   144

1. The numbered items are single-spaced with a double space between   157
items.   159

2. The second and succeeding lines of numbered items are blocked   172
immediately under the number.   178

When enumerations appear within a <u>report</u>, they should be indented and 194
blocked five spaces from the left margin. The block format is recom-   207
mended, since the items receive emphasis by being single-spaced and   221
indented.   223

    xx   223

4
Figure Keyreaches

Learning goals:
1 To master selected symbol (top-row) keyreaches.
2 To edit (proofread) and revise copy.
3 To key from statistical copy.
4 To key from script copy.
5 To improve staying power.

Formatting guides:
1 Default margins or 60-space line.
2 Single-space drills; double-space paragraphs.

18a   7'

Skill-building warmup

each line twice SS; DS between 2-line groups

Note: Margins for a 60-space line are pica, 12-72; elite, 21-81.

alphabet 1 Jessie Quick believed the campaign frenzy would be exciting.
shift keys 2 L. K. Coe, M.D., hopes Dr. Lopez can leave for Maine in May.
third row 3 We were quietly prepped to write two letters to Portia York.
easy 4 Kale's neighbor works with a tutor when they visit downtown.

| 1 | 2 | 3 | 4 | 5 | 6 | 7 | 8 | 9 | 10 | 11 | 12 |

18b   14'

Learn 1 and 8

each line twice SS; DS between 2-line groups

Note: The digit "1" and the letter "l" have separate values on a computer keyboard. Do not interchange these characters.

Abbreviations: Do not space after a period within an abbreviation, as in Ph.D., U.S., C.O.D., a.m.

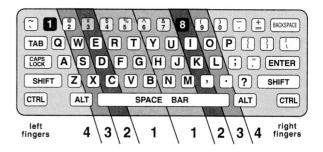

left fingers   4 3 2 1   1 2 3 4   right fingers

1   Reach *up* with *left little* finger.
5 1 1a a1 1 1; 1 and a 1; 1 add 1; 1 aunt; 1 ace; 1 arm; 1 aye
6 1 and 11 and 111; 11 eggs; 11 vats; Set 11A; May 11; Item 11
7 The 11 aces of the 111th Corps each rated a salute at 1 p.m.

8   Reach *up* with *right second* finger.
8 8 8k k8 8 8; 8 kits; ask 8; 8 kites; kick 8; 8 keys; spark 8
9 OK 88; 8 bags; 8 or 88; the 88th; 88 kegs; ask 88; order 888
10 Eight of the 88 cars score 8 or better on our Form 8 rating.

all figures learned
11 She did live at 818 Park, not 181 Park; or was it 181 Clark?
12 Put 1 with 8 to form 18; put 8 with 1 to form 81. Use 1881.
13 On May 1 at 8 a.m., 18 men and 18 women left Gate 8 for Rio.

44b (continued)

words

THE IMPORTANCE OF BUSINESS COMMUNICATION

THE IMPORTANCE OF BUSINESS   5
COMMUNICATION   8
QS

Probably no successful enterprise   15
exists that does not rely for its success upon   24
the ability of its members to communicate   33
with each other and with third   39
parties. The role that effective communica-   48
tion plays in business success cannot be   56
stressed too strongly; it is essential that   65
strict attention be paid to the application,   74
implementation, and administration of   81
communication within a business venture.   90

Effective communication results   96
when information is transmitted from   104
a sender to a receiver, and the   110
message is understood. It is not nec-   118
essary that the message result in any   125
specific outcome, only that it be sent,   133
received, and understood (Estevez,   140
1994, 12).   143

Business communication falls into two   150
main categories, written and verbal. More   159
time is spent by most business firms   166
studying and perfecting their written com-   175
munications. It is verbal communication,   183
however, that makes up a major portion of   192
all communication and deserves more   200
attention than is typically the case. "Suc-   208
cessful businesses have long known the   217
importance of good verbal communication,   225
yet many of them still give written com-   234
munication greater emphasis" (Hunter,   242
1993, 29).   244

Written communication confirms facts   252
and intentions, and any important verbal   260
conversation should be confirmed in   267
writing. Written communication also   275
constitutes proof; a letter signature can have   284
the same effect as a contract signature. Fur-   293
ther, written communications can be retained   302

for later reference, affirmation being as close as   312
the filing cabinet. Written communication avoids   322
some of the natural barriers of verbal communi-   332
cation. Shyness, speech problems, and other   341
distractions are not found in a letter.   349

Since verbal communication often involves   357
encounters on a one-on-one basis, it can bring   367
quicker results. Misunderstandings are avoided;   377
questions are answered. It is usually less   385
formal and friendlier; moods, attitudes, and   394
emotions are more easily handled. Verbal com-   404
munication is augmented with facial expressions   413
and gestures, assuring greater clarity of the mes-   423
sage. Words and phrases can be given special   432
emphasis not possible in a written message,   441
where emphasis is given by the receiver, not the   451
sender.   453

Murphy points out the importance of   460
communication: 463

Make no mistake; both written and   470
verbal communication are the stuff upon   478
which success is built. Both forms de-   485
serve careful study by any business that   494
wants to grow. Successful businesspeople   502
must read, write, speak, and listen with   511
skill (Murphy, 1994, 57).   516
QS

REFERENCES

REFERENCES   518
QS

Estevez, Ted. "The Art of Communicating in   527
Business." <u>New Age Magazine</u>, July 1994.   538
DS

Hunter, Dake R. <u>Business Communications   550
Today</u>. Fort Worth: Big Bend Publishers,   560
Inc., 1993.   562

Murphy, Grace. "Sharp Management Tools."   571
<u>Modern Business</u>, May 1994.   579

SKILL BUILDING

Improve figure keyreaches

Control your reading speed; read only slightly ahead of what you are keying. Key each line once DS; repeat lines 15, 17, and 19.

14 The 8 men in 8 boats left Dock 1 at 1 p.m. June 1.

15 *On August 1, I saw 8 mares and 8 foals in Field 1.*

16 The 81 boxes on Pier 18 left at 8 p.m. on March 1.

17 *Jan is 18 and Sean is 18; their grandfather is 81.*

18 Our 18 trucks moved 188 tons on May 18 and June 1.

19 *Send Mary 18 No. 1 panes for her home at 8118 Oak.*

18d   13'

SKILL BUILDING

Reach for new goals

Key each sentence twice as "Return" is called every 30".
Goal: To reach the end of each line as "Return" is called.

Goals for 1'
14-15 *gwam*, acceptable
16-17 *gwam*, good
18-20 *gwam*, very good
  22+ *gwam*, excellent

		gwam 1'	30"
20	I paid for six bushels of rye.	6	12
21	Risk a penalty; this is a big down.	7	14
22	Did their form entitle them to the land?	8	16
23	Did the men in the field signal for us to go?	9	18
24	I may pay for the antique bowls when I go to town.	10	20
25	The auditor did the work right, so he risks no penalty.	11	22
26	The man by the big bush did signal us to turn down the lane.	12	24

18e   8'

SKILL BUILDING

Improve keying techniques

each line twice; DS between 2-line groups

first row
27 Can Max Babbs, my zany cousin, raze Ms. Mann's vacant manor?
home row
28 Sada and Jake had a dish of salad; Gail had a glass of soda.
third row
29 At our party, Roy quietly poured tea for our worried guests.
top row
30 In July, 81 men visited 8 cities and 18 towns on 11 islands.
| 1 | 2 | 3 | 4 | 5 | 6 | 7 | 8 | 9 | 10 | 11 | 12 |

44 ◆ Unbound Report

44a 7'

each line 3 times SS
(work for fewer than
3 errors per group);
DS between 3-line
groups

alphabet 1 Joyce Wexford left my squad after giving back the disputed prize.
figures 2 Reply to Items 4, 5, and 6 on page 39 and 1, 7, and 8 on page 20.
double letters 3 A committee supplied food and coffee for the Mississippi meeting.
easy 4 In Dubuque, they may work the field for the profit paid for corn.

| 1 | 2 | 3 | 4 | 5 | 6 | 7 | 8 | 9 | 10 | 11 | 12 | 13 |

44b 43'

FORMATTING

Two-page report with direct quotations

Read "Moving to a second page" and "Direct quotations" at the right. Then key the 2-page report on page 103 DS. Use appropriate format.

Moving to a second page

1 Number second and subsequent pages at the right margin 1" from the top; DS below number.
2 Try to leave at least a 1" margin at the foot of a previous page.
3 Avoid dividing the last word on a page.

4 Avoid carrying over a single line of a paragraph to a subsequent page or leaving a single line on a page.
5 Key references on the last page of a report only if all references can be confined to that page. Otherwise, use a separate, numbered page.

Direct quotations

Word-for-word quotations from published works of other authors must be acknowledged with an internal citation.

Short quotations: Short quotations are simply enclosed in quotation marks followed (or preceded) by an internal citation.

> and deserves more attention than is typically the case. "Successful businesses have long known the importance of good verbal communication, yet many of them still give written communication greater emphasis" (Hunter, 1993, 29).

Long quotations: A quotation that runs to four or more lines of text should be set off in single spacing and indented 5 spaces (10 spaces for the first line of the paragraph) from the left report margin. No quotation marks are used.

> application, implementation, and administration of communication within a business venture.
>
>> Effective communication results when information is transmitted from a sender to a receiver, and the message is understood. It is not necessary that the message result in any specific outcome, only that it be sent, received, and understood (Estevez, 1994, 12).
>
> Business communication falls into two main categories, verbal and written. More time is spent in most organizations

19 ▸ 5 and 0

19a 7'

each line twice; DS between 2-line groups

alphabet 1 John Quigley packed the zinnias in twelve large, firm boxes.
figures 2 Idle Motor 18 at 8 mph and Motor 81 at 8 mph; avoid Motor 1.
shift/lock 3 Lily read BLITHE SPIRIT by Noel Coward. I read VANITY FAIR.
easy 4 Did they fix the problem of the torn panel and worn element?

| 1 | 2 | 3 | 4 | 5 | 6 | 7 | 8 | 9 | 10 | 11 | 12 |

19b 9'

SKILL BUILDING

Improve response patterns

each line once SS; DS between 2-line groups

word response: read word by word

5 el id la or by doe so am is go us it an me ox he of to if ah
6 Did the air corps hang a map of the glens on the big island?

stroke response: read stroke by stroke

7 up you be was in at on as oh are no ad pop fad pun cad hi ax
8 Face bare facts, we beg you; read a free tract on star wars.

combination response: vary speed but maintain rhythm

9 be a duty|as junk|to form|at rest|of corn|do work|he read it
10 Doria paid the taxes on six acres of rich lake land in Ohio.

| 1 | 2 | 3 | 4 | 5 | 6 | 7 | 8 | 9 | 10 | 11 | 12 |

19c 14'

Learn 5 and 0

each line twice SS; DS between 3-line groups

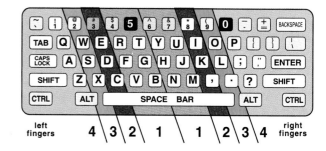

5 Reach *up* with *left first* finger.

11 5 5f f5 5 5; 5 fans; 5 feet; 5 figs; 5 fobs; 5 furs; 5 flaws
12 5 o'clock; 5 a.m.; 5 p.m.; is 55 or less; buy 55; 5 and 5 is
13 Call Line 555 if 5 fans or 5 bins arrive at Pier 5 by 5 p.m.

0 Reach *up* with *right little* finger.

14 0 0; ;0 0 0; skip 0; plan 0; left 0; is below 0; I scored 0;
15 0 degrees; key 0 and 0; write 00 here; the total is 0 or 00;
16 She laughed at their 0 to 0 score; but ours was 0 to 0 also.

all figures learned

17 I keyed 550 pages for Invoice 05, or 50 more than we needed.
18 Pages 15 and 18 of the program listed 150, not 180, members.
19 On May 10, Rick drove 500 miles to New Mexico in car No. 08.

DS

and thus oxygen becomes a crucial part of any aquatic ecosystem.

Dissolved oxygen is derived from the atmosphere as well as from

the photosynthetic processes of aquatic plants. Oxygen, in turn,

is consumed through the life activities of most aquatic animals

and plants (Bruce, 1994, 129). When dissolved oxygen reaches

very low levels in the aquatic environment, unfavorable condi-

tions for fish and other aquatic life can develop.

<u>Conclusion</u>

The absence of dissolved oxygen may give rise to unpleasant

odors produced through anaerobic (no oxygen) decomposition. On

the other hand, an adequate supply of oxygen helps maintain a

healthy environment for fish and other aquatic life and may help

prevent the development of unacceptable conditions that are

caused by the decomposition of municipal and industrial waste

(Ryn, 1993, 29).
QS

REFERENCES
QS

Book reference   Beard, Fred F. <u>The Fulford County Dilemma</u>. Niagara Falls:
                Dawn General Press, 1992.
DS
Periodical reference   Bruce, Lois L. "Hazardous Waste Management: A History." <u>State
                of Idaho Bulletin No. 7312</u>. Boise: State of Idaho Press,
                1994.
DS
Periodical reference   Ryn, Jewel Scott. "But Please Don't Drink the Water." <u>Journal
                of Environmental Science</u>, Winter 1993.

19d 8'

SKILL BUILDING

Improve figure keyreaches

Work to avoid pauses; each line once DS; repeat 21, 23, and 25.

20 After May 18, French 050 meets in Room 185 at 10 a.m. daily.

21 *Read pages 5 and 8; duplicate page 18; omit pages 50 and 51.*

22 We have Model 80 with 10 meters or Model 180 with 15 meters.

23 *Between 8 and 10 that night, 5 of us drove to 580 Park Lane.*

24 Flight 508 left Reno at 1 on May 10; it landed in Lima at 8.

25 *They need to use Rooms 10 and 11; lock Rooms 50, 80, and 85.*

19e 12'

OS

SKILL BUILDING

Improve speed

Follow the procedures at the right.

Guided writing procedures

1 Take a 1' writing on ¶1. Determine *gwam*.

2 Add 4 words to your 1' *gwam* to determine your goal rate.

3 From the table at the right, select from Column 4 the speed nearest your goal rate.

Note the ¼' points at the left of that speed.

4 Take two 1' writings on each ¶ at your goal rate guided by the quarter-minute calls (15", 30", 45", and 1').

5 Take a 2' and 3' timing without the guide.

¼'	½'	¾'	*gwam* 1'
4	8	12	16
5	10	15	20
6	12	18	24
7	14	21	28
8	16	24	32
9	18	27	36
10	20	30	40

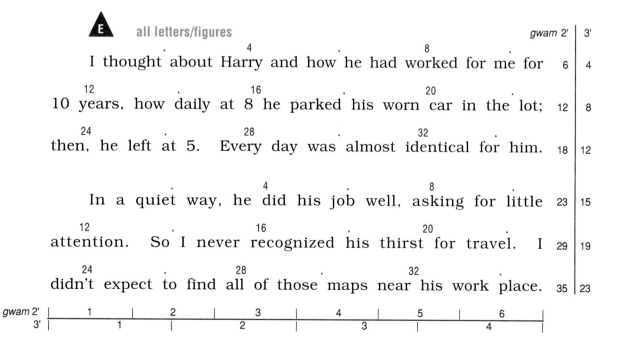

E all letters/figures
gwam 2' | 3'

.   4   .   8   .
I thought about Harry and how he had worked for me for   6 | 4

12   .   16   .   20   .
10 years, how daily at 8 he parked his worn car in the lot;   12 | 8

24   .   28   .   32   .
then, he left at 5.   Every day was almost identical for him.   18 | 12

.   4   .   8   .
In a quiet way, he did his job well, asking for little   23 | 15

12   .   16   .   20   .
attention.   So I never recognized his thirst for travel.   I   29 | 19

24   .   28   .   32   .
didn't expect to find all of those maps near his work place.   35 | 23

gwam 2' | 1 | 2 | 3 | 4 | 5 | 6
3' | 1 | 2 | 3 | 4

43 Unbound Report

43a 7'

each line 3 times
SS; DS between 3-
line groups; work for
fewer than 3 errors
per group

alphabet 1 Jacki might analyze the data by answering five complex questions.
figures 2 Memo 67 asks if the report on Bill 35-48 is due the 19th or 20th.
double letters 3 Aaron took accounting lessons at a community college last summer.
easy 4 Hand Bob a bit of cocoa, a pan of cod, an apricot, and six clams.

| 1 | 2 | 3 | 4 | 5 | 6 | 7 | 8 | 9 | 10 | 11 | 12 | 13 |

43b 13'

COMMUNICATION

Compose at the keyboard

Construct an outline that could have been used in the composition of the report on page 99. Use the same main heading as was used for the report.

43c 30'

FORMATTING

Unbound report: second page with references

1 Read "Report documentation" at the right.
2 Study the model showing the second page of a report. Note especially the top margin and page number position.
3 Key the last page of a report shown on page 101. (Your lines might not match those in the copy.)

Report documentation

Documentation shows sources of quotations or other information cited in a report.

Internal citations are an easy and practical method of documentation. The last name of the author(s), the publication date, and the page number(s) of the cited material are shown in parentheses within the body of the report; as, **(Bruce, 1994, 129)**. This information cues a reader to the name Bruce in the references listed at the end of the report.

References cited in the report are listed in alphabetical order by authors' last names at the end of the report. The list may be titled **REFERENCES** or **BIBLIOGRAPHY**.

References are keyed single-spaced in "hang indent" style; that is, with the first line flush left and each additional line indented 5 spaces. DS between references.

A book reference includes the name of the work (underlined), city of publication, publisher, and copyright date. A magazine reference shows the name of the article (in quotation marks), magazine title (underlined), and time of publication.

> 2
>
> and thus oxygen becomes a crucial part of any aquatic ecosystem.
> Dissolved oxygen is derived from the atmosphere as well as from
> the photosynthetic processes of aquatic plants. Oxygen, in turn,
> is consumed through the life activities of most aquatic animals
> and plants (Bruce, 1994, 129). When dissolved oxygen reaches
> very low levels in the aquatic environment, unfavorable condi-
> tions for fish and other aquatic life can develop.
>
> Conclusion
>
> The absence of dissolved oxygen may give rise to unpleasant
> odors produced through anaerobic (no oxygen) decomposition. On
> the other hand, an adequate supply of oxygen helps maintain a
> healthy environment for fish and other aquatic life and may help
> prevent the development of unacceptable conditions that are
> caused by the decomposition of municipal and industrial waste
> (Ryn, 1993, 29).
>
> REFERENCES
>
> Beard, Fred F. The Fulford County Dilemma. Niagara Falls:
> Dawn General Press, 1992.
>
> Bruce, Lois L. "Hazardous Waste Management: A History." State
> of Idaho Bulletin No. 7312. Boise: State of Idaho Press,
> 1994.
>
> Ryn, Jewel Scott. "But Please Don't Drink the Water." Journal
> of Environmental Science, Winter 1993.

20 ▷ 2 and 7

20a **7'**

each line once; then
take two 1' writings on
line 4; determine *gwam*

alphabet 1   Perry might know I feel jinxed because I have missed a quiz.

figures 2   Channels 5 and 8, on from 10 to 11, said Luisa's IQ was 150.

shift/lock 3   Ella Hill will see Chekhov's THE CHERRY ORCHARD on Czech TV.

easy 4   The big dog by the bush kept the ducks and hen in the field.

| 1 | 2 | 3 | 4 | 5 | 6 | 7 | 8 | 9 | 10 | 11 | 12 |

20b **14'**

Learn 2 and 7

each line twice SS; DS
between 2-line groups

left fingers   4   3   2   1   1   2   3   4   right fingers

2   Reach *up* with *left third* finger.

5   2 2s s2 2 2; has 2 sons; is 2 sizes; was 2 sites; has 2 skis

6   add 2 and 2; 2 sets of 2; catch 22; as 2 of the 22; 222 Main

7   Exactly at 2 on August 22, the 22d Company left from Pier 2.

7   Reach *up* with *right first* finger.

8   7 7j j7 7 7; 7 jets; 7 jeans; 7 jays; 7 jobs; 7 jars; 7 jaws

9   ask for 7; buy 7; 77 years; June 7; take any 7; deny 77 boys

10   From May 7 on, all 77 men will live at 777 East 77th Street.

all figures learned

11   I read 2 of the 72 books, Ellis read 7, and Han read all 72.

12   Tract 27 cites the date as 1850; Tract 170 says it was 1852.

13   You can take Flight 850 on January 12; I'll take Flight 705.

20c **10'**

SKILL BUILDING

Improve keying techniques

fingers curved, wrists low;
each line twice SS; DS
between 2-line groups;
repeat as time permits

shift/lock

14   Our OPERATOR'S HANDBOOK says to use either AC or DC current.

adjacent reaches

15   He said that poised talk has triumphed over violent actions.

direct reaches

16   Murvyn must not make any decisions until Brad has his lunch.

double letters

17   He will tell all three cooks to add a little whipped butter.

combination

18   Kris started to blend a cocoa beverage for a shaken cowhand.

1.5" top margin

BASIC STEPS IN REPORT WRITING

QS

1" side margin   The effective writer makes certain that reports that leave   1" side margin
her or his desk are technically correct in style, usable in con-
tent, and attractive in format.

DS

Side headings The First Step

DS

Information is gathered about the subject; the effective
writer takes time to outline the data to be used in the report.
This approach allows the writer to establish the organization of
the report. When a topic outline is used, order of presentation,
important points, and even various headings can be determined and
followed easily when writing begins.

The Correct Style

The purpose of the report often determines its style. Most
academic reports (term papers, for example) are double-spaced
with indented paragraphs. Most business reports, however, are
single-spaced; and paragraphs are blocked. When a style is not
stipulated, general usage may be followed.

The Finished Product

The most capable writer will refrain from making a report
deliberately _impressive_, especially if doing so makes it less
expressive. The writer does, however, follow the outline carefully as a first draft is written. Obvious errors are ignored
momentarily. Refinement comes later, after all the preliminary
work is done. The finished document will then be read and reread to ensure it is clear, concise, correct, and complete.

20d   9'

Compare skill sentences

1 Take a 1' writing on line 19.

2 Take 1' writings on lines 20 and 21; try to match the number of lines completed with line 19.

3 Repeat Steps 1 and 2 with lines 22-24.

19 Both towns bid for six bushels of produce down by the docks.

20 *The cowl of the formal gown is held down by a bow.*

21 I work 18 visual signals with 2 turns of the lens.

22 Did he fix the shape of the hand and elbow of the clay form.

23 *The ivy bowl is a memento of their visit to Japan.*

24 Did 7 of them fix the signals for the 50 bicycles?

| 1 | 2 | 3 | 4 | 5 | 6 | 7 | 8 | 9 | 10 | 11 | 12 |

20e   (Optional)

Reach for new goals

Key each line once as "Return" is called every 30".

Goal: To reach the end of the line just as "Return" is called.

		30"	20"
25	Pam visited the island in May.	12	18
26	The auditor may handle the problem.	14	21
27	He bid by proxy for the bushels of corn.	16	24
28	Did a man by a bush signal Ken to turn right?	18	27
29	If they wish, she may make the form for the disks.	20	30
30	Did the chap focus the lens on the airy downtown signs?	22	33
31	The formal gowns worn by the girls hang in the civic chapel.	24	36
32	Di paid us to go to town to bid for an authentic enamel owl.	26	39
33	Busy firms burn coal; odor is a key problem in the city air.	28	42

20f   10'

Review centering

full sheet; 2" top margin; DS; center each line horizontally

The Surprise of 1870

Sadie's 25 Days in London

WHY THE 75 FROGS LEFT FOR POUGHKEEPSIE

1207 Rue Martinique

88 Keys and Me

BETTY KEYES' 85 LOW-CALORIE LUNCHES

FORMATTING

The underline

Read the information at the right and then key Drills 1 and 2.

See Reference Guide page RG3 for rules for using underline.

Electric typewriter
1 Find the underline key in the upper right of the keyboard.
2 To underline a word, backspace to its first letter and strike the underline key once for each character to be underlined.

MicroAssistant
Strike **Alt + U** to turn underline on and off.

Word processing/electronic typewriter
1 Turn on the underline feature by striking the underline key or combination of keys.
2 Key the text.
3 Turn off the underline feature by striking the same keys used to turn it on.

WP Word processors may underline text that has already been keyed. Often this is done by blocking existing text and then keying the underline command.

Drill 1
Key the line as shown.

I saw the movie <u>once</u>; they saw it <u>three</u> times.

Drill 2
Titles of books may be shown either underlined or in ALL CAPS. Key the paragraph once DS; as you key, change the book titles from ALL CAPS to underlined with main words capitalized. Correct errors.

When Daniels wrote his popular book, REASONING WITH THE UNREASONABLE, he was fulfilling a desire of some years standing. When he was younger, he had read Traczewsky's MINDS UNLIMITED and Grbak's NO ROOM FOR ARGUMENT; and these books had created in his mind the necessity for a rebuttal based on his own theories. His earlier book, THE IMMATURITY CRISIS, would indeed prove to be a worthy prelude to REASONING WITH THE UNREASONABLE.

FORMATTING

Unbound report with main and side headings

Read carefully "Unbound reports" at right. Follow these guidelines as you key the report on page 99. (Your lines may not end as shown in the illustration.)

Unbound reports
Reports are often prepared without covers or binders. Reports longer than one page are usually attached with a staple or paper clip in the upper left corner. Such reports are called **unbound reports**. Follow these formatting guidelines for unbound reports:
1 **Top margins:** 1.5" for the first page; 1" for second and succeeding pages.
2 **Side margins:** 1" on all pages.
3 **Bottom margins:** At least 1" and not more than 2" on all pages but the last one, which might be deeper.
4 **Spacing:** Double-space educational reports and indent paragraphs 5 spaces. Business reports are usually single-spaced; paragraphs are blocked with a double space between them.
5 **Page numbers:** Number the second and subsequent pages 1" from top edge. DS below page number to the first line of the body. The first page is not numbered.
6 **Main headings:** Center in ALL CAPS; follow with a QS (3 blank lines).
7 **Side headings:** Begin at left margin and underline; capitalize first letters of main words; DS above and below.

BASIC STEPS IN REPORT WRITING

The effective writer makes certain that reports that leave her or his desk are technically correct in style, usable in content, and attractive in format.

<u>The First Step</u>

Information is gathered about the subject; the effective writer takes time to outline the data to be used in the report. This approach allows the writer to establish the organization of the report. When a topic outline is used, order of presentation, important points, and even various headings can be determined and followed easily when writing begins.

<u>The Correct Style</u>

The purpose of the report often determines its style. Most academic reports (term papers, for example) are double-spaced with indented paragraphs. Most business reports, however, are single-spaced; and paragraphs are blocked. When a style is not stipulated, general usage may be followed.

<u>The Finished Product</u>

The most capable writer will refrain from making a report deliberately <u>impressive</u>, especially if doing so makes it less <u>expressive</u>. The writer does, however, follow the outline carefully as a first draft is written. Obvious errors are ignored momentarily . Refinement comes later, after all the preliminary work is done. The finished document will then be read and reread to ensure it is clear, concise, correct, and complete.

21 ▷ 4 and 9

21a 7'

each line twice; DS
between 2-line
groups; 1' writings on
line 4 as time permits

alphabet 1 Bob realized very quickly that jumping was excellent for us.
figures 2 Has each of the 18 clerks now corrected Item 501 on page 27?
space bar 3 Was it Mary? Helen? Pam? It was a woman; I saw one of them.
easy 4 The men paid their own firms for the eight big enamel signs.

◁ | 1 | 2 | 3 | 4 | 5 | 6 | 7 | 8 | 9 | 10 | 11 | 12 | ▷

21b 14'

Learn 4 and 9

each line twice SS; DS
between 2-line groups

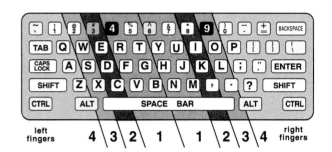

4 Reach *up* with *left first* finger.

5 4 4f f4 4 4 4; if 4 furs; off 4 floors; gaff 4 fish; 4 flags
6 44th floor; half of 44; 4 walked 44 flights; 4 girls; 4 boys
7 I order exactly 44 bagels, 4 cakes, and 4 pies before 4 a.m.

9 Reach *up* with *right third* finger.

8 9 9l 19 9 9 9; fill 9 lugs; call 9 lads; Bill 9 lost; dial 9
9 also 9 oaks; roll 9 loaves; 9.9 degrees; sell 9 oaks; Hall 9
10 Just 9 couples, 9 men and 9 women, left at 9 on our Tour 99.

all figures learned

11 Memo 94 says 9 pads, 4 pens, and 4 ribbons were sent July 9.
12 Study Item 17 and Item 28 on page 40 and Item 59 on page 49.
13 Within 17 months he drove 85 miles, walked 29, and flew 490.

21c 9'

S K I L L B U I L D I N G

Improve figure keyreaches

each line twice; DS between
2-line groups

14 My staff of 18 worked 11 hours a day from May 27 to June 12.
15 There were 5 items tested by Inspector 7 at 4 p.m. on May 8.
16 Please send her File 10 today at 8; her access number is 97.
17 Car 47 had its trial run. The qualifying speed was 198 mph.
18 The estimated score? 485. Actual? 190. Difference? 295.

Document 2

Use 1" side margins and a 2" top margin. Roman numerals I and II must be placed appropriately so the periods will align with III.

PLANTING GRASS SEED

Space forward twice from maargin ➤I.   PREPARING THE SOIL FOR SEEDING

     A.   Breaking Up and Pulverizing Soil
        1.   Spade, rake, hoe
        2.   Power tiller
           a.   Purchase
           b.   Rent
     B.   Soaking Area to **Be** Planted
     C.   Adding Nutrients

Space forward once from margin ➤II.   SMOOTHING OUT/PREPARING THE SEEDBED FOR PLANTING

     A.   Leveling the Soil
     B.   Eliminating High Spots
        1.   "Homemade" drag
        2.   Weighted roller
        3.   Rake

  III.   SEEDING AND SUBSEQUENTLY PROTECTING THE PLANTED
       AREA AGAINST EROSION

     A.   Manual Seeding
     B.   Mechanical Seeding
     C.   Adding Protective Cover
        1.   Straw
        2.   Cloth
     D.   Sprinkling to Set Seed

41c   13'

C O M M U N I C A T I O N

Compose at the keyboard

Compose a short outline on a subject of your choice; for example, MY CURRENT CLASSES, in which you show the class name, instructor, location, etc., on appropriate levels. Other possible subjects include RECENT BOOKS READ or PLANS FOR THE MONTH.

42 ◆ Unbound Report

Skill-Building Warmup

42a   7'

each line 3 times SS (work for fewer than 2 errors per group); DS between 3-line groups

alphabet 1	Di quickly won several junior prizes at the Foxburgh swim trials.
figures 2	From July 13 to 20, the extension numbers will be 45, 67, and 89.
shift/lock 3	Ms. Ing keyed the notations REGISTERED and CERTIFIED in ALL CAPS.
easy 4	Did he visit a city to handle the authentic enamel dish and bowl?

| 1 | 2 | 3 | 4 | 5 | 6 | 7 | 8 | 9 | 10 | 11 | 12 | 13 |

S K I L L B U I L D I N G

Improve keying techniques

key smoothly; repeat 20, 22, and 24

1st finger

19 Hagen, after her July triumph at tennis, may try volleyball.
20 Verna urges us to buy yet another of her beautiful rag rugs.

2d finger

21 Did Dick ask Cecelia, his sister, if she decided to like me?
22 Suddenly, Micki's bike skidded on the Cedar Street ice rink.

3d/4th finger

23 Paula has always allowed us to relax at La Paz and at Quito.
24 Please ask Zale to explain who explores most aquatic slopes.

| 1 | 2 | 3 | 4 | 5 | 6 | 7 | 8 | 9 | 10 | 11 | 12 |

21e   12'

S K I L L B U I L D I N G

Reach for new goals

1 Key each ¶ for a 1' writing. Compute *gwam*.
2 Take two 2' writings on all ¶s. Reach for a speed within two words of 1' *gwam*.
3 Take a 3' writing on all ¶s. Compute *gwam*. Reach for a speed within four words of 1' *gwam*.

E all letters   gwam 2' | 3'

We consider nature to be limited to those things, such   6 | 4
as air or trees, that we humans do not or cannot make.   11 | 7

For most of us, nature just exists, just is. We don't   17 | 11
question it or, perhaps, realize how vital it is to us.   22 | 15

Do I need nature, and does nature need me? I'm really   28 | 19
part of nature; thus, what happens to it happens to me.   33 | 22

gwam 2' | 1 | 2 | 3 | 4 | 5 | 6 |
     3' | 1 | 2 | 3 | 4 |

9

Simple Reports

Learning goals:
1 To format topical outlines.
2 To format unbound reports with side headings, internal citations, and reference lists.
3 To concentrate on data as you key.
4 To compose at the keyboard.

Formatting guides:
1 Default margins or a 65-space line.
2 Single-space drills; double-space paragraphs.

41a 7'

Skill-building warmup

each line 3 times SS
(concentrate on copy
to avoid errors); DS
between 3-line groups

alphabet 1 Jakob will save the money required for your next big cash prizes.
fig/sym 2 I saw Vera buy 16 7/8 yards of #240 cotton denim at $3.95 a yard.
3d/4th fingers 3 Zone 12 is impassable; quickly rope it off.   Did you wax Zone 90?
easy 4 Did an auditor handle the formal audit of the firms for a profit?

| 1 | 2 | 3 | 4 | 5 | 6 | 7 | 8 | 9 | 10 | 11 | 12 | 13 |

41b 30'

FORMATTING

Outlines

Study "Preparing outlines"; then study the example below.

Document 1

1 Format the outline below with 2" side margins and a 1.5" top margin.
2 Set 3 tab stops—4 spaces, 8 spaces, and 12 spaces—from the Roman numeral I.

Preparing outlines

Outlining is a critical first step in the process of organizing data, especially for reports. Making an outline clarifies a writer's thinking and helps her or him give ideas appropriate emphasis. A good outline has the following format features:

1 Capitalize topics as follows: first level, ALL CAPS; second level, main words; third level, first word only.

2 Single-space outlines; double-space above and below first-level topics.

3 Include at least two parts within each level.

4 Align all numbers, Roman and Arabic, at the period.

5 Indent each successive level four spaces under the previous level.

6 If a level has a second line, begin it under the first word of the line above, not under the number or letter.

7 Use 1" margins unless an outline is narrow and a shorter line length is more appropriate.

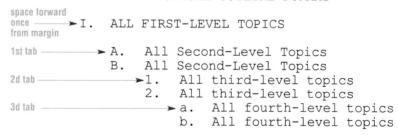

```
                    TOPICAL OUTLINE FORMAT

space forward
once ─────────►I.   ALL FIRST-LEVEL TOPICS
from margin

1st tab ─────────►  A.   All Second-Level Topics
                    B.   All Second-Level Topics
2d tab ──────────────►1.   All third-level topics
                      2.   All third-level topics
3d tab ─────────────────────►a.   All fourth-level topics
                             b.   All fourth-level topics

                   II.  ALL FIRST-LEVEL TOPICS

                    A.   All Second-Level Topics
                         1.   All third-level topics
                         2.   All third-level topics
                    B.   All Second-Level Topics
```

22 ▶ 3 and 6

22a   7'

each line twice SS;
DS between 2-line
groups

alphabet 1   Jim Kable won a second prize for his very quixotic drawings.
figures 2   If 57 of the 105 boys go on July 29, 48 of them will remain.
shift/lock 3   Captain Jay took HMS James and HMS Down on a Pacific cruise.
easy 4   With the usual bid, I paid for a quantity of big world maps.

| 1 | 2 | 3 | 4 | 5 | 6 | 7 | 8 | 9 | 10 | 11 | 12 |

22b   14'

Learn 3 and 6

each line twice SS; DS
between 2-line groups

3   Reach *up* with *left second* finger.

5   3 3d d3 3 3; had 3 days; did 3 dives; led 3 dogs; add 3 dips
6   we 3 ride 3 cars; take 33 dials; read 3 copies; save 33 days
7   On July 3, 33 lights lit 33 stands holding 33 prize winners.

6   Reach *up* with *right first* finger.

8   6 6j 6j 6 6; 6 jays; 6 jams; 6 jigs; 6 jibs; 6 jots; 6 jokes
9   only 6 high; on 66 units; reach 66 numbers; 6 yams or 6 jams
10   On May 6, Car 66 delivered 66 tons of No. 6 shale to Pier 6.

all figures learned

11   At 6 p.m., Channel 3 reported the August 6 score was 6 to 3.
12   Jean, do Items 28 and 6; Mika, 59 and 10; Kyle, 3, 4, and 7.
13   Cars 56 and 34 used Aisle 9; Cars 2 and 87 can use Aisle 10.

22c   10'

SKILL BUILDING

Improve keying techniques

each line twice; do not pause
at the end of lines; DS
between 2-line groups

shift/lock
14   The USS San Simon sent an SOS; the USS McVey heard it early.
adjacent reaches
15   Ersa Polk sang three hymns before we lads could talk to her.
direct reaches
16   Brace Oxware hunted for a number of marble pieces in Greece.
double letters
17   Tell the cook to add eggs and cheese to Ann's dinner entree.
one hand
18   Jimmy's drab garage crew tests gears fastest, in my opinion.

Drill 8
Develop/measure skill growth
Key 3' and 5' writings.

 all letters

gwam | 3' | 5'

Writing 11: **Straight copy**

Even the experienced authors know when they write that their | 4 | 2 | 25
original copy often is not the best copy. Of course, the first | 8 | 5 | 27
try will be readable; but there usually are a few areas that will | 13 | 8 | 30
need polishing. An excellent method for you as a creative writer | 17 | 10 | 33
is to sit down at your keyboard and place your ideas on paper as | 21 | 13 | 35
quickly as possible, then reorganize as needed. Read your paper | 26 | 15 | 38
aloud; if it sounds good to you, chances are it will sound just | 30 | 18 | 40
as good to a reader. Time will not allow you to be overly fussy. | 35 | 21 | 43
Learn when to polish--and when to finish. | 37 | 22 | 45

Writing 12: **Statistical copy**

One stormy night last winter, just 29 days before Christmas, | 4 | 2 | 28
I was driving my little Bentley automobile to South Ionia, a town | 8 | 5 | 31
about 75 miles away. I had been invited by Major Bill Jellison, | 13 | 8 | 34
just mustered out of the U. S. Marines, where I too had served 10 | 17 | 10 | 36
years as a captain, to see a new English play in the City Center. | 22 | 13 | 39
The night was quite dark; snow had started lazily to fall. After | 26 | 16 | 42
going about 38 miles, I remembered that Bill had said to me: "Be | 30 | 18 | 44
sure to turn east at the corner of Level and South Essex roads. | 35 | 21 | 47
Do not take a chance and turn west"; or, at least I thought that | 39 | 23 | 49
was what he said. So, I turned east on Level Road, Route 46. | 43 | 26 | 52

Writing 13: **Rough-draft copy**

According to studies done at a State University, one quick method | 4 | 2 | 25
way to get rid of physical tiredness, given the opportunity, is to | 8 | 5 | 28
jump into a cold shower. while we still don't exactly know which | 13 | 8 | 30
this has the affect that it does, it seems to do the trick. The | 17 | 10 | 33
researchers have discovered also the that average person can work | 21 | 13 | 36
both harder and harder if she or she takes short, frequent rests. | 26 | 15 | 38
They have found also that some music, any kind from classical to | 30 | 18 | 41
jazz, usually have some affect on the amount and quality of work | 34 | 21 | 43
completed, as well as upon the well-being of the workers. | 38 | 23 | 46

gwam 3' | 1 | 2 | 3 | 4 | 5
5' | 1 | 2 | 3

22d 10'

Improve response patterns

each line once SS; DS
between 2-line groups;
repeat

word response: think and key words

19 he el id is go us it an me of he of to if ah or bye do so am
20 Did she enamel emblems on a big panel for the downtown sign?

stroke response: think and key each stroke

21 kin are hip read lymph was pop saw ink art oil gas up as mop
22 Barbara started the union wage earners tax in Texas in July.

combination response: vary speed but maintain rhythm

23 upon than eve lion when burley with they only them loin were
24 It was the opinion of my neighbor that we may work as usual.

| 1 | 2 | 3 | 4 | 5 | 6 | 7 | 8 | 9 | 10 | 11 | 12 |

22e 9'

OS

SKILL BUILDING

Build staying power

Work for good rhythm; key
two 1' writings, then a 2'
writing and a 3' writing.

Goals:

1', 17-23 *gwam*
2', 15-21 *gwam*
3', 14-20 *gwam*

  all letters

gwam 2' | 3'

I am something quite precious. Though millions of   5 | 3

people in other countries might not have me, you likely do.   11 | 7

I have a lot of power. For it is I who names a new   16 | 11

president every four years. It is I who decides if a tax   22 | 15

shall be levied. I even decide questions of war or peace.   28 | 19

I was acquired at a great cost; however, I am free to all   34 | 23

citizens. And yet, sadly, I am often ignored; or, still   40 | 27

worse, I am just taken for granted. I can be lost, and in   46 | 30

certain circumstances I can even be taken away. What, you   52 | 34

may ask, am I? I am your right to vote. Don't take me   57 | 38

lightly.   58 | 39

gwam 2' | 1 | 2 | 3 | 4 | 5 | 6 | 7 |
3' | 1 | 2 | 3 | 4 | 5 |

Drill 7
Measure skill growth: straight copy

1 Key 1' writings on each ¶ of a timing. Note that ¶s within a timing increase by 2 words. **Goal:** to complete each ¶.
2 Key a 3' timing on the entire writing.

 To access writings on MicroPace Plus, key **W** and the timing number. For example, key **W8** for Writing 8.

Writing 8: **34, 36, 38** *gwam*

	gwam 1'	3'
Any of us whose target is to achieve success in our professional	13	4
lives will understand that we must learn how to work in harmony	26	8
with others whose paths may cross ours daily.	35	12
We will, unquestionably, work for, with, and beside people, just	13	16
as they will work for, with, and beside us. We will judge them,	26	20
as most certainly they are going to be judging us.	38	24
A lot of people realize the need for solid working relations and	13	28
have a rule that treats others as they, themselves, expect to be	26	33
treated. This seems to be a sound, practical idea for them.	40	37

Writing 9: **36, 38, 40** *gwam*

I spoke with one company visitor recently; and she was very much	13	4
impressed, she said, with the large amount of work she had noted	26	9
being finished by one of our front office workers.	36	12
I told her how we had just last week recognized this very person	13	16
for what he had done, for output, naturally, but also because of	26	21
its excellence. We know this person has that "magic touch."	38	25
This "magic touch" is the ability to do a fair amount of work in	13	29
a fair amount of time. It involves a desire to become ever more	26	34
efficient without losing quality--the "touch" all workers should	39	38
have.	40	38

Writing 10: **38, 40, 42** gwam

Isn't it great just to untangle and relax after you have keyed a	13	4
completed document. Complete, or just done? No document is	25	8
quite complete until it has left you and passed to the next step.	38	13
There are desirable things that must happen to a document before	13	17
you surrender it. It must be read carefully, first of all, for	26	22
meaning to find words that look right but aren't. Read word for	39	26
word.	40	26
Check all figures and exact data, like a date or time, with your	13	31
principal copy. Make sure format details are right. Only then,	26	35
print or remove the work and scrutinize to see how it might look	39	39
to a recipient.	42	40

gwam 3' | 1 | 2 | 3 | 4 | 5 |
5' | 1 | 2 | 3 |

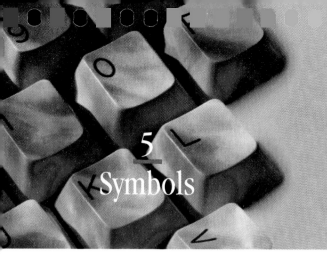

5
Symbols

Learning goals:
1 To master figure reaches.
2 To edit (proofread) and revise copy.
3 To key from statistical and script copy.
4 To improve staying power.

Formatting guides:
1 Default margins or 60-space line.
2 Single-space drills; double-space paragraphs.

23a 7'

Skill-building warmup

each line twice SS (slowly, then faster); DS between 2-line groups

alphabet 1 Why did the judge quiz poor Victor about his blank tax form?
figures 2 J. Boyd, Ph.D., changed Items 10, 57, 36, and 48 on page 92.
third row 3 To try the tea, we hope to tour the port prior to the party.
easy 4 Did he signal the authentic robot to do a turn to the right?

| 1 | 2 | 3 | 4 | 5 | 6 | 7 | 8 | 9 | 10 | 11 | 12 |

23b 14'

Learn $ and - (hyphen)

each line twice SS; DS between 2-line groups

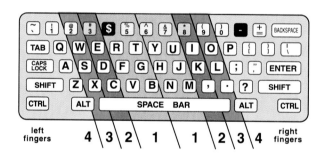

left fingers   4 3 2   1   1   2 3 4   right fingers

$ Shift; then reach *up* with *left first* finger.

5 $ $f f$ $ $; if $4; half $4; off $4; of $4; $4 fur; $4 flats
6 for $8; cost $9; log $3; grab $10; give Rolf $2; give Viv $4
7 Since she paid $45 for the item priced at $54, she saved $9.

- (hyphen)   Reach *up* with *right little* finger.

8 - -; ;- - - -; up-to-date; co-op; father-in-law; four-square
9 pop-up foul; big-time job; snap-on bit; one- or two-hour ski
10 My sister-in-law paid a top-rate fee for a first-class trip.

all symbols learned

11 I paid $10 for the low-cost disk; high-priced ones cost $40.
12 Le-An spent $20 for travel, $95 for books, and $38 for food.
13 Mr. Loft-Smit sold his boat for $467; he bought it for $176.

Drill 4
Build production skill

1 Key 1' writings (18 *gwam*) on the letter parts, arranging each line in correct format. Ignore top margin requirements.
2 Return 5 times between drills.
Reference: pages 72 and 78.

1 May 15, 19-- | Mr. Brad Babbett | 811 Wier Avenue, W. | Phoenix, AZ 83018-8183 | Dear Mr. Babbett

2 May 3, 19-- | Miss Lois J. Bruce | 913 Torch Hill Road | Columbus, GA 31904-4133 | Dear Miss Bruce

3 Sincerely yours | George S. Murger | Assistant Manager | xx | Enclosures: Warranty Deed | Invoice

4 Very cordially yours | Marvin J. Cecchetti, Jr. | Assistant to the Comptroller | xx | Enclosures

Drill 5
Reach for new goals

1 From the second or third column at the right, choose a goal 2-3 *gwam* higher than your best rate on either straight or statistical copy.
2 Take 1' writings on that sentence; try to finish it the number of times shown at the top of the goal list.
3 If you reach your goal, take 1' writings on the next line. If you don't reach your goal, use the preceding line.

	words	1' timing 6 times gwam	5 times gwam
Did Dixie go to the city?	5	30	25
I paid $7 for 3 big maps.	5	30	25
Do they blame me for the goal?	6	36	30
The 2 men may enamel 17 oboes.	6	36	30
The auditor may handle the problem.	7	42	35
Did the 4 chaps focus the #75 lens?	7	42	35
She did vow to fight for the right name.	8	48	40
He paid 10 men to fix a pen for 3 ducks.	8	48	40
The girl may cycle down to the dormant field.	9	54	45
The 27 girls paid their $9 to go to the lake.	9	54	45
The ensign works with vigor to dismantle the auto.	10	60	50
Bob may work Problems 8 and 9; Sid did Problem 40.	10	60	50
The form may entitle a visitor to pay for such a kayak.	11	66	55
They kept 7 panels and 48 ivory emblems for 29 chapels.	11	66	55

| 1 | 2 | 3 | 4 | 5 | 6 | 7 | 8 | 9 | 10 | 11 |

Drill 6
Build accuracy with figures

Choose a line (they get progressively more difficult) and key that line for one minute. The number of correct groups is approximately your correct *gwam*.

1849 3729 4016 4039 1616 2758 4820 3736 5656 4910 2838 5057

2393 3562 7050 9047 4293 5461 7856 6719 1504 3582 8037 9618

1518 6965 1420 6892 5247 7682 4310 8073 4349 7982 5317 9063

4132 8709 5143 6708 5132 9067 8690 4132 7087 4235 8086 1452

COMMUNICATION

Edit as you key

Read carefully; each line contains two errors, but only one is circled. Correct both errors as you key.

14 (i) asked Ty for a loan of $40; his interest rate is two high.

15 Please advise me how I can spent $18 for a second-hand book(?)

16 I'm sorry I lost (you) first-balcony tickers for the concert.

17 Lynda saws 3659 Riley (rode) is her daughter-in-law's address.

18 She can key 100 (storkes) a mintue at a 20-word-a-minute rate.

23d   20'

COMMUNICATION

Learn number-usage rules

Study the rules at right, then key the sample sentences below.

Numbers expressed as words

Good writers know how to use numbers in their writing. The following rules illustrate when numbers should be expressed as words. Key as words:

• a number that begins a sentence.

• numbers ten and lower, unless they are part of a series of numbers any of which is over ten.

• the smaller of two adjacent numbers.

• isolated fractions and approximate numbers.

• round numbers that can be expressed as one or two words.

• numbers that precede "o'clock."

Note: Hyphenate spelled-out numbers between 21 and 99 inclusive. Also, hyphenate fractions expressed as words.

19 **Six** or **seven** older players were cut from the **37**-member team.

20 I have **2** of **14** coins I need to start my set.   Elia has **nine**.

21 Of **nine 24**-ton engines ordered, we shipped **six** last Tuesday.

22 Shelly has read just **one-half** of about **forty-five** documents.

23 The **six** boys sent well over **two hundred** printed invitations.

24 **One** or **two** of us will be on duty from **two** until **six** o'clock.

23e   (Optional)   OS

COMMUNICATION

Revise as you key

Change figures to words as needed.

25 The meeting begins promptly at 9.   We plan 4 sessions.

26 The 3-person crew cleaned 6 stands, 12 tables, and 13 desks.

27 The 3d meeting is at 3 o'clock on Friday, September 2.

28 6 members, half of the team, were early for the 10 a.m. game.

Skill-Building Workshop 2

Drill 1
Compare skill sentences

1 Take a 1' writing on line 1; determine *gwam* and use this score for your goal as you take two 1' writings each on lines 2 and 3.

2 Take a 1' writing on line 4; determine *gwam* and use this score for your goal as you take two 1' writings each on lines 5 and 6.

1 Did the visitor on the bicycle signal and turn to the right?

2 The 17 girls kept 30 bushels of kale and 29 bushels of yams.

3 *The hen and a lamb roam down the field of rocks to the corn.*

4 The penalty she had to pay for the bogus audit is a problem.

5 Do 10 ducks, 46 fish, and 38 hams for the big island ritual.

6 *We got the usual quantity of shamrocks for Pamela to handle.*

| 1 | 2 | 3 | 4 | 5 | 6 | 7 | 8 | 9 | 10 | 11 | 12 |

Drill 2
Review number and symbol reaches

each line twice SS; DS between 2-line groups; repeat difficult lines

1 The inn opened at 6789 Brentt; rooms are $45 (May 12 to July 30).

2 I paid $1.56 for 2% milk and $97 for 48 rolls of film on June 30.

3 Order #4567-0 (dated 2/18) was shipped on May 30 to Spah & Erven.

4 Send Check #3589 for $1,460--dated the 27th--to O'Neil & Company.

5 Ann's 7% note (dated May 13) was just paid with a check for $285.

6 Send to The Maxi-Tech Co., 3489 D Drive, our Bill #10 for $25.67.

7 I wrote "Serial #1830/27"; I should have written "Serial #246/9."

| 1 | 2 | 3 | 4 | 5 | 6 | 7 | 8 | 9 | 10 | 11 | 12 | 13 |

Drill 3
Improve keying techniques

concentrate on each word as you key it; key each group twice; DS between 3-line groups

direct reaches

1 runny cedar carver brunt numbs humps dunce mummy arbor sects hymn

2 Irvyn jumped over a clump of green grass; he broke my brown pump.

3 My uncle Cedric carved a number of brown cedar mules in December.

adjacent reaches

4 trios where alert point buyer spore milk sands sagas treads ports

5 There were three points in Porter's talk on the ports of Denmark.

6 Has Bert Welker prepared loin of pork as her dinner on Wednesday?

double letters

7 glass sells adder offer room sleek upper errors inner pretty ebbs

8 The committee soon agreed that Bess's green wool dress looks odd.

9 Three sweet little moppets stood happily on a green grassy knoll.

| 1 | 2 | 3 | 4 | 5 | 6 | 7 | 8 | 9 | 10 | 11 | 12 | 13 |

24 ▸ # and /, Number Expression

24a 7'

each line twice SS;
DS between 2-line
groups

alphabet 1 Freda Jencks will have money to buy six quite large topazes.
symbols 2 I bought 10 ribbons and 45 disks from Cable-Han Co. for $78.
home row 3 Dallas sold jade flasks; Sal has a glass flask full of salt.
easy 4 He may cycle down to the field by the giant oak and cut hay.

| 1 | 2 | 3 | 4 | 5 | 6 | 7 | 8 | 9 | 10 | 11 | 12 |

24b 14'

Learn # and /

each line twice SS; DS
between 2-line groups

Note:
= number sign, pounds
/ = diagonal, slash

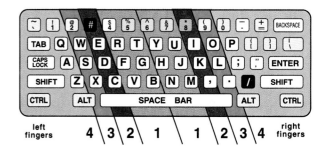

left fingers 4 3 2 1   1 2 3 4 right fingers

  #   Shift; then reach *up* with *left second* finger.

5 # #e e# # # #; had #3 dial; did #3 drop; set #3 down; Bid #3
6 leave #82; sold #20; Lyric #16; bale #34; load #53; Optic #7
7 Notice #333 says to load Car #33 with 33# of #3 grade shale.

  /   Reach *down* with *right little* finger.

8 / /; ;/ / / /; 1/2; 1/3; Mr./Mrs.; 1/5/94; 22 11/12; and/or;
9 to/from; /s/ William Smith; 2/10/n,30; his/her towels; 6 1/2
10 The numerals 1 5/8, 3 1/4, and 60 7/9 are "mixed fractions."

all symbols learned

11 Invoice #737 cites 15 2/3# of rye was shipped C.O.D. 4/6/95.
12 B-O-A Company's Check #50/5 for $87 paid for 15# of #3 wire.
13 Our Co-op List #20 states $40 for 16 1/2 crates of tomatoes.

24c 7'

SKILL BUILDING

Reach for new goals

Key 30" writings on both
lines of a pair. Try to key
as many words on the
second line of each pair.
Work to avoid pauses.

gwam 30"

14 She did the key work at the height of the problem.   20
15 Form #726 is the title to the island; she owns it.   20

16 The rock is a form of fuel; he did enrich it with coal.   22
17 The corn-and-turkey dish is a blend of turkey and corn.   22

18 It is right to work to end the social problems of the world.   24
19 If I sign it on 3/19, the form can aid us to pay the 40 men.   24

Drill 3
Review capitalization rules

1 Follow general format guides on page 90.
2 Set a tab 39 spaces from left margin for examples.
3 Study each line and its example from your printed copy.

CAPITALIZATION GUIDES

Capitalize

Specific persons or places:	She lives in Tudor Hall.
First words of sentences:	He had some good news.
Weekdays, months, holidays:	Friday, May 1, is May Day.
First words of direct quotes:	Dan shouted, "He's home."
Titles preceding personal names:	Dr. Iki phoned Lt. Moe.
Adjectives drawn from proper nouns:	Don likes Italian sausage.
Political/military organizations:	A Democrat has a Navy map.
Nouns followed by numbers:	Pack Order 7 in Bin 9.

Do not capitalize

Titles following a name:	Jan is our secretary.
Plurals of geographic designations:	I saw Ice and Swan lakes.
Compass points not part of a name:	Ride west to North Dakota.
Common nouns such as page or line followed by a number:	Copy the words on page 7.
Seasons (unless personified):	Next is fall, then spring.
Generic names of products:	He likes Flavorite coffee.
Commonly accepted derivatives:	I ordered french toast.

Drill 4
Apply capitalization rules

Provide capitalization as you key. Check your copy with Writing 12 on page 95 when you finish.

one stormy night last winter, just 29 days before christmas, I was driving my little bentley automobile to south ionia, a town about 75 miles away. i had been invited by major bill jellison, just mustered out of the u. s. marines, where i too had served 10 years as a captain, to see a new english play in the city center. the night was quite dark; snow had started lazily to fall. after going about 38 miles, i remembered that bill had said to me: "be sure to turn east at the corner of level and south essex roads. do not take a chance and turn west"; or, at least i thought that was what he said. so, I turned east on level road, route 46.

COMMUNICATION

Review number usage

DS; decide whether the circled numbers should be keyed as figures or as words and make needed changes. Check your finished work with 23d, page 53.

20 Six or ⑦ older players were cut from the ㊲-member team.

21 I have ② of 14 coins needed to start my set. Elia has ⑨.

22 Of ⑨ 24-ton engines ordered, we shipped ⑥ last Tuesday.

23 Shelly has read just ① half of about ㊺ documents.

24 The ⑥ boys sent well over ⑳⓪ printed invitations.

25 ① or ② of us will be on duty from ② until ⑥ o'clock.

24e 14' OS

SKILL BUILDING

Improve speed

1 Take 1' guided writings (see page 45 for guided writing procedures).
2 Take a 2' and 3' timing.

gwam

¼'	½'	¾'	1'
4	8	12	16
5	10	15	20
6	12	18	24
7	14	21	28
8	16	24	32
9	18	27	36
10	20	30	40

E all letters   *gwam* 2' | 3'

Some of us think that the best way to get attention is   6 | 4
to try a new style, or to look quixotic, or to be different 12 | 8
somehow. Perhaps we are looking for nothing much more than 18 | 12
acceptance from others of ourselves just the way we now are. 24 | 16

There is no question about it; we all want to look our 29 | 19
best to impress other people. How we achieve this may mean 35 | 23
trying some of this and that; but our basic objective is to 41 | 27
take our raw materials, you and me, and build up from there. 47 | 31

gwam 2' | 1 | 2 | 3 | 4 | 5 | 6 |
3' | 1 | 2 | 3 | 4 |

Communication Workshop 1

Format guides

1 1" side margins; 1.5" top margin.
2 Center title; DS; use bold as shown.
3 Proofread carefully; correct errors.

Drill 1
Review spacing skills

1 Set a tab 36 spaces from the left margin for the examples.
2 Key a spacing guide beginning at the left margin; tab; key the example.
3 Study each line and its example from your printed copy.

PUNCTUATION SPACING GUIDES

Space twice after

A sentence period:	Jo ran. Peter walked alone.
A question mark:	Who is it? Someone called.
A colon (except in time):	The way to win: go, go, go.
An exclamation point:	Oh! It can't be!

Space once after

An abbreviation period:	Mr. Coe met Adm. A. T. Brum.
A semicolon:	Meg met us; she visits daily.
A comma (except in numbers):	Rae, Lu, and I joined a team.

Do not space before or after

A hyphen:	We saw a first-rate ballet.
A dash:	He--I mean Bo--left early.
A comma in large numbers:	Key $1,000,000 or $1 million.
A colon in time figures:	We closed at 5:30 p.m.
A period within an abbreviation:	At 3 p.m. the meeting begins.

Drill 2
Improve spelling skills

1 Set tabs 25 and 50 spaces from left margin.
2 Center the title.
3 Key the first word at the left margin; tab and key the word again; then tab and key it a third time without looking at the word.
4 Study the words that you often misspell.

FREQUENTLY MISSPELLED WORDS

installation	installation	installation
committee		
corporate		
employees		
immediately		
interest		
necessary		
opportunity		
personnel		
received		
services		

25 ▸ % and --, Word Division

25a 7'

each line twice SS;
DS between 2-line
groups; take 1'
writings on line 4 if
time permits

alphabet 1 Merry will have picked out a dozen quarts of jam for boxing.
symbols 2 Jane-Ann bought 16 7/8 yards of #249 cotton at $3.59 a yard.
first row 3 Can't brave, zany Cave Club men/women next climb Mt. Zamban?
easy 4 Did she rush to cut six bushels of corn for the civic corps?

| 1 | 2 | 3 | 4 | 5 | 6 | 7 | 8 | 9 | 10 | 11 | 12 |

25b 14'

Learn % and -- (dash)

each line twice SS; DS
between 2-line groups

Note:
% = percent sign
Use % with business forms or where
space is restricted; otherwise, use
the word "percent."

-- = dash
No space precedes or follows the
dash.

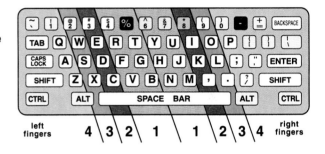

left fingers 4 3 2 1   1 2 3 4 right fingers

% Shift; then reach up with *left first* finger.

5 % %f f% % %; off 5%; if 5%; of 5% fund; half 5%; taxes of 5%
6 7% rent; 3% tariff; 9% F.O.B.; 15% greater; 28% base; up 46%
7 Give discounts of 5% on rods, 50% on lures, and 75% on line.

-- Reach *up* with *right little* finger.

8 -- --; ;-- --; one--not all--of us; Hap--our brother--drives
9 look--really look--and; why--and, indeed, why not--deny that
10 We--I mean the entire group--saw the movie--and we liked it.

all symbols learned

11 The total class--by "total" I mean 95% to 100%--voted to go.
12 Invoice #20--it was dated 3/4--billed $17, less 5% discount.
13 I did my CPR cases--1-6 yesterday, 7-9 today--and rated 89%.

25c 4'

SKILL BUILDING

Practice speed runs with
numbers

Take 1' writings; the last
number you key when you
stop is your approximate
gwam.

1 and 2 and 3 and 4 and 5 and 6 and 7 and 8 and 9 and 10 and

11 and 12 and 13 and 14 and 15 and 16 and 17 and 18 and 19

and 20 and 21 and 22 and 23 and 24 and 25 and 26 and 27 and

40b 15'

Key edited copy

Key as shown; make marked changes.

Time is money. In fact, I talked with a ~~person~~ *friend* last week ~~to~~ *for* whom this is an heart-felt sentiment. She explained to me that if her salary were $10 an hour, waiting *15 minutes* in line in a grocery store could theoretically add $2.50 to her grocery bill. She looses that much she says waiting at stoplights on her way to work and tardy friends cost her she figures $10 a week. Waiting in her doctors office cost her a fortune. To her, punctuality is a genuine virtue.

40c 13'

Compare skill sentences

1 Take a 1' writing on line 5 DS; determine *gwam* and use this score for your goal as you take two 1' writings on line 6 and then on line 7.
2 Repeat Step 1 for lines 8-10.

5 A cozy island Jan and Pamela visit is a land of enchantment.
6 A man got 62 of the fish, 26 cod and 36 sockeye, at Dock 10.
7 *An auditor may handle the fuel problems of the ancient city.*
8 Blame me for their penchant for the antique chair and panel.
9 The 20 girls kept 38 bushels of corn and 59 bushels of yams.
10 *It is a shame to make such emblems of authentic whale ivory.*

| 1 | 2 | 3 | 4 | 5 | 6 | 7 | 8 | 9 | 10 | 11 | 12 |

40d 15'

Build staying power

Take two 1' writings on each ¶, then two 3' writings on all ¶s; avoid pauses.

  all letters/figures

gwam 1' | 3'

Julia had a garden near her house at 4728 Western. She gave 12 | 4 | 35
it expert care--not one single plant ever went without its water 25 | 8 | 39
or fertilizer. And due to all this attention, nature was kind; a 38 | 12 | 43
bit of new growth became evident each day. 47 | 15 | 46

Now, Julia knew that she had several tomatoes here, 9 squash 12 | 19 | 50
over there, and 36 limas on down the line. What she did not know 25 | 23 | 54
was that two small beady eyes were also looking over her garden; 38 | 27 | 58
and at 5:10 that evening, some brown fur sat down to dinner. 50 | 31 | 62

| *gwam* 1' | 1 | 2 | 3 | 4 | 5 | 6 | 7 | 8 | 9 | 10 | 11 | 12 | 13 |
| 3' | | 1 | | 2 | | 3 | | 4 | | 5 | | |

SKILL BUILDING

Improve speed

1 Take 1' guided writings.
2 Take a 2' writing; try to maintain 1' rate.
3 Key one 3' writing.
Goals: 2', 15-22 *gwam*
3', 14-20 *gwam*

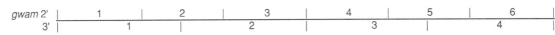

	gwam					*gwam*		
¼'	½'	¾'	1'		¼'	½'	¾'	1'
4	8	12	16		8	16	24	32
5	10	15	20		9	18	27	36
6	12	18	24		10	20	30	40
7	14	21	28					

E all letters

	gwam 2'	3'
As a member of Group #1 in my car club, I get $1--or	6 · 4	19
10%--off on each $10 I spend--at top-quality motels/inns as	12 · 8	23
I travel; I expect, too, my card will soon be recognized by	18 · 12	27
most major city department stores. The cost is only $45.	24 · 16	31

gwam 2' | 1 | 2 | 3 | 4 | 5 | 6 |
3' | 1 | 2 | 3 | 4 |

25e 15'

FORMATTING

Learn to divide words

Study "Word division guides" at the right; then key the problem below.
1 Set 1" side margins and 1" top margin; DS.
2 Clear tabs; set three new tabs 15 spaces apart. Center WORD DIVISION PRACTICE.
3 Key the first line, striking the tab key to move to the second, third, and fourth columns.
4 Key the words in Columns 2 and 4 with a hyphen to indicate the first correct division.

Word division guides

To achieve a more even right margin, long words (over five letters) must occasionally be divided. Follow these rules when dividing words:

1 Divide between syllables. One-syllable words cannot be divided. Consult a dictionary when in doubt.

cor- rect   weighed   planned

2 Key at least two strokes on the first line and carry at least three strokes to the next line.

ex- plain   enough   crafty

3 Divide between double consonants except when dividing a syllable from a root word that ends in double consonants.

chal- lenge   enroll- ment   set- tled

4 Divide after a single-letter syllable within a word; divide between consecutive one-letter syllables.

resi- dent   situ- ation   usa- ble

5 Divide compound words with a hyphen after the hyphen. Compound words without a hyphen are best divided between the word elements.

son- in-law   dead- lines   self- help

6 Do not divide a contraction, abbreviation, or most numbers.

wouldn't   NAACP   1,680,900

7 Avoid dividing nouns that should be read as a group such as proper nouns, dates, or places. When a division must be made, divide at a logical break.

Mr. John / Langford   July 27, / 1997
Austin, / Texas   1539 Madison / Avenue

WORD DIVISION PRACTICE

DS

telescope	tab	tele-scope	tab	catalog	tab	cata-log
deposit				first-class		
situation				spelling		
through				987,900		
membership				swimming		

pica margin 10   tab 25   tab 40   tab 55
elite margin 12   tab 27   tab 42   tab 69

COMMUNICATION

Edit as you key
DS; correct as marked

Someone has said, "you are what you eat?." the speaker did not mean to imply that fast food make fast people, or that a hearty [meal makes a person heart, or even that good food makes a perso good? On the other hand, though, a health full diet does indeed make person healthier; and good health is one of the most often over looked treasures within human existance.

SKILL BUILDING

Reach for new goals

1 Key a 1' timing; note *gwam.*

2 Add 4 *gwam* to this rate. Mark your ½' and 1' goals in the copy.

3 Take three 1' timings; try to reach your goals as your instructor calls ½' guides.

4 Take two 3' timings. Use Step 1 *gwam* as your goal.

LA all letters   gwam 3'

	4	8	12		
So now you are operating a keyboard. And don't you find it				4	38

So now you are operating a keyboard. And don't you find it   4 38
                    16   20   24
amazing that your fingers, working with very little visual help,   8 43
            28   32   36
move easily and quickly from one key to the next, helping you to 13 47
        40   44   48
change words into ideas and sentences. You just decide what you 17 51
        52   56   60   64
want to say and the format in which you want to say it, and your 21 56
                68   72   76
keyboard will carry out your order exactly as you enter it. One 26 60
            80   84   88
operator said lately that she sometimes wonders just who is most 30 64
        92   96   100
responsible for the completed product--the person or the machine. 34 69

gwam 3' | 1 | 2 | 3 | 4 | 5 |

40 ◆ Skill Building

each line 2 times
SS; repeat as
time permits

Skill-Building Warmup

alphabet 1 When Jorg moves away, quickly place five-dozen gloves in the box.
figures 2 Flight 372 leaves at 10:46 a.m. and arrives in Omaha at 9:58 p.m.
direct reaches 3 I obtain unusual services from a number of celebrated decorators.
easy 4 She may sign an authentic name and title to amend this endowment.

| 1 | 2 | 3 | 4 | 5 | 6 | 7 | 8 | 9 | 10 | 11 | 12 | 13 |

26 ▸ (and)

26a   7'

each line twice SS;
DS between 2-line
groups; take 1'
writings on line 4; try
for 18 *gwam*

Skill-Building Warmup

alphabet 1 Avoid lazy punches; expert fighters jab with a quick motion.
symbols 2   Be-Low's Bill #483/7 was $96.90, not $102--they took 5% off.
shift/lock 3 Report titles may be shown in ALL CAPS; as, BOLD WORD POWER.
easy 4   Do they blame me for their dismal social and civic problems?

| 1 | 2 | 3 | 4 | 5 | 6 | 7 | 8 | 9 | 10 | 11 | 12 |

26b   14'

Learn (and) (parentheses)

each line twice SS; DS
between 2-line groups

Note:
( ) = parentheses
Parentheses indicate offhand,
aside, or explanatory messages.

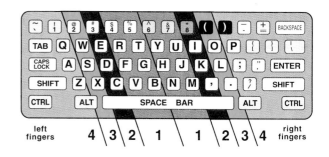

left fingers 4 3 2 1   1 2 3 4 right fingers

5 ((1 1(((; Reach from l for the left parenthesis; as, (((.
6)); ;))); Reach from ; for the right parenthesis; as,)).

( )

7 Learn to use parentheses (plural) or parenthesis (singular).
8 The red (No. 34) and blue (No. 78) cars both won here (Rio).
9 We (Galen and I) dined (bagels) in our penthouse (the dorm).

all symbols learned

10 The jacket was $35 (thirty-five dollars)--the tie was extra.
11 Starting 10/29, you can sell Model #49 at a discount of 25%.
12 My size 8 1/2 shoe--a blue pump--was soiled (but not badly).

26c   6'

SKILL BUILDING

Review numbers and symbols

Key each line twice, keeping
eyes on copy. DS between
pairs.

13 Jana has one hard-to-get copy of her hot-off-the-press book.
14 The invoice read: "We give discounts of 10%, 5%, and 3.5%."
15 The company paid Bill 3/18 on 5/2/95 and Bill 3/1 on 3/6/95.
16 The catalog lists as out of stock Items #230, #710, and #13.
17 Elyn had $8; Sean, $9; and Cal, $7. The cash total was $24.

8
Skill Building

Learning goals:
1 To improve keystroking.
2 To gain skill in keying numbers and symbols.
3 To improve ability to work with script and rough-draft copy.

Formatting guides:
1 Default or 65 space line.
2 Single-space drills; double-space ¶ writings.
3 5-space ¶ indention for writings and all DS copy.

39a 7'

Skill-building warmup

each line 2 times SS; DS between 2-line groups; take a 1' writing on line 4 as time permits

alphabet 1 Which oval jet-black onyx ring blazed on the queen's prim finger?
figures 2 Cy will be 19 on May 4; Jo, 27 on May 6 or 8; Mike, 30 on June 5.
adjacent reaches 3 We acquire few rewards for walking short treks to Union Terminal.
easy 4 To augment and enrich the visual signal, I turn the right handle.

| 1 | 2 | 3 | 4 | 5 | 6 | 7 | 8 | 9 | 10 | 11 | 12 | 13 |

39b 10'

SKILL BUILDING

Improve keystroking technique

fingers curved, hands quiet; each line twice as shown

1st finger
5 My 456 heavy brown jugs have nothing in them; fill them by May 7.
6 The 57 bins are numbered 1 to 57; Bins 5, 6, 45, and 57 are full.

2d finger
7 Ed decided to crate 38 pieces of cedar decking from the old dock.
8 Mike, who was 38 in December, likes a piece of ice in cold cider.

3d/4th finger
9 Polly made 29 points on the quiz; Wex, 10 points.   Did they pass?
10 Sally saw Ezra pass 200 pizza pans to Sean, who fixed 10 of them.

| 1 | 2 | 3 | 4 | 5 | 6 | 7 | 8 | 9 | 10 | 11 | 12 | 13 |

39c 10'

SKILL BUILDING

Practice figures and symbols

each line 2 times SS, then DS; work for smooth, fluid keying

"   %
11 Use "percent," not "%," for most writing.   Use "%" to save space.
/
12 On 7/3, fill Hoppers #10/1, #3/7, and #19/9 each with #27 gravel.
$ -
13 My son-in-law gets up-to-date $35-value lamps for $27, saving $8.
$
14 Policies #7301 and #8448 for $50,000 and $20,000 run for 4 years.
%   -
15 She--Ms. Borek--said we lost "9%, 7%, 5%, and 3%" on those deals.
&   /
16 Bort & Lee sold 2 tons on 6/9 and 6/13; J & J sold 9 tons on 7/5.
$ ( )
17 Serial #15 (40) marks his (Ron's) motor (this is not Model #206).
/
18 See reference to Invoice #14/910; the date, 8/27; the file, #359.

| 1 | 2 | 3 | 4 | 5 | 6 | 7 | 8 | 9 | 10 | 11 | 12 | 13 |

26d 14'

Learn number-usage rules

Study the rules at the right;
then key lines 18-23.

Numbers expressed as figures

In most business communications, some numbers are expressed in figures, while others are expressed in words. The following guidelines indicate instances when writing numbers as figures is preferred practice. Key as figures:

• numbers coupled with nouns.

• house numbers (except house number One) and street names (except ten and under); if street name is a number, separate it from the house number with a dash (--).

• time when expressed with a.m. or p.m.

• a date following a month; a date preceding the month (or standing alone) is expressed in figures followed by "d" or "th".

• money amounts and percents, even when approximate, are written as figures (use the $ symbol and/or the words "cents" or "percent").

• round numbers in the millions or higher with their word modifiers (with or without a dollar sign).

Note: When speaking or writing numbers (as in writing numbers on a check), the word "and" should be used only to signify a decimal point. Thus, 850 is spoken or written as "eight hundred fifty," not "eight hundred and fifty."

18 Ask **Group 1** to read **Chapter 6** of **Book 11 (Shelf 19, Room 5)**.

19 All **six** of us live at **One Bay Road**, not at **126--56th Street**.

20 At **9 a.m.** the owners decided to close from **12 noon** to **1 p.m.**

21 Ms. Vik leaves **June 9**; she returns the **14th or 15th of July**.

22 The **16 percent** discount saves **$115**. A stamp costs **35 cents**.

23 Elin gave **$3 million** to charity; our gift was only **75 cents**.

26e 9'

Paragraph review

1 Set 1.5" side margins and a 2" top margin; DS.
2 Key ¶ once; your lines will not match those in the text.
3 Divide words appropriately.

KEYBOARD--TOOL OR TOY?

Like most other mechanical devices, a keyboard is nothing more than a tool; and, like most other tools, the skill with which it is used defines the caliber of what is accomplished with it. The wise student, therefore, works to gain fast, accurate skill combined with knowledge of how, when, and where to use that skill.

Document 1
Business letter

block format (average
length); envelope

Current date | AMASTA Company, Inc. | 902 Greenridge Drive | Reno, NV   13
69505-5552 | Ladies and Gentlemen   19

We sell your video cassettes and have since you introduced them. Follow-   33
ing instructions in your recent flyer, we tell customers who buy your Super   48
D video cassettes to return to you the coupon we give them; and you will   63
refund $1 for each cassette.   69

Several of our customers now tell us they are unable to follow the direc-   83
tions on the coupon. They explain, and we further corroborate, that there   98
is no company logo on the box to return to you as requested. We are not   113
sure how to handle our unhappy customers.   121

What steps should we take? A copy of the coupon is enclosed, as is a   135
Super D container. Please read the coupon, examine the box, and then let   150
me know your plans for extricating us from this problem.   161

Sincerely | John J. Long | Sales Manager | xx | Enc. 2   170

Document 2
Business letter

modified block format
(average length); envelope

Current date | Mr. John J. Long | Sales Manager | The Record Store | 12
9822 Trevor Avenue | Anaheim, CA 92805-5885 | Dear Mr. Long   23

With your letter came our turn to be perplexed, and we apologize. When   37
we had our refund coupons printed, we had just completed a total   50
redesign program for our product boxes. We had detachable logos put on   64
the outside of boxes, from which each could be peeled and placed on a   78
coupon.   80

We had not anticipated that our distributors would use back inventories   94
with our promotion. The cassettes you sold were not packaged in our   108
new boxes; therefore, there were no logos on them.   118

I'm sorry you or your customers were inconvenienced. In the future,   132
simply ask your customers to send us their sales slips; and we will honor   147
them with refunds until your supply of older containers is depleted.   161

Sincerely yours | Bruna Wertz | Sales and Promotions Dept. | BW:xx   173

Document 3
Interoffice memo

plain paper; bold headings

TO: Brenda Hull | **FROM:** Bruna Wertz | **DATE:** Current | **SUBJECT:**   13
Current Promotion   16

We have a problem, Brenda. I have learned that some of our distributors   31
are using older stock with our latest promotion. As you know, our older   46
boxes have no logos; but our refund plan asks for them.   57

Nothing can be done now to rectify the situation. I believe you will agree,   72
however, that we must honor those coupons that arrive without logos.   86
There should not be many of them. Please alert your staff.   98

xx   98

27 & and :, Proofreaders' Marks

27a 7'

each line twice SS;
DS between 2-line
groups

Skill-Building Warmup

alphabet 1 Roxy waved as she did quick flying jumps on the trapeze bar.
symbols 2 Ryan's--with an A-1 rating--sold Item #146 (for $10) on 2/7.
space bar 3 Mr. Fyn may go to Cape Cod on the bus, or he may go by auto.
easy 4 Susie is busy; may she halt the social work for the auditor?

| 1 | 2 | 3 | 4 | 5 | 6 | 7 | 8 | 9 | 10 | 11 | 12 |

27b 14'

Learn & and : (colon)

each line twice SS; DS
between 2-line groups

Note:
& = ampersand, "and" sign
The & is used only as part of
company names.

: = colon
Space twice after a colon.

& (ampersand) Shift, then reach *up* with *right first* finger.

5 & &j j& & & &; J & J; Haraj & Jay; Moroj & Jax; Torj & Jones
6 Nehru & Unger; Mumm & Just; Mann & Hart; Arch & Jones; M & J
7 Rhye & Knox represent us; Steb & Doy, Firm A; R & J, Firm B.

: (colon) Left shift; strike key.

8 : :; ;: : : :; as: for example: notice: To: From: Date:
9 in stock: 8:30; 7:45; Age: Experience: Read: Send: See:
10 Space twice after a colon, thus: To: No.: Time: Carload:

all symbols learned

11 Consider these companies: J & R, Brand & Kay, Uper & Davis.
12 Memo #88-899 read as follows: "Deduct 15% of $300, or $45."
13 Bill 32(5)--it got here quite late--from M & N was paid 7/3.

27c 9'

SKILL BUILDING

Improve response patterns

1 Key each line once; check
difficult lines.
2 Key again each line
checked.
3 Take a 1' writing on line 16;
then on line 19. Determine
gwam on each writing.

word response

14 Did the busy girl also fix the torn cowl of the formal gown?
15 Clement works with proficiency to make the worn bicycle run.
16 They may pay the auditor the duty on eighty bushels of corn.

stroke response

17 Lou served a sweet dessert after a caterer carved oily beef.
18 After noon, a battered red streetcar veers up a graded hill.
19 Jim gave up a great seat; give him a few cases of free soap.

| 1 | 2 | 3 | 4 | 5 | 6 | 7 | 8 | 9 | 10 | 11 | 12 |

38 ◆ Measurement

38a 7'

each line 2 times
SS; DS between
2-line groups

Skill-Building Warmup

alphabet 1 Two exit signs jut quietly above the beams of a razed skyscraper.

figures 2 At 7 a.m., I open Rooms 18, 29, and 30; I lock Rooms 4, 5, and 6.

direct reaches 3 I obtain many junk pieces dumped by Marvyn at my service centers.

easy 4 The town may blame Keith for the auditory problems in the chapel.

◄ | 1 | 2 | 3 | 4 | 5 | 6 | 7 | 8 | 9 | 10 | 11 | 12 | 13 | ►

38b 10'

SKILL BUILDING

Measure straight-copy skill

Take two 3' writings;
key fluently, confi-
dently; determine
gwam; proofread;
count errors.

LA all letters   *gwam 3'*

Whether or not a new company will be a success will depend	4 | 62
on how well it fits into our economic system. Due to the demands	8 | 71
of competition, only a company that is organized to survive will	13 | 75
likely ever get to be among the best. Financial success, the	17 | 79
reason why most companies exist, rests on some unique ideas that	21 | 84
are put in place by a management team that has stated goals in	25 | 88
mind and the good judgment to recognize how those goals can best	30 | 92
be reached.	31 | 93
It is in this way that our business system tries to assure	34 | 97
us that, if a business is to survive, it must serve people in the	39 | 101
way they want to be served. Such a company will have managed to	43 | 106
combine some admirable product with a low price and the best ser-	47 | 110
vice--all in a place that is convenient for buyers. With no	51 | 114
intrusion from outside forces, the buyer and the seller benefit	56 | 118
both themselves and the economy.	58 | 120

gwam 3' | 1 | 2 | 3 | 4 | 5 |

38c 33'

FORMATTING

Measurement: basic business correspondence

(LM pp. S27-S29) or 4 plain
sheets

Time schedule

Planning time .... 3'
Timed production .... 25'
Final check; proofread;
   determine *g-pram* ..... 5'

1 Organize your supplies.

2 On the signal to begin, key the documents in sequence; use the current date and your reference initials.

3 Repeat Document 1 if time allows.

4 Proofread all documents; count errors; determine *g-pram*.

  g-pram = total words keyed
             25'

27d   8'

Edit as you key

each drill line once DS;
repeat if time permits

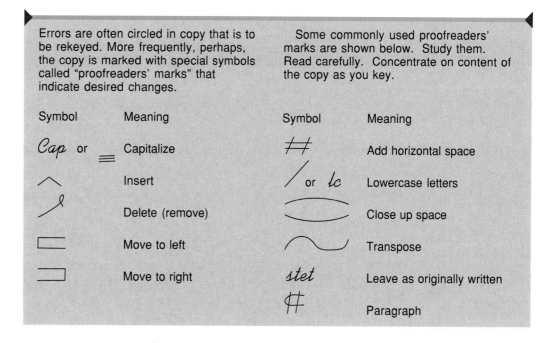

Errors are often circled in copy that is to be rekeyed. More frequently, perhaps, the copy is marked with special symbols called "proofreaders' marks" that indicate desired changes.

Some commonly used proofreaders' marks are shown below. Study them. Read carefully. Concentrate on content of the copy as you key.

Symbol	Meaning	Symbol	Meaning
Cap or ≡	Capitalize	⌗	Add horizontal space
⌃	Insert	/ or *lc*	Lowercase letters
⌿	Delete (remove)	‿	Close up space
⊏	Move to left	∿	Transpose
⊐	Move to right	*stet*	Leave as originally written
		⌗	Paragraph

20 We miss 50% in life's rewards by refusingto new try things.

21 do it now--today--then tomorrow's load will be 100%% lighter.

22 Satisfying work--whether it pays $40 or $400--is the pay off.

23 Avoid mistakes: confusing a #3 has cost thousands.

24 Pleased most with a first-rate job is the person who did it.

25 My wife and/or me mother will except the certificate for me.

26 When changes for success are 1 in 10, try a new approach.

27e   12'

Build staying power

Key two 1' writings on each ¶; then two 3' writings on both ¶s; compute *gwams*.

Goals: 1', 20-27 *gwam*
      3', 17-24 *gwam*

E   all letters   *gwam* 3'

Is how you judge my work important? It is, of course;			4	26
I hope you recognize some basic merit in it. We all expect			8	30
to get credit for good work that we conclude.			11	33
I want approval for stands I take, things I write, and			14	37
work I complete. My efforts, by my work, show a picture of			18	41
me; thus, through my work, I am my own unique creation.			22	44

gwam 3' | 1 | 2 | 3 | 4 |

37c 22'

FORMATTING

Interoffice
memorandums

Document 1
Key the memo; bold headings; correct errors.

words

TO:	John J. Lo **DS**	3
FROM:	Rosetta Kunzel	7
DATE:	Current	11
SUBJECT:	ZIP Code Information **DS**	17

Please stress information about ZIP Code use 26
when you meet with our office staff next Fri- 35
day: The ZIP Code follows the city and state 45
on the same line one space after the approved 54
two-letter state abbreviation. Encourage full 63
use of 9-digit ZIP Codes on our mail. 71

Also, be sure everyone has a copy of the 81
approved two-letter state abbreviations and the 91
USPS booklet ADDRESSING FOR AUTOMATION. 99
DS

xx 99

Document 2
Key the three *TO* names on one line. Correct errors.

words

TO:	Hollis Carver, Maxine Findlay, and	8
	Dorcas Washington	12
FROM:	T. R. McRaimond	16
DATE:	Current	20
SUBJECT:	Gym Benefits	24

As part of a special contract with the propri- 33
etors of HEALTH GLOW, Inc., our employees 41
can now use without charge the HEALTH GLOW 50
gym facilities at 27 Boone Drive each Tuesday 59
and Thursday afternoon after 4 p.m. 66

This privilege is an extension of the better- 75
health policy this company adopted last Janu- 84
ary. You will receive more information as it 93
becomes available. 97

xx 97

37d 11'

COMMUNICATION

Compose as you key

(plain sheet)

Refer to Document 2 above. Assume you are Hollis Carver or Maxine Findlay. Compose a memo to T. R. McRaimond. State in one or two paragraphs how you think your department members will react to the HEALTH GLOW program.

28 ▸ Other Symbols

28a 7'

each line twice SS;
DS between 2-line
groups; 30" writings
on line 4 (try to
complete the line)

alphabet 1   Pfc. Jim Kings covered each of the lazy boxers with a quilt.
figures 2   Do Problems 6 to 29 on page 175 before class at 8:30, May 4.
" 3   They read the poems "September Rain" and "The Lower Branch."
easy 4   When did the busy girls fix the tight cowl of the ruby gown?

◄   1 | 2 | 3 | 4 | 5 | 6 | 7 | 8 | 9 | 10 | 11 | 12   ►

28b 14'

Note location of <, >, [,],
@, *, +, =, and !

each pair of lines twice SS;
DS between 2-line groups

These keys are less commonly used, but they are needed in special circumstances. Unless your instructor tells you otherwise, you may key these reaches with visual help.

* = asterisk, star
+ = "plus sign" (use a hyphen for "minus"; x for "times")
@ = "at sign"
= = "equals sign"
< = "less than"
> = "more than"
[= "left bracket"
] = "right bracket"
! = exclamation point

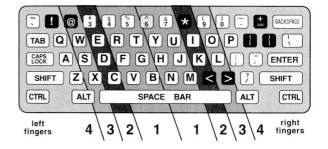

left fingers   4 3 2 1   1 2 3 4   right fingers

*   Shift; reach up with right second finger to *.

5   * *k k8* * *; aurelis*; May 7*; both sides*; 250 km.**; aka*
6   Note each *; one * refers to page 29; ** refers to page 307.

\+   Shift; reach up with right little finger to +.

7   + ;+ +; + + +; 2 + 2; A+ or B+; 70+ F. degrees; +xy over +y;
8   The question was 8 + 7 + 51; it should have been 8 + 7 + 15.

@   Shift; reach up with left third finger to @.

9   @ @s s@ @ @; 24 @ .15; 22 @ .35; sold 2 @ .87; were 12 @ .95
10   Ship 560 lbs. @ .36, 93 lbs. @ .14, and 3 lbs. @ .07 per lb.

=   Reach up with right little finger to =.

11   = =; := = =; = 4; If 14x = 28, x = 2; if 8 = 16, then 1 = 2.
12   Change this solution (where it says "= by") to = bx or = BX.

<   Shift; reach down with right second finger to <.   >   Shift; reach down with right third finger to >.

13   Can you prove "a > b"?   If 28 > 5, then 5a < x.   Is a < > b?
14   Is your answer < > .05?   Computer programs use < and > keys.

[ ]   Reach up with right little finger to [and].

15   Mr. Wing was named.   [That's John J. Wing, ex-senator.   Ed.]
16   Mr. Lanz said in his note, "I am moving to Filly [sic] now."

!   Shift, reach up with left little finger to !.

17   Yes!   My new clubs are in!   Just watch my score go down now!
18   I got the job!   With Ross & Myer!   Please call Lonal for me!

Document 2

Key the memorandum, using bold mode for headings; proofread and correct errors.

words

TO:	Tyrone A. Bledsoe, Production	6
	DS	
FROM:	Kim Bressuyt, Human Resources	12
DATE:	Current	15
SUBJECT:	Vacation Time and Pay	19
	DS	

When an employee's vacation coincides with a national holiday, the   32
employee will receive one additional day added to the scheduled vaca-   46
tion time. The maximum number of employees who may schedule a   59
vacation during a particular holiday period will be based upon the   72
production schedule set for the period.   80

Employees may pick up vacation pay on the last payday before the   93
scheduled vacation time. Any other adjustment to an employee's sched-   107
uled vacation must be approved by the department manager at least one   121
month prior to the month in which the vacation falls.   132

xx   132

37 ▸ Review Standard Memo

each line 2 times
SS; DS between
2-line groups

Skill-Building Warmup

alphabet 1 The explorer questioned Jack's amazing story about the lava flow.
fig/sym 2 I cashed Cartek & Bunter's $2,679 check (Check #3480) on June 15.
adjacent reaches 3 As Louis said, few questioned the points asserted by the porters.
easy 4 The eighty firms may pay for a formal audit of their field works.

| 1 | 2 | 3 | 4 | 5 | 6 | 7 | 8 | 9 | 10 | 11 | 12 | 13 |

37b   10'

SKILL BUILDING

Build staying power
Take two 3' writings.

 all letters

gwam 1' | 3'

When you write, how does the result portray you? Some of us   12 | 4 | 38
seem to take on some unique personality when we write. We forget   25 | 8 | 42
writing is just another way of talking, and what we write may   38 | 13 | 47
project an image that is not natural. Some writers, on the other   51 | 17 | 51
hand, try to humanize what they write so that it extends genuine   64 | 22 | 56
warmth and makes one want to read it. Apparently, correct format   77 | 26 | 60
and language, common sense, and some idea that a writer is still   90 | 30 | 64
among the living can add up to be very fine writing.   101 | 34 | 68

gwam 1' | 1 | 2 | 3 | 4 | 5 | 6 | 7 | 8 | 9 | 10 | 11 | 12 | 13 |
3' | 1 | 2 | 3 | 4 | 5 |

28c 10'

SKILL BUILDING

Troublesome reaches

Key smoothly, unrushed; avoid pauses, and allow your fingers to work. Repeat difficult lines.

n/m
19 Call a woman or a man who will manage Minerva Manor in Nome.

q/?
20 When did Marq Quin go? Did Quentin or Quincy Quin go? Why?

v/b
21 Barb Abver saw a vibrant version of her brave venture on TV.

w/q
22 We were quick to squirt a quantity of water at Quin and Wes.

4/5
23 On July 5, 54 of us had only 45 horses; 4 of them were lame.

9/0
24 Back in '90, Car 009 traveled 90 miles, getting 9 to 10 mpg.

28d 7'

COMMUNICATION

Edit as you key

Read carefully and key each line twice at a controlled pace; edit as indicated by proofreaders' marks; compare your completed lines with those of 26e, page 59.

25 Ask Group 1 to read Chater 6 of Book 11 (Shelf 19, Room 5).

26 All 6 of us live at One Bay road, not at 126-56th Street.

27 At 9 a.m. the owners decided to close form 12 noon to 1 p.m.

28 Ms. Vik leaves June 9; she returns the 14 or 15 of July.

29 The 16 per cent discount saves 115. A stamp costs 35 cents.

30 Elin gave $300,000,000; our gift was only 75 cents.

28e 12'

SKILL BUILDING

Build staying power

Keep eyes on copy, wrists low. Key a 1' writing on each ¶; then key two 3' writings on both ¶s.

E all letters   *gwam* 3'

Why don't we like change very much? Do you think that   4 | 26

just maybe we want to be lazy; to dodge things new; and, as   8 | 30

much as possible, not to make hard decisions?   11 | 33

We know change can and does extend new areas for us to   15 | 37

enjoy, areas we might never have known existed; and to stay   18 | 41

away from all change could curtail our quality of life.   22 | 44

gwam 3' | 1 | 2 | 3 | 4 |

36d 23'

FORMATTING

Interoffice memos

Document 1

1 Read "Interoffice memos"; then study the memorandum below.

2 Key the memo, using bold mode for form headings.

3 Take three 1' writings on opening lines and ¶1. Do not use the bold mode for timings.

Document 2 is on the next page.

Interoffice memos

Not all business correspondence is "outside mail." Mail is often sent between offices within an organization in the form of interoffice memorandums.

In this section, you will learn one acceptable memo format. See Reference Guide RG7 for an example of a simplified memo format.

Memos are sent in plain envelopes or in interoffice envelopes, which can be reused several times. The receiver's name and department are included on the outside of the envelope. "Confidential" tabs may be attached to seal the envelope when appropriate.

Format: Interoffice memos may be formatted on memohead, plain paper, or printed forms. Follow these guides when using plain paper or memohead stationery:

1 Use 1" side margins and 1.5" top margin (or begin a DS below the memohead).

2 Set a tab 10 spaces from the left margin to accommodate the longest line in the headings (**SUBJECT:** plus two spaces).

3 Key the form headings in bold. The recipient's and sender's personal and/or official titles are optional.

4 DS headings and between ¶s; SS body.

5 Include reference initials and enclosure notations when appropriate.

Set tab
10 spaces
from
margin

gwam 1'

TO:	Manuel E. Muni 1.5" (line 10)	3
	DS	
FROM:	Brett Luxward	6
DATE:	February 9, 19--	9
SUBJECT:	Company Newspaper	13
	DS	

1" This fall, the Human Resources Department begins a monthly news- 1" 26
paper that will report company announcements and activities   38
directly to each employee, bypassing much bulletin-board and   51
word-of-mouth communications.   56

The paper will contain personal news about employees, also.   65
Sports achievements, volunteer work, prizes won, and other news-   78
worthy activities will be included.   85

Please give this project some thought. Then report to me within   98
the next ten days the name of a person in your area willing (and   111
able) to accept responsibility for reporting such news to Denise   124
Byung, Human Resources Department, who will edit the paper.   136
                                                            DS
xx   136

6
Review/Measurement

Learning goals:
1 To achieve smoother, more continuous keying.
2 To key script and rough-draft copy smoothly.
3 To measure ability to key production, straight copy, and copy with figures.

Formatting guides:
1 Default margins or 60-space line.
2 Single space drills; double-space paragraphs.
3 Indent paragraphs 5 spaces.

29a 7'

Skill-building warmup

each line twice SS; DS between 2-line groups; 1' writings on line 4 as time permits

alphabet 1 My wife helped fix a frozen lock on Jacque's vegetable bins.
figures 2 Sherm moved from 823 West 150th Street to 9472--67th Street.
double letters 3 Will Scott attempt to sell his bookkeeping books to Elliott?
easy 4 It is a shame he used the endowment for a visit to the city.

| 1 | 2 | 3 | 4 | 5 | 6 | 7 | 8 | 9 | 10 | 11 | 12 |

29b 10'

SKILL BUILDING

Practice figure and symbol keyreaches

Work for fluency; key each line twice SS; DS between 2-line groups; repeat lines that seemed difficult.

$
5 He spent $25 for gifts, $31 for dinner, and $7 for cab fare.

/
6 As of 6/28, my code number is 1/k; Mona's, 2/k; John's, 3/k.

#
7 Bill #773 charged us for 4# of #33 brads and 6# of #8 nails.

%
8 He deducted 12% instead of 6%, a clear saving of 6%, not 7%.

( )
9 All of us (including Vera) went to the game (and it rained).

29c 7'

SKILL BUILDING

Improve keying techniques

Concentrate on quiet hands, curved fingers; key each line twice SS; DS between 2-line groups.

first row
10 Mr. Caz, an excited man, visits a monument to the brave men.

home row
11 Hal had a glass of soda; Jas had half a dish of fresh salad.

third row
12 You were to key quietly three erudite reports that were due.

top row
13 On April 2, Flight 89 left at 1:30 with 47 men and 65 women.

| 1 | 2 | 3 | 4 | 5 | 6 | 7 | 8 | 9 | 10 | 11 | 12 |

36 Standard Memo; Bold

36a   7'

each line 2 times SS;
DS between 2-line
groups

alphabet 1	Perhaps Max realized jet flights can quickly whisk us to Bolivia.
fig/sym 2	Send 24 Solex Cubes, Catalog #95-0, price $6.78, before April 31.
1st finger 3	The boy of just 6 or 7 years of age ran through the mango groves.
easy 4	The auditor did sign the form and name me to chair a small panel.

1 | 2 | 3 | 4 | 5 | 6 | 7 | 8 | 9 | 10 | 11 | 12 | 13

36b   10'

SKILL BUILDING

Build staying power

Take a 1' writing on
each ¶, then a 3'
writing on all ¶s.

LA   all letters   gwam 1' | 3'

		1'	3'
All of us can be impressed by stacks of completed work; yet,		12	4	39
we should recognize that quality is worth just as much praise, or		25	8	44
maybe even more, than the quantity of work done.		35	12	47
Logically, people expect a fair amount of work will be fin-		12	16	47
ished in a fair amount of time; still, common sense tells us a		24	20	55
bucket of right is better than two wagonloads of wrong.		35	24	59
The logic of the situation seems lucid enough: Do the job		12	27	63
once and do it right. If we plan with care and execute with		24	32	67
confidence, our work will have the quality it deserves.		35	35	70

gwam 1' | 1 | 2 | 3 | 4 | 5 | 6 | 7 | 8 | 9 | 10 | 11 | 12 | 13 |
3' | 1 | 2 | 3 | 4 | 5 |

36c   10'

FORMATTING

Bold mode

1 Set 1" margins; set a tab
10 spaces from left margin;
DS.
2 Do Drill 1; if your equipment will bold existing text, do
Drill 2 also.

Bold mode

The bold mode emphasizes text by
printing characters darker than normal
print. To key copy in bold:

Computers or electronic typewriters

1 Turn on the bold feature by striking the
bold key or combination of keys.
2 Key the text.
3 Turn off the bold feature by striking the
same key(s) used to turn it on.

MicroAssistant: Strike **Alt + B** to turn bold
on and off.

Word processing programs also enable bold
to be added to text that is already keyed.
This is often done by blocking the existing
text and then keying the bold command.

The proofreaders' mark for bold is a wavy
underline ($\sim\!\sim\!\sim$).

Drill 1

1 Turn on bold; key **TO:**; turn off bold.
2 Tab and key the information at the tab
stop. Repeat for each line of the heading.

TO:	Arthur Abt
FROM:	Bette Ashmyer
DATE:	January 23, 19--
SUBJECT:	Sick Leave Policy

Drill 2

1 Key text as shown:

No other vendor keeps you "in the
know" like FIRST SOLUTIONS.

2 Revise the text as shown.

No other vendor keeps you "in the
know" like FIRST SOLUTIONS.

29d 13'

SKILL BUILDING

Measure figure skill

Key with controlled speed three 3' writings.
Goals: 3', 16-24 *gwam*

E all letters/figures   *gwam* 3'

Do I read the stock market pages in the news? Yes; and	4 | 35
at about 9 or 10 a.m. each morning, I know lots of excited	8 | 39
people are quick to join me. In fact, many of us zip right	12 | 43
to the 3d or 4th part of the paper to see if the prices of	16 | 47
our stocks have gone up or down. Now, those of us who are	19 | 51
"speculators" like to "buy at 52 and sell at 60"; while the	23 | 55
"investors" among us are more interested in a dividend we	27 | 59
may get, say 7 or 8 percent, than in the price of a stock.	31 | 62

gwam 3' | 1 | 2 | 3 | 4 |

29e 13'

COMMUNICATION

Key edited copy

1.5" top and side margins; DS Make corrections as indicated by proofreaders' marks; divide words as appropriate or as directed.

	words
First Impressions	4
take time to evaluate your completed work. Look	13
caefully at what you have done. Would be you impressed	25
with it ifyou wre a reader? Is it attractive in form and	37
accurate in content? Does it look like something you wou	49
pick up because it looks interesting? Does the title	60
attract you? Do the first couple of lines catch your	70
attention? Personal appraisal of your own work is very	82
important. For if it does not impress you,	91
it will not impress any one else.	96

Document 2

1 Key the letter at right (average) in modified block format. Add closing notations. Correct errors. If necessary, review proofreaders' marks on page 61.

2 Address an envelope with this return address:

**METAL ENGINEERING INC
198 SANTA YNEZ DRIVE
LAS VEGAS NV 89105-9808**

Document 3

Key Document 2 again with these changes:

1 Address the letter to:

**Mr. Charles B. Onehawk
139 Via Cordoniz
Santa Barbara, CA 93105-0319**

2 Use an appropriate salutation.

3 Omit the final paragraph.

Current date　　3

Mr. Herbert *Brackmun*　　7
747 Myrtle Street　　11
Evansville, IN 47710-*3277*　　16

Dear Mr. *Brackmun*　　20

Your recent letter has us more than a little intrigued.　　31

In it, you describe a back yard squirrel feeder you　　41
have built, one that keeps out birds. This is certainly　　52
a the turnaround from the usual winter ~~animal~~ feeding *bird*-　　62
situation, and we believe it may have some apeal for　　73
many of our customers. We are interested.　　82

We are interested enough, in matter of fact, to　　90
invite you to send or bring to our office plans for your　　101
new feeder. If it can be built at a reasonable cost, we　　112
want to talk with you about representation in the market　　123
place.　　124

We have a several agency plans that we used have with　　134
success in representing clients like you for a number of　　145
years. We shall be happy to explain them to you.　　155

A copy of our recent catalog is enclosed.　　163

Very truly yours　　166

Miss Debra Stewert　　170
Sales manager　　176

on . . . Protocol in Addresses

Specific protocol is demanded by letter writers as they compose appropriate letter addresses and salutations. Use a courtesy title before the recipient's name or a professional title after the name. Do not use both.

Ms. Rachel Lindsey	not	Rachel Lindsey
Dr. William Jones or William Jones, M.D.	not	Dr. William Jones, M.D.
Dr. Susan Chain or Susan Chain, Ph.D.	not	Dr. Susan Chain, Ph.D.
The Honorable Steven Combs	not	Mr. Steven Combs

The woman's movement challenges us to ask why we distinguish between married and single women when we don't make the distinction in men. As a result, the use of *Miss* and *Mrs.* has decreased. Just as we use *Mr.* for men, *Ms.* is becoming the preferred title by many women. However, if you know that a woman has a different preference, use it.

30 Measurement

30a   7'

each line twice SS;
DS between 2-line
groups; 1' writings
on line 4 as time
permits

alphabet 1 Jewel quickly explained to me the big fire hazards involved.
symbols 2 Her $300 note (dated May 3) was paid (Check #1343 for $385).
- (hyphen) 3 Pam has an up-to-the-minute plan to lower out-of-town costs.
easy 4 Did the girl make the ornament with fur, duck down, or hair?

| 1 | 2 | 3 | 4 | 5 | 6 | 7 | 8 | 9 | 10 | 11 | 12 |

30b   10'

SKILL BUILDING

**Measure skill growth:
straight copy**

Key with controlled speed
two 3' writings DS.
Goals: 3', 19-27 *gwam*

 E all letters   *gwam* 1' | 3'

	1'	3'
I have a story or two or three that will carry you away	11	4
to foreign places, to meet people you have never known, to	23	8
see things you have never seen, to feast on foods available	35	12
only to a few. I will help you to learn new skills you want	47	16
and need; I will inspire you, excite you, instruct you, and	59	20
interest you. I am able, you understand, to make time fly.	71	24
I answer difficult questions for you. I work with you	11	27
to realize a talent, to express a thought, and to determine	23	31
just who and what you are and want to be. I help you to	35	35
know words, to write, and to read. I help you to comprehend	47	40
the mysteries of the past and the secrets of the future. I	59	44
am your local library. We ought to get together often.	70	47

gwam 1' | 1 | 2 | 3 | 4 | 5 | 6 | 7 | 8 | 9 | 10 | 11 | 12 |
     3' | | 1 | | 2 | | 3 | | 4 |

30c   33'

FORMATTING

Measure formatting skills

3 full sheets

Time schedule

Assemble materials; check
   marked references .... 2'
Timed production .... 25'
Final check: Proofread;
   mark any format errors
   you see .... 6'

1 Organize your supplies.
2 When the signal to begin
is given, insert paper (if
using a typewriter) and
begin keying Document 1.
Key the documents in
sequence until the signal to
stop is given. Repeat

Document 1 if you have time
after completing Document 3.
3 Scan for format errors and
mark any that you find.
Do the best, not the most,
you can do; and you will have
better results.

35 ◆ Review Modified Block

35a 7'

each line 2 times SS;
DS between 2-line
groups

alphabet 1	Melva Bragg required exactly a dozen jackets for the winter trip.	
figures 2	The 1903 copy of my book had 5 parts, 48 chapters, and 672 pages.	
shift/lock 3	THE LAKES TODAY, published in Akron, Ohio, comes in June or July.	
easy 4	Did he vow to fight for the right to work as the Orlando auditor?	

◄ | 1 | 2 | 3 | 4 | 5 | 6 | 7 | 8 | 9 | 10 | 11 | 12 | 13 | ►

35b 10'

SKILL BUILDING

Build production skill

1 Key 1' writings on the letter parts, arranging each drill line in correct letter format.

2 Use 1" or default top and side margins; return 5 times between drills. Use your reference initials.

gwam 1'

5 May 28, 19--   3
    QS
Ms. Dora Lynn   6
128 Avon Lane   9
Macon, GA 31228   11
    DS
Dear Ms. Lynn   13

gwam 1'

6 Cordially   2
    QS
Rebecca Dexter   5
Engineer   7
    DS
xx   8
    DS
Enclosures: Draft 251   13
               Area maps   15

7 February 4, 19--|Mr. Bill Bargas|3945 Park Avenue|Racine, WI 53404-3822   14

8 Miss Lois Bruce | 8764 Gold Plaza | Lansing, MI 48933-8121 | Dear Miss Bruce   14

9 Sincerely yours | Manuel Garcia | Council President | MG:xx | c Ron N. Nesbit   14

10 Yours truly | Ms. Loren Lakes | Secretary General | xx | Enclosure | c Libby Uhl   14

35c 33'

FORMATTING

Business letters: modified block

(LM pp. S21-S25)

Document 1

1 Key the (short) letter in modified block format. Correct errors.

2 Address an envelope with this return address:

GREATER BIRMINGHAM INC
163 UNION DRIVE
BIRMINGHAM AL 16303-3636

words

Current date | Dr. Burtram M. Decker | 800 Barbour   9
Avenue | Birmingham, AL 35208-5333 | Dear Dr. Decker   19

The Community Growth Committee offers you its sincere   30
thanks for taking an active part in the sixth annual Youth   42
Fair. We especially appreciate your help in judging the   53
Youth of Birmingham Speaks portion of the Fair and of   64
contributing to the prize bank.   70

Participation of community leaders such as you makes this   82
event the annual success it has become. We sincerely hope   94
we can seek your help again next year.   102

Cordially | Grace Beebe Hunt | Secretary | GBH:xx   111

Document 1
Center lines
2" top margin; DS;
center each line
horizontally

	words
The	1
City of	2
Los Portales	5
Mencken Public Library	10
New Books for July and August	16
LIFE IN ARGENTINA TODAY (Carmody)	22
ACHILLES AND THE DARDANELLES (Dodds)	30
BODY BUILDING: FOR EVERYBODY? (Szakely)	38
MARYE, THE WILL-O'-THE-WISP (O'Hargan)	46
LOST ON THE LOST ISLAND (Loupoin)	53
Hours:	54
10-10	55
Daily	56

Document 2
Key paragraph from script
1.5" top and side margins;
DS; 5-space ¶ indention;
center title; divide words
appropriately

COMMUNICATION SKILLS = EARNING POWER   7

The story in the newspaper emphasized one fact: 17
Ability to communicate is vital. An area survey reveals   29
that young people recently hired to staff jobs in local   40
offices have more chances for promotion and wage in-   50
creases if they have better-than-average ability to   61
communicate. Apparently, language and grammar are   71
still important for one reason: They earn money!   82

Document 3
Key paragraph from rough draft
2" top and side margins;
SS; 5-space ¶ indention;
center title; divide words
appropriately

A MODERN FABLE   3

, but unhappy,

There| was once a rich man who was not very happy; He had   13
spend large sums of for fancy clothes, a beautiful home,   25
money   lovely
luxurious cars--even his own plane--but none of it brought   37
him happiness. his psychiatrist, after weeks oftherapy,   48
DS { finally explained that happiness can't be bought; it must be   60
found. And--you guessed it--the unhappy man paid for these   72
words of wisdom with another large sum.   80
stet

Octagon Club
3851 Farmington Avenue
Flint, MI 48521-9109

Dateline

November 27, 19--
QS

Letter address Mr. Jose E. Morales, Director
Flint Business Association
584 Brabyn Avenue
Flint, MI 48508-5548
DS

Salutation Dear Mr. Morales
DS

Body The Octagon Club is concerned about Baker House.

As you know, Baker House was built on Calumet Road in
1797 by Zaccaria Baker; he and his family lived there
for many years. It was home for various other families
until 1938, when it became an attractive law and real
estate office. Flint residents somehow assumed that
Baker House was a permanent part of Flint. It wasn't.

Baker House was torn down last week to make room for a
new mall. It's too late to save Baker House. But what
about other Flint landmarks. Shall we lose them, too?
Shopping malls may indicate that a community is grow-
ing, but need growth destroy our heritage?

We ask for your help. Will you and Mr. Wilkes include
20 minutes on your January meeting agenda for Myrna
Targlif, president of the Flint Octagon Club, to present our views on this problem? She has information
that I guarantee you will find interesting; a brief
outline is enclosed.
DS

Complimentary
close

Sincerely yours
QS

Writer's name

Barbara Brahms

Title

Secretary, Octagon Club
DS

Reference initials BB:xx
DS

Enclosure notation Enclosure
DS

Copy notation c Andrew Wilkes

Level Two
Formatting
Basic Business
Documents

34 — Modified Block with Notations

34a   7'

each line 2 times SS;
DS between 2-line groups

alphabet 1   Johnny Willcox printed five dozen banquet tickets for my meeting.

fig/sym 2   Check #3589 for $1,460--dated the 27th--was sent to O'Neill & Co.

1st finger 3   It is true Greg acted bravely during the severe storm that night.

easy 4   In the land of enchantment, the fox and the lamb lie by the bush.

| 1 | 2 | 3 | 4 | 5 | 6 | 7 | 8 | 9 | 10 | 11 | 12 | 13 |

34b   10'

COMMUNICA...

Compose at the keyboard

1 Compose an answer to each question in one or two sentences. Join the sentences into 3 paragraphs (as shown). Center the title **MY CAREER** over the paragraphs. Divide words if necessary.

2 Proofread; identify errors with proofreaders' marks; rekey in final form.

¶1
1 What is your present career goal?
2 Why do you think you will enjoy this career?

¶2
3 Where do you think you would most like to pursue your career?
4 Why do you think you would enjoy living and working in that area?

¶3
5 What civic, political, or volunteer activities might you enjoy?
6 What other careers may lie ahead for you?

34c   33'

FORMATTING

Business letters: modified block format

(LM pp. S17-S19)

Read the information at the right; then study the letter on page 78.

Document 1

Key the letter (average) on page 78; address an envelope. Proofread; correct errors.

Document 2

Rekey Document 1 on page 71 in modified block format.

Modified block format

The modified block format is a variation of the block format. It is "modified" by moving the dateline and the closing lines from the left margin to the center point of the page. Paragraphs may be indented, but it is more efficient not to indent them. Do not indent paragraphs in Section 7.

Reference initials: If the writer's initials are included with those of the keyboard operator, the writer's initials are listed first in ALL CAPS followed by a colon:

  BB:xx

Enclosure notation: If an item is included with a letter, an enclosure notation is keyed a DS below the reference initials. Acceptable variations include:

  Enclosure
  Enclosures: Check #8331
        Order form
  Enc. 2

Copy notation: A copy notation *c* indicates that a copy of the document has been sent to person(s) named. Key it a DS below reference initials (or enclosure notation):

  c Andrew Wilkes

Express Rapid Delivery
8000 Iliff Avenue
Denver, CO 80237-4512

October 19, 19--

Miss Latanya Denny
208 Humboldt Street
Denver, CO 80218-8828

Dear Miss Denny

Today our delivery service tried unsuccessfully a second time to deliver at the above address the merchandise you ordered. The merchandise is now at our general warehouse at 8000 Iliff Avenue.

We regret that no further attempts at delivery can be made. You may claim your merchandise at the warehouse if you will show a copy of your order (a duplicate is enclosed) to John Kimbrough at the warehouse.

We shall hold your merchandise for 30 days. After that time, it will be transferred to our main warehouse at 218 Harvard Avenue, East; unfortunately, we must charge a rental fee for each day the goods are stored there.

Yours very truly

Elizabeth A. LeMoyne
Dispatcher

BB:xx

Enclosure

c John Kimbrough

Learning goals:
1 To format business letters in block and modified block format on letterhead stationery.
2 To address business envelopes.
3 To format standard inter-office memorandums.
4 To correct keyboarding errors.
5 To develop composing skills.

Formatting guides:
1 Margins: Default or 1" (65 spaces).
2 Single-space drills; double-space ¶ writings.
3 5-space ¶ indention for writings and all DS copy.

31a   7'

Skill-building warmup

each line twice SS; DS
between 2-line groups

alphabet 1 Buddy Jackson is saving the door prize money for wax and lacquer.
figures 2 I have fed 47 hens, 25 geese, 10 ducks, 39 lambs, and 68 kittens.
one hand 3 You imply Jon Case exaggerated my opinion on a decrease in rates.
easy 4 I shall make hand signals to the widow with the auditory problem.

| 1 | 2 | 3 | 4 | 5 | 6 | 7 | 8 | 9 | 10 | 11 | 12 | 13 |

31b   7'

S K I L L   B U I L D I N G

Straight copy

Key two 1' writings on each ¶. Each ¶ contains 2 more words than the previous one. Try to complete each ¶ within 1'.
Optional: Take 2' and 3' timings to build staying power.

LA all letters used   gwam 2' 3'

Have you thought about time? Time is a perplexing commod-   6   4
ity. Frequently we don't have adequate time to do the things we   12   8
must, yet we all have just the same amount of time.   17 12

We seldom refer to the quantity of time; to a great extent,   24 16
we cannot control it. We can try to set time aside, to plan,   30 20
and therefore, to control portions of this valuable asset.   36 24

We should make an extra effort to fill each minute and hour   42 28
with as much quality activity as possible. Time, the most pre-   47 32
cious thing a person can spend, can never be realized once it   54 36
is lost.   55 36

gwam 2' | 1 | 2 | 3 | 4 | 5 | 6 | 7 |
     3' | 1 | 2 | 3 | 4 | 5 |

33c   21'

Business letters and envelopes
(LM pp. S13-S15)

> **Personal titles**
>
> Personal titles (for example, Mr. or Ms.) should be included in the letter address unless a professional title (Dr.) is appropriate.
>
> **1** Use Mr. when the recipient's first name is obviously masculine.
>
> **2** Use Ms. when the recipient's first name is obviously feminine and no other title (Mrs., Miss) is indicated.
>
> **3** A short job title may follow the name; key a long job title as the second line of the address.

words

Document 1

Key the (short) letter in block format; proofread and correct errors; address an envelope.

Current date | Mr. Trace L. Brecken | 4487 Ingram Street | Corpus Christi,   14
TX 78409-8907 | Dear Mr. Brecken   20

We have received the package you sent us in which you returned goods   34
from a recent order you gave us. Your refund check, plus return postage,   49
will be mailed to you in a few days.   56

We are sorry, of course, that you did not find this merchandise personally   71
satisfactory. It is our goal to please all of our customers, and we are   86
always disappointed if we fail.   92

Please give us an opportunity to try again. We stand behind our mer-   106
chandise, and that is our guarantee of good service.   117

Cordially yours | Margret Bredewig | Customer Service Department | xx   129

Document 2

Use directions in Document 1 for this average letter.

Current date | Mrs. Rose Shikamuru | 55 Lawrence Street | Topeka, KS   13
66607-6657 | Dear Mrs. Shikamuru   19

Thank you for your recent letter asking about employment opportunities   33
with our company. We are happy to inform you that Mr. Edward Ybarra,   47
our recruiting representative, will be on your campus on April 23, 24, 25,   62
and 26 to interview students who are interested in our company.   75

We suggest you talk soon with your student placement office, as all   89
appointments with Mr. Ybarra will be made through that office. Please   103
bring with you the application questionnaire they provide.   115

Within a few days, we will send you a company brochure and more   128
information about our offices; plant; salary, bonus, and retirement plans;   143
and the beautiful community in which we are located. We believe a close   158
study of this information will convince you, as it has many others, that   173
our company builds futures as well as small motors.   183

If there is any other way we can help you, please write to me again.   197

Yours very truly | Miss Myrle K. Bragg | Human Services Director | xx   210

33d   10'

Compose at the keyboard

2" top margin; 1" side margins; 5-space indention; DS
1 Center your name horizontally; then QS.

2 Key a complete sentence to answer each question. Avoid beginning all answers with "I" or "My." Then combine sentences into a paragraph.
3 Proofread; make pencil corrections; rekey the ¶.

1 What is your birth date?

2 What do you enjoy doing during the summer?

3 What are your favorite winter activities?

4 What is your favorite food?

5 What sports activities do you like to watch or play?

6 What is your favorite shopping trip?

31c 6'

Compose at the keyboard

1" top and side margins; DS
1 Key the ¶, inserting the missing information. Do not correct errors.
2 Remove the paper and make pencil corrections. Rekey the ¶ from the marked copy. Proofread; circle errors.

My name is (your name). I am now a (class level) student at (name of your school) in (city and state) where I am majoring in (major area of study). I was graduated from (name of your high school) in (name of town) in (year), where my favorite subject was (name of subject). My hobby is (name of hobby). In my free time, I like to (name a free-time activity you enjoy). I operate a keyboard at approximately (state the *gwam* rate in figures).

31d 30'

FORMATTING

Business letters in block format

Study carefully the information about business letter placement on this page and about letter parts on the next page. Then key Documents 1 and 2 as directed on page 71.

Business letters

Business letters are prepared on letterhead stationery, which has the company name, address, telephone number, and logo (the company trademark or symbol) printed at the top of the page. Most letterheads are between 1" and 2" deep. If a letter is sent on plain stationery, a return address must be keyed immediately above the date.

Letter placement: Placing a letter attractively on the page requires learning to judge its length. An average-length letter has at least three paragraphs and about 100 to 200 words. A short letter, however, may have one or two paragraphs and fewer than 100 words. A long letter has four or more paragraphs and more than 200 words.

Margins and dateline: The letter placement table serves as a guide for placement of letters of varying lengths. Using standard (default) side margins is efficient, but variable side margins often provide better placement. Variable side margins will be used for letters in Section 7.

Letter Placement Table

Letter length	Variable side margins	Standard side margins	Dateline
Short	2"	1"	line 18
Average	1.5"	1"	line 16
Long	1"	1"	line 14

Short letter

Average-length letter

33 ▸ Block Format and Envelopes

33a 7'

each line 2 times SS;
DS between 2-line
groups

alphabet	1
figures	2
one hand	3
easy	4

Jim Daley gave us in that box the prize he won for his quick car.
Send 346 of the 789 sets now; send the others on April 10 and 25.
I deserve, in my opinion, a reward after I started a faster race.
Enrique may fish for cod by the dock; he also may risk a penalty.

| 1 | 2 | 3 | 4 | 5 | 6 | 7 | 8 | 9 | 10 | 11 | 12 | 13 |

33b 12'

F O R M A T T I N G

Address large envelopes/insert letters

(LM pp. S9-S11) or 3 large
envelopes

1 Read placement information at the right.

2 Address a business envelope to each addressee listed below; proofread; correct errors.

3 Fold three sheets correctly and insert them into the envelopes.

Envelope address: Set a tab about .5" left of center. Space down to about line 14 from the top edge of the envelope and begin keying at the tab. Learn to visualize this position so that you can address envelopes quickly.

Use ALL CAPS, block format, and no punctuation. Leave one space between the state and ZIP Code.

Return address: When a return address is printed on the envelope, the writer's name may be keyed above the company address. If the return address is not printed, key it in ALL CAPS on line 2, beginning about 3 spaces from the left edge.

Special notations: Key special notations for the addressee (as PLEASE FORWARD, HOLD FOR ARRIVAL, PERSONAL) in ALL CAPS a DS below the return address. Key mailing notations for postal authorities (as SPECIAL DELIVERY and REGISTERED) in ALL CAPS a DS below the stamp position on line 8 or 9.

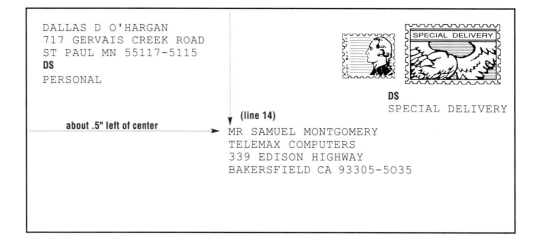

```
DALLAS D O'HARGAN
717 GERVAIS CREEK ROAD
ST PAUL MN 55117-5115
DS
PERSONAL
```

SPECIAL DELIVERY

DS
SPECIAL DELIVERY

about .5" left of center   ↓ **(line 14)**

```
MR SAMUEL MONTGOMERY
TELEMAX COMPUTERS
339 EDISON HIGHWAY
BAKERSFIELD CA 93305-5035
```

Envelope 1
From T L LEWIS | 1594 EASY STREET | MOUNTAIN VIEW CA 90756-8765 to MS GERTRUDE SCHUYLER | 633 SLEEPY HOLLOW AVENUE | TAMPA FL 33617-6711

Envelope 2
From (supply your own return address) to MR ALBERT CHUNG | 254 SHERBORN DRIVE | CINCINNATI OH 45231-5112. Include the special notation CONFIDENTIAL.

Envelope 3
Assume the company address of the writer is printed on the envelope. From C VOLTZ to MISS CELIA PEREZ | 399 RED BRIDGE ROAD E | KANSAS CITY MO 64114-2344. Include the mailing notation SPECIAL DELIVERY.

Folding and inserting letters into large envelopes

Step 1
With letter face up, fold slightly less than 1/3 of sheet up toward top.

Step 2
Fold down top of sheet to within 1/2 inch of bottom fold.

Step 3
Insert letter into envelope with last crease toward bottom of envelope.

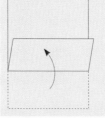

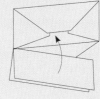

Document 1

(LM p. S1) LM page references refer to the Laboratory Materials, Lessons 1-60.

Format and key the letter on page 72 (average length); proofread; circle errors.

Document 2

(LM p. S3)

Format and key the short letter at the bottom of this page; proofread; circle errors.

Parts of a business letter

Business letters contain a variety of parts that serve very specific purposes. Listed below are basic parts of a typical business letter:

Dateline: The letter is dated the day it is mailed.

Letter address: The address of the person who will receive the letter begins a quadruple space (QS) below the dateline. Include a personal title (for example, Mr. or Ms.) unless a professional title (Dr.) is appropriate.

Salutation: Key the salutation, or greeting, a double space (DS) below the letter address. The salutation should correspond to the first line of the letter address. Use Ladies and Gentlemen when the first line of the address is a company name.

Body: The body is the message of the letter. Begin the body a double space (DS) below the salutation. Single-space the body and double-space between paragraphs.

Complimentary close: The complimentary close, which is the formal closing of the letter, begins a double space below the body.

Writer's name and title: Leave three blank lines (QS) for the writer's signature, keying the name on the fourth line. Women generally include a personal title with their names. If the writer's title is short, it may follow the name; if the title is long, key it on the next line.

Reference initials: When business letters are keyed by someone other than the writer, the keyboard operator's initials are keyed in lowercase a double space below the writer's keyed name and/or title. Initials are not included when the writer keys the letter.

Long letter

Document 2

	words
May 1, 19--	2
QS	
Mr. John M. Browert	6
1403 Poplar Lane	10
Annapolis, MD 21403-0314	15
DS	
Dear Mr. Browert	18
DS	
Please stop at your convenience to pick up	28
your travel tickets. You are scheduled to sail	38
for one week on the SS CONTESSA, leaving	48
Pier 40, Miami, May 21, at 2 p.m. We under-	57
stand you have made your own arrangements	66
for travel to and from Annapolis.	70

	words
Thanks very much for allowing us to serve	77
you.	78
DS	
Ship ahoy!	80
QS	
Frances Westburg	83
General Agent	86
DS	
xx	86

32c 12'

SKILL BU[ ]

Practice letter parts

1 Key the letter parts, spacing correctly between each. Use 1" or default top and side margins. Return 5 times between exercises. Do not correct errors.

2 Take a 2' writing on 1 and 2, then 1' writings on 3 and 4, following the directions above.

1 April 15, 19--　　2
　　　QS
Miss Joyce Bohn, Treasurer　　4
Stapex Stamping Co.　　6
118 Lehigh Parkway　　8
Allentown, PA 18103-8181　　11
　　　DS
Dear Miss Bohn　　12

2 March 21, 19--　　14

Parkway Construction Company　17
2188 Hawthorne Place, E.　　19
Niagara Falls, NY 80206-2006　22

Ladies and Gentlemen　　24

3 Very sincerely yours　　2
　　　QS
Marianne R. Robert　　4
District Attorney　　6
　　　DS
xx　　6

4 Thank you for your help.　　9

Sincerely　　10

F. E. Dravis　　11
President　　12

xx　　12

32d 18'

F O R M A T T I N G

Business letters: block format
(LM pp. S5-S7)

Document 1
Key the (short) letter; proofread carefully; correct errors.

　　　words

Current date　　3
　　QS
Mr. Grady Atgood　　6
Personnel Director　　10
Letter Beams, Inc.　　14
2112 Smythe Road, N.　　19
Arlington, VA 22201-1201　　23
　　　DS
Dear Mr. Atgood　　26
　　DS
Miss Carolyn Carvere, an employee of Letter　35
Beams, Inc. from 1990 to 1993, has applied　44
for a position with our company as a com-　52
puter analyst. She has given us your name　60
and her permission to ask you about her work　69
history with Letter Beams, Inc.　　76

Will you, therefore, please verify Carolyn　84
Carvere's employment with you and respond　93
as you desire about her performance with your　102
organization. Thank you, Mr. Atgood.　　109
　　　DS
Sincerely yours　　113
　　QS
A. Alonzo Cruz, Director　　118
Personnel Services　　121
　　　DS
xx　　122

Document 2
Follow directions in Document 1 for this average-length letter.

　　　words

Current date　　3

Dr. Myron Moilion　　7
690 Edward Place　　10
Stamford, CT 06905-5069　　15

Dear Dr. Moilion　　18

Thank you for your letter regarding the　26
mislabeled tree. We are certainly embarrassed　35
that one of the "white birch" we planted for　44
you two years ago has matured into a wild　52
cherry tree. While birch and cherry trees look　62
quite similar when they are immature, there is　71
a remarkable difference as they grow older.　80

We will be happy to replace the wild cherry　89
tree with a similarly matured white birch at　98
your convenience. Call us to set a date for the　108
planting. We will also, if you desire, remove　117
the cherry tree at that time.　　123

We appreciate your patience.　　129

Very truly yours　　132

Ms. Lynn Harley, President　　137

xx　　137

The Henderson Company

6677 Farmington Avenue
West Hartford, CT 06119-7284
(203) 555-6941

Dateline May 6, 19-- **(Line 16)**
QS

Letter address Ms. Sara Arbecki, Editor
Alpha Communications
676 Hundley Drive
St. Joseph, MO 64506-6766
DS

Salutation Dear Ms. Arbecki
DS

Body Your article "Efficient Correspondence" described the
block format letter as "effective, economical, and easy
to read." I can see from the illustration that the
block format is efficient.
DS

Your article made me aware of the parts of a business
letter and the importance of arranging the parts in a
particular order. The examples you gave helped me
realize that attractive letter placement is a "hidden
message" in every letter I send.

I have attempted to follow all of your directions in
formatting my letter in block style. In your article,
you offered to answer readers' questions about block
format letters. My question: How did I do?

Personal business and civic responsibilities require me
to write letters quite often. I shall appreciate any
advice you can give me to improve my communications.
DS

Complimentary close Sincerely yours
QS

Writer's name Miss Muriel Werter
Title Administrative Assistant
DS

Reference initials jrm

32 ► Block Format and Error Correction

Skill-Building Warmup

alphabet	1	I quickly explained to two managers the grave hazards of the job.
figures	2	All channels--16, 25, 30, and 74--reported the score was 19 to 8.
shift keys	3	Maxi and Kay Pascal expect to be in breezy South Mexico in April.
easy	4	Did the man fight a duel, or did he go to a chapel to sign a vow?

1 | 2 | 3 | 4 | 5 | 6 | 7 | 8 | 9 | 10 | 11 | 12 | 13

32b   13'

FORMATTING

Error correction procedures

Study the information at the right. Do the drill below.

Proofread: Before documents are complete, they must be carefully proofread and all errors must be corrected. Error-free documents send the message that you are detailed-oriented and capable.

Proofreading tips
✓ Never assume work is error free.
✓ Read each line carefully for keying errors.

✓ Check for misused words; repair faulty sentence structure.
✓ Read the document once for meaning/content.
✓ Check documents for format errors.
✓ Compare the printed copy to the original, checking for omissions.

Computers: Correct errors using either the backspace key or the delete key. Strike the backspace key to delete characters to the left of the cursor. Striking the delete key erases characters at the cursor. Correct on-screen errors before the document is printed.

Typewriters: Most typewriters have a correction key located at the right of the keyboard coded with an *x*. Backspacing to the error and depressing this key activates a tape or ribbon that "lifts off" incorrect characters.

Drill

1.5" top and side margins; DS; divide words appropriately; correct errors; proofread

Work that contains careless errors almost always has exactly the opposite effect from the one intended by a writer. So, for example, if what we key is meant to earn a top grade, to gain a job interview, or to impress someone important in our lives, it must be error free. When we write on behalf of someone else, such as a business, our letter at once becomes representative of that company; and our responsibility for error detection is compounded.

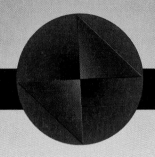

CONTENTS

APPENDIX

A

WELCOME TO WINDOWS

Exploring Windows

Before using a *Windows*-based software, you will need to know a few basic concepts of *Windows*, which is the operating system software you are using. *Windows* controls the operation of the computer and the peripherals such as the mouse and printer. Software that runs under *Windows* has several features in common. All *Windows* application programs use similar icons, and the menus are consistent. Once you learn the basics of *Windows 3.1* or *Windows 95*, you can apply that knowledge to every *Windows* application. On the next few pages, you will start *Windows 3.1* or *Windows 95*, use the mouse, and learn a few of the basic operations.

Using the Mouse

Windows software requires the use of a mouse or other pointing device. You will use the mouse to select items, to find and move files, to execute or cancel commands, to move and size items, and to draw images. The mouse pointer changes in appearance depending on its location on the screen and the task that it is doing.

I   The I-beam indicates that the mouse is located in the text area. When you pause, it blinks. As you use your software, most of the time you will see the I-beam.

↖   The arrow selects items. It displays when the mouse is located outside the text area.

⌛   The hourglass indicates that *Windows* is processing your command. You must wait until *Windows* finishes what it is doing before keying text or entering another command.

Move the mouse on a padded, flat surface. If you run out of space, pick up the mouse and place it in another spot. The mouse performs the following actions:

Point: Move the mouse so that the pointer touches the icon or text.

Click: Point to the desired item, then press and release the left mouse button once.

Double-click: Point to the desired item and quickly press and release the left mouse button twice.

Click with the right mouse button: Press and release the right mouse button once. A shortcut menu appears (*Windows 95*).

Drag: Point to the desired item; hold down the mouse button; drag the item to a new location; then release the button.

Windows 3.1

Program Manager: The name of the program that is currently running appears on the top line of the window, called the title bar.

Group icons: Each software program installed on the computer should be identified with a group icon. For instance, the group icon for *Word* will either be *Microsoft Word for Windows* or *Microsoft Office*. *Microsoft Office* includes *Word, Excel, PowerPoint,* and *Scheduler.*

Control-Menu bar: Click on this bar to display a menu allowing you to manipulate the windows.

Minimize and Maximize buttons: The Minimize button reduces a window, and the Maximize button expands a window.

Scroll bars: Move the window display in the direction of the arrow.

Menu bar: Click any item on the Menu bar to display a pull-down menu.

1. Turn on the computer and monitor.
2. Open *Windows*:

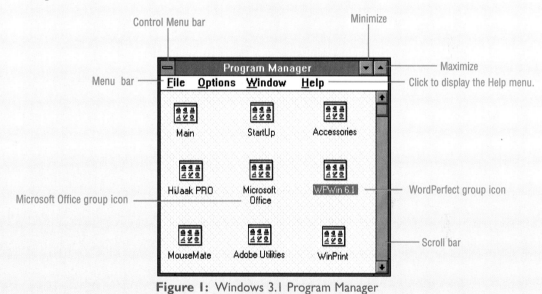

Figure 1: Windows 3.1 Program Manager

Starting Windows 3.1

- If your screen resembles Figure 1, you are already in *Windows*.
- If only the Program Manager icon is displayed at the bottom left of the screen, double-click on the icon.
- If the DOS prompt C> is displayed on your screen, key **win** and press ENTER.

If you are not familiar with *Windows*, complete the Windows Tutorial.

1. Click **Help** in the Menu bar.

Windows 3.1 Tutorial

2. Click **Windows Tutorial**.
3. Key **m** to begin the Mouse lesson. After completing the Mouse lesson, continue with the Windows Basics lesson.

Windows 95

The opening screen of *Windows 95* simulates a *desktop* working environment. The icons displayed on the screen are symbols of items on your desk. Your screen may have additional icons besides those listed below.

My Computer displays the disk drives, CD-ROM, and printers that are attached to the computer.

Network Neighborhood allows you to view the available resources if you are connected to a network environment.

Recycle Bin stores documents that have been deleted from the hard drive. Documents deleted in error can be retrieved and returned to their folders. When the recycle bin is emptied, however, the files are gone.

Start displays the Start menu. From the Start menu, you can open a program, open Help, change system settings, close and exit *Windows 95*, and more.

The Start button is located on the *taskbar* at the bottom of the desktop (Figure 2). It is always visible when *Windows 95* is running. When you click Start, a menu displays with the commands for using *Windows 95* (Figure 3). Each time you open a program, a button with the name of the program displays on the taskbar. The taskbar in Figure 2 shows that *Microsoft Word* is open.

Start   Taskbar

Figure 2: *Windows 95* Opening Screen

Start menu

Figure 3: Start Menu

Exercise I
Open *Windows 95*

1. Turn on the computer and monitor.
2. *Welcome to Windows 95* screen displays with a tip. Read the screen as it offers helpful tips, then click the **Close** button.
3. Click the **Start** button to display the Start menu. (Your Start menu may not look exactly like the illustration.)
4. Point to the Programs menu; a submenu displays to the right listing all software programs loaded on your system.

B APPENDIX

WORD PROCESSING WORKSHOP

Getting Familiar with the Work Screen

When you open word processing software, the screen contains a blank document just waiting to be created. The work screen shown is *Microsoft Word 7*. Your work screen may vary, but all *Windows*-based word processing programs are similar.

> **Menu bar:** Click to access any feature of the software.
>
> **Toolbar:** Click for quick access to common commands. The name of the button displays when you point to it.
>
> **Insertion point:** The blinking insertion point shows where the text you key will appear. The insertion point moves to the right as you key.
>
> **Ruler:** Change tabs, margins, and indents on the ruler. Default tabs are set every half inch.

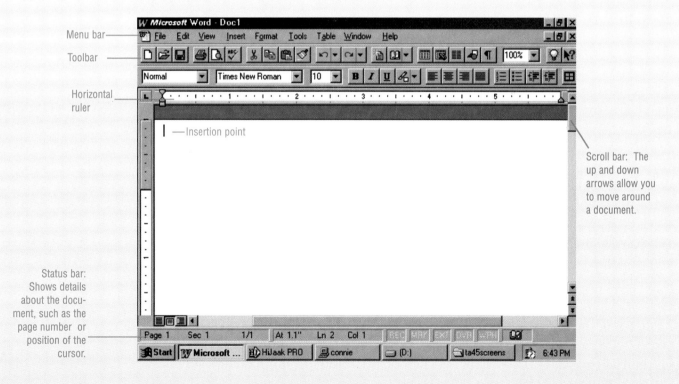

Menu bar

Toolbar

Horizontal ruler

Insertion point

Scroll bar: The up and down arrows allow you to move around a document.

Status bar: Shows details about the document, such as the page number or position of the cursor.

Document I
Use menus

1. Click **File** in the Menu bar. Observe the items in the File menu.
2. Click **Open** to display the Open dialog box. An ellipsis (...) following a command indicates that a dialog box will display. If a command is not available, it appears dimmed. From the Open dialog box, click **Cancel** to close the dialog box.
3. Click all other menus to view the items on them.
4. Move the mouse over the buttons. *Windows 95* software displays their names.

Creating a New Document

As you key a new document, word wrap automatically moves text to the next line. Strike the ENTER key only between paragraphs. Wavy red lines may appear on the screen as you key, indicating that an error has been keyed. The red lines will not print if you do not correct the error. If you make a mistake, use the Insert or Delete functions.

Insert — Position the insertion point where the new text should appear and key. If text is replaced as you key, press the Insert key to turn on Insert mode.

Delete — Erases text to the right of the insertion point. To delete text to the left of the insertion point, strike the BACKSPACE key.

Undo — Reverses the last change made. Certain commands such as Save cannot be undone. You can click on the down arrow next to Undo (or Redo) to view previous actions or select a specific action.

Redo — Reverses the last Undo.

Save As — Select the appropriate folder and then key the filename. Click the **Save** button to save an existing document.

Print — When you click the Print button, a dialog box may display. Options are available for choosing pages that you print, number of copies, etc. Click **Print** from the dialog box.

Select — Identifies text that has been keyed so that it can be changed. Selected text appears black on the screen. Select text using the mouse. Cancel Select by clicking the mouse button again.

To select:	Microsoft	WordPerfect
a word	Double-click	Double-click
a paragraph	Triple-click	Quadruple-click
several lines	Click the mouse and drag through the lines.	

Writing concise responses, formulating competitive bids, creating effective business plans, answering customer feedback, composing messages and letters to clients, responding to customers and staff, maintaining relations with coworkers and supervisors, interpreting messages, and persuading customer—these are just a few examples of written and oral communication that is handled by everyday by competent business people. Communicating skills and a keen knowledge of business are valuable assets for anyone seeking success in business.

Accidents on the job can often be avoided if each employee is aware of the hazards involved in his or her duties. Employees should be informed of things that they may inadvertently do or leave undone that may jeopardize others. It is always better to play it safe when working with others. Remember, accidents don't just happen; they are caused.

Document 2
Create and save document
1. Key ¶ 1.
2. Apply word wrap as you key; do not strike ENTER key.
3. Save as Doc2.
4. Key ¶ 2 following Step 2 within the paragraph. Save as Doc4 above.

Document 3
Edit text

1. Open the file **Doc2** that you keyed earlier.
2. Select and delete the text that is marked. Save as **Doc3**. Print.
3. Undo the last edit. Print.
4. Redo the last edit.

Writing ~~concise~~ responses, formulating ~~competitive~~ bids, creating ~~effective~~ business plans, answering ~~customer~~ feedback, composing messages ~~and letters~~ to clients, responding to customers and staff, maintaining relations with coworkers and supervisors, interpreting messages, and persuading customers these are just a few examples of written and oral communication that *are* ~~is~~ handled ~~by~~ everyday by competent business people. ~~Communicating skills and a keen knowledge of business are valuable assets for anyone seeking success in business~~

Formatting a Document

Formats such as line spacing, bold, italic, font styles and sizes, and alignment enhance the appearance of a document and provide emphasis. Many of these formats are available as buttons on the toolbar. If an arrow appears on the button, click the arrow to see other options. Other font options, such as font color or SMALL CAPS, are available by choosing *Fonts* from the Format menu.

Formats can be applied as you key or after the text is keyed.

- *To apply formats as you key*, click the appropriate button and key the text. The function will stay on until you click the button to turn it off.
- *To apply formats to text that has already been keyed*, select the text and then click the format button.

Numbers and bullets emphasize listed information. Use numbered items if the list requires sequential order. Use bullets or symbols for unordered items. Bullets and numbers may be added as text is keyed or after. Bullets and numbers are available on the toolbar or from a menu such as the Insert menu or Format menu.

Document 4
Apply formats

1. Open the file **Doc4** that you keyed earlier.
2. Key the title PLAY IT SAFE. Select the title and apply 14-point size.
3. Edit the text as marked.
4. With the insertion point in the paragraph, apply a different font.

italic

Accidents on the job can often be (avoided) if each employee is (aware) of the hazards involved in his or her duties. Employees should be informed of things that they may (inadvertently) do or leave undone that may (jeopardize) others. It is always better to play it safe when working with others. Remember, accidents don't just happen; they are caused.

Document 5
Use Align
1. Select Left align; key ¶ 1.
2. Select Center align; key ¶ 2.
3. Select Right Align; key ¶ 3.
4. Save as Doc5.

Text is traditionally keyed **left-aligned**. The first letter of each line begins at the left margin, making an even left margin and a ragged right margin. Left-aligned text is easy to read.

Center Align
Center align automatically centers each line between the left and right margins. Center align is often used in keying announcements.

Right Align
All text lines up with the right margin. This produces a ragged left margin.

Document 6
Review formats
1. Set the line spacing to 2 or DS.
2. Key the title. Select it and apply 14-point size.
3. Key the ¶s using word wrap. Correct errors.
4. Single-space and italicize the last two lines.

NEW MISSION FOR EDUCATION ← 14 pt.

In a time of increasing emphasis on diversity, schools must find a way to focus on conveying common human and democratic values and to validate their expressions in a multicultural context.

As reflected in our mission statement, the fundamental expectations of our schools are to develop:

Well-Informed Citizens

A Professional, Adaptive, World-Class Workforce

Document 7
Add Bullets and Numbers
1. Format the list using the Numbers feature. DS between items.
2. Save and print. Then select the numbers and change them to bullets.
3. Use the Spelling feature, proofread, and print.

Recording an appropriate voice mail greeting is very important as we provide our clients with excellent and friendly service. Please study the following essential parts of an effective voice mail greeting.

1. State your name.
2. Include the day and date you are recording the greeting.
3. Describe why you are not available to take the call.
4. Request caller to leave a message or directions for obtaining personal assistance.
5. Provide an approximate time when the call will be returned.

Editing a Document

You have learned to modify text that has already been keyed. Other common edits include copying and moving text, changing text from all caps to lower case or vice versa, and finding text and replacing it with other text.

✂	**Cut**	Deletes blocks of text. Select the text and click the **Cut** button.
📋	**Paste**	Paste is often used with Cut to move blocks of text. First, cut the block; then move the insertion point to the new location and click the **Paste** button. The text has now moved to the new location. Text can be cut and pasted between documents.
📑	**Copy**	When you need another copy of text, select the text and click **Copy.** The text is copied to the clipboard. Position the insertion point where the copy is needed and paste the text. Text can be copied between documents.
📄	**New**	Takes you to a fresh, new document. If two documents are open, click the name of the other document from the Windows menu.
	Change Case	Changes text keyed in all capital letters to lower case or to initial caps or title case. This option is available from a menu. (*Word:* Format menu, Change Case; *WordPerfect:* Edit menu, Convert Case.)
	Hard Page Break	Hold down the Control Key and strike ENTER to move text to the next page.
	Spell Check	The Spell Check command looks for misspelled words in your document.

Document 8
Change Case

1. Key the lines shown.
2. Save the document as **Doc8**.
3. Copy the entire document to a new screen. Save as **Doc8b**.

1. Add the side heading facilities and equipment.

2. Cindy Sturzenberger is chairman and ceo.

3. Britt Burge, president, ASSOCIATED TRAVEL SERVICES

4. DM POMMERT, ASSOCIATES

5. ms. margarita valadez

   1130 confederation dr.

   saskatoon sk s71 4k5

4. Edit **Doc8b** as shown at the right.

1. Add the side heading facilities and equipment.
2. Cindy Sturzenberger is chairman and ceo. ⌐ person
3. Britt Burge, president, ASSOCIATED TRAVEL SERVICES
4. DM POMMERT, ASSOCIATES
5. ms. margarita valadez
   1130 confederation dr.
   saskatoon sk s71 4k5

initial caps

Indent

Indent moves the current paragraph to the first tab position. Hanging Indent places the first line of a paragraph at the left margin and indents remaining lines to the first tab. Hanging indent is commonly used in bibliographic entries, glossaries, and bulleted and enumerated items. Indent is available by choosing *Paragraph* from the Format menu. In *Word*, you choose the type of indention from the Indents and Spacing tab.

Document 9
Apply Indent
1. Key the following text, using Indent or Hanging Indent as shown.
2. Check the spelling and proofread.
3. Save as **Doc9** and print.

Cheating has become a more wide-spread problem in colleges and universi-

ties than was originally thought.

Indent ——→ In a poll of 15,000 juniors and seniors at 31 universities, more than 87 percent of business majors admitted to cheating at least once in college, the largest such percentage.

The same poll showed that less cheating took place among Engineering and

Humanities students.

Hanging Indent ——→ Holtinger, Richard C. "Suggestions on Referencing Using MLA Style." *National Education Journal,* February 1997, pp. 36-40.

Publication Manual of the American Psychological Association. 4th ed. Washington, D.C.: American Psychological Association, 1994.

Document 10
Indent

Word: Key the entire document, pressing TAB after the headings Presiding and Participants. Allow the names in the second line to wrap to the left margin.
- Position the insertion point at the beginning of the first name "Lanete Garriga." Drag the bottom marker on the ruler to align with "Cynthia Housely" in the heading above.

WordPerfect: After keying "Participants," press Indent (**F7**) to indent the runover lines.

SYSTEMS FOR EMPLOYMENT TRAINING
March 1, 19-- _DS
Action Minutes

{ Bold and center

Presiding: Cynthia Housely _DS
Participants: Lanete Garriga, Diane Rodgers, Cary Tabb, Nancy Riser, Ricky Boler, W. C. Wax, Jr., and Anne Stokes

Cynthia Housely welcomed the group and announced that Systems Training, Inc. was the host for the meeting. In addition, Systems invited the group to serve as consultants in the development of computer-based training systems.

APPENDIX

SELKIRK COMMUNICATIONS, PROJECT

Project objectives:
1. Apply your keyboarding, formatting, and word processing skills.
2. Work with few specific directions.

Selkirk Communications is a training company that is relocating its office from Spokane, Washington, to Nelson, Canada. As an administrative assistant, you will prepare a number of documents using many of the formatting skills you have learned. Selkirk Communications uses the block letter format and unbound report style.

Document 1 **S C**
Invitation

Format this document attractively. Use bold for the main heading and callouts (PLACE, TIME, etc.). DS between listed items; position the document attractively on the page.

WP Vary font sizes. Use bullets for the listed items.

		words
OPEN HOUSE		2
PLACE: Selkirk Communications		8
1003 Baker St.		11
Nelson BC V1L 5N7		15
TIME: 1:00-4:00 p.m.		20
DATE: Saturday and Sunday, April 27 and 28		29

Selkirk Communications is excited to open its tenth international communications office in downtown Nelson. Please plan to attend the Open House.   43 / 57 / 58

Come in and meet our friendly staff. Learn how we can help meet your training needs.   72 / 76

Selkirk Communications specializes in: 84

* Instructor-Led Training in Our Classroom or Your Facility   96

* Newsletters Designed to Meet Your Needs   104

* Authorized Training Center for *Microsoft Office* and *Corel Suite 7*   118

* Oral and Written Communication Refresher Courses   128

words

Document 2
Block letter

This letter includes the company name. Key it a DS below the complimentary closing in ALL CAPS. QS to the writer's name.

February 8, 19-- | Chamber of Commerce | 225 Hall St. | Nelson BC V1L 13
5X4 | CANADA 15

Selkirk Communications will be relocating its headquarters from 32
Spokane, Washington, to downtown Nelson on April 1. We are an inter- 46
national communications company, offering the following services: 59

1. Written and oral communications refresher workshops 70
2. Customized training on-site or in our training center 82
3. Mail-order newsletters 87
4. Computer training on popular business software 97
5. Individualized or group training sessions 106

I would like to attend the Nelson Chamber of Commerce meeting in 119
March to share some of the exciting ways we can help Chamber members 133
meet their training needs. Is there time available for us on your March 147
agenda? Please contact Anthony Baker, public relations coordinator, at 162
our Nelson office at (604) 555-1093. 169

Selkirk Communications will be holding an open house during the month 183
of April, and we will be inviting you and the Nelson community to attend. 198
We look forward to becoming actively involved with the business com- 212
munity of Nelson. 216

Yours truly | SELKIRK COMMUNICATIONS | Richard R. Holmes, President 229

Document 3
Memorandum

TO: Marilyn Smith, Public Relations Media Assistant | **FROM:** Anthony 14
Baker, Public Relations Coordinator | **DATE:** February 16, 19-- | 26
SUBJECT: Electronic Presentation 33

Richard Holmes has been invited to introduce our company at the March 47
15 meeting of the Nelson Chamber of Commerce. Please prepare a 20- 60
minute electronic presentation for this meeting by extracting the key 74
points from Richard's speech, which is attached. 84

As you prepare the presentation, remember these key points: 96

1. Write phrases, not sentences, so that listeners focus on the key points. 111
2. Use parallel structure and limit wraparound lines of text. 124
3. Create *builds* to keep the audience alert. 133
4. Add transitions between slides (suggest fade in and out). 145
5. Add graphics and humor--we want them to remember us. 156

Please have the presentation ready for Richard to review by February 24. 171
After he has made his revisions and the presentation is final, print the 186
presentation as a handout. | xx | Attachment 194

Note: Word counts for missing parts have been added to appropriate lines.

PURCHASE ORDER				3
(Current date)				7

Quantity	Description	Unit Price	Total Price	15
2	Ergonomic Comfort computer chairs	$ 455.00		26
2	Slide-out keyboard shelf	54.00		33
36	3 1/2" high-density/double-sided formatted disks	1.99		46
1	10-ream carton laser printer paper (20 lb.)	54.25		57
3	HP LaserJet Series 4 toner cartridge #92298A	145.89		69
2	Address labels 1" x 2 5/8", white, #5160	24.95		80
	Total			83

Document 4
Table

1. Format the purchase order as a 4-column table. Center the table vertically and horizontally.
2. Calculate all totals.

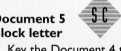 Use table formatting options to add lines and shading.

Document 5
Block letter

1. Key the Document 4 table again as part of this order letter.
2. Make the letter fit on one page.
3. Use the current date.
4. Add an appropriate salutation.
5. Format the company name in closing lines in ALL CAPS.

Copy Document 4 and place in letter.

You can adjust vertical placement of a document after it is keyed.

West Coast Office Supplies — 9
3245 Granville St. — 12
Vancouver BC V6B 5J8 — 17

Please ship the following items, which are listed in — 32
your current office supplies catalog. — 39

Insert the table here (Document 4)

Please bill this to our account number 4056278. This — 50
order is urgent; therefore, ship it overnight by Loomis. — 62

Yours truly — 64
Selkirk Communications — 69

Allan Burgess, Purchasing Agent — 75

Document 6
Table

1. Select an attractive format for the table.
2. Add at least 2 words that you frequently misspell.
3. Supply the correct spellings in the right-hand column.

Frequently Misspelled Words — 6

Misspelled	Correct Spelling	
recieve		14
accomodate		19
conveience		23
similiar		27
to (meaning also)		31
congradulations		38
envelop		41
inclosure		45

— 11

Document 7
Standard memo with table

1. DS heading lines.
2. Alphabetize the list before keying the table.
3. Format the table attractively. Center it horizontally.

		words
TO:	All Staff, Spokane Branch	6
FROM:	Marilyn Josephson, Office Manager	14
DATE:	Current	19
SUBJECT:	American versus Canadian Spelling	28

All correspondence addressed to our Canadian office should now include 42
Canadian spelling. Some of the differences are shown in the following 56
table. We'll need to get a list of other words that differ as well. 70

U.S. Spelling	Canadian Spelling	
		77
counseling	counselling	81
honor	honour	84
endeavor	endeavour	88
defense	defence	91
center	centre	94
check (meaning money)	cheque	99
color	colour	102
marvelous	marvellous	106
z	"zed"	107

Document 8
Multiple-page report with table and appendix

1. Format the report as a DS unbound report. Proofread carefully; not all errors are marked.
2. Include the agenda as an appendix in the report. (See the directions, p. A16.)
3. Prepare a title page. Assume that the report was prepared for Nelson Chamber of Commerce by Richard R. Holmes, President. Date the report March 15.

WP Use the spelling feature to help you proof your document.

PROPOSAL FOR COMMUNITY GOALS CONFERENCE 8

The Steering Committee for the chamber of commerce com- 19
munity enhancement proposes the sponsorship of a goals con- 31
ference for all citizens of Nelson. This recommendation is 43
based on research data compiled from conferences sponsored 55
in other cities similar to Nelson. Also, the recommendation 66
is supported by the committee's combined experience in work- 79
ing with varied groups of citizens and commitment to 90
progress. The report presents a proposed outline for a 101

goals conference. 105

Purpose of Conference 109

The purposes of this conference are (1) to improve educa- 121
tion, economic development, youth services, and recreation and 133
(2) to reduce crime in the Nelson and district. All members 145
of the community will be invited to attend this conference and 157

contribute ∧to ~~the~~ the achievement of these goals. ∧a ~~P~~ublicity com- 170

mittee will be resonsible for informing the community. 181

Goals Conference Format 186

    The Steering Committee recommends that the confence be 197

held at ∧*Marion Hall,* Canadian International College (CIC) ∧ on *May* ~~March~~ 18, 211

19--, from 9:30 a.m. to 4:00 p.m. Facilities can be 222

reserved by calling Patzy Frazier at (606) 555-3789. 233

    The conference would begin with an opening session and 244

should inlcude introductions of key leaders in the community 256

as well as Chamber of Commerce officers. The keynote 267

∧*speaker* should be a prominent state leader who has vision for 279

quality communities. 284

    Following the opening sessions, participants will 294

choose from one of the following five breakout groups: edu- 306

cation, youth services, *recreation* ~~education~~, economic development, 317

~~youth services, recreation~~ and crime. Breakout sessions 323

will be directed by facilitators trained in working with 335

diverse groups. *¶ Groups will brainstorm and then set* ~~Lunch will follow and be served in the~~ 345

goals and prepare plans for achieving the specific ~~Banquet Room of the college. The afternoon~~ sessions will be 355

goals of the conference. The sessions will run for
~~a repeat of the workshops so that participants may attend~~ 366

one hour.
~~different sessions.]~~ 368

Recommended facilitators include: *team leaders and the following* 381

Team	Team Leaders	Facilitators	
Education	Dale Coppage, Nelson BC	Ellen Obert, Spokane WA	399
Youth Services	Lawrence Riveria, Portland, OR	Jack Jones, Vancouver BC	413
Recreation	Bradley Greger, Nelson BC	Carlos Pena, Calgary AB	425
Economic Development	Jon Guyton, Nelson BC	Harvey Lewis, *Nelson BC*	439
Crime	Monica Brigham, Toronto ON	Shawn McNullan, ~~NC~~ ''	450

words

DS

After the first breakout sessions, participants will join   462
for lunch in the H. L. Calvert Union Building. The Steering 474
Committee recommends that Mayor Alton johnson address the   486
topic of meeting educational challenges of the next century. P.M. 498
A repeat of the morning breakout sessions will begin at 1:30. 512
This repeat will allow participants to contirube to antoher   524
topic. In the closing session, breakout facilitators will   536
present the goals and plans to the audience.   546
During

Sponsors   547

The Steerting Committee has discussed the sponsorhsip of   559

a goals conference with a number of partners in the Nelson   570

area. The following organizations have agreed to serve as   582

sponsors: Nelson Economic Development Foundation, Bank of   594

Canada, Northeast Bottling Company, and Bank of Nelson, and 605

Farthington's Clothiers.   610

Summary   612

The Steering Committee strongly recommends this goals   623

conference. The committee will be avilable at the Camber   635

of commerce meeting to answer any questions.   644

**Document 9
Agenda**

SC

1. Prepare a sheet that will precede the agenda. Use 1.5" top margin; center-align APPENDIX; DS and center the title of the agenda. Number this page in sequence.
2. DS between items of the agenda.

Goals Conference Agenda   5

9:30 a.m.-9:45 a.m.   Welcome   11

9:45 a.m.-10:15 a.m.   Opening Remarks   19
                             Overview of Community Quality   25
                                Initiative   27
                          SS Purpose of Goals Conference   33
                             Process   34
                             Introduction of Community Leaders 41
                                and Chamber Officers   45

10:15 a.m.-10:35 a.m.   Refreshment Break   54
10:35 a.m.-12 noon   Breakout Sessions: List the 5 sessions SS 62
12 noon-1:00 p.m.   Lunch   79
                          SS Speaker on Educational Challenges 86
                                of the 21st Century   90

Breakout Sessions   DS between items
1:00 p.m.-2:30 p.m.   Goals Setting Workshops   98
2:30 p.m.-2:45 p.m.   Refreshment Break   106
2:45 p.m.-4:00 p.m.   Presentation of Goals   115

APPENDIX

TIMED WRITINGS

Writing 51

Key two 3' writings with controlled speed.

E all letters
gwam 3'

The term careers can mean many different things to	3	51
different people. As you know, a career is much more than a	8	55
job. It is the kind of work that a person has through life.	12	59
It includes the jobs a person has over time. It also involves	16	63
how the work life affects the other parts of our life. There	20	67
are as many types of careers as there are people.	23	71
Almost all people have a career of some kind. A career	27	74
can help us to reach unique goals, such as to make a living	31	79
or to help others. The kind of career you have will affect	35	83
your life in many ways. For example, it can determine where	39	87
you live, the money you make, and how you feel about yourself.	44	91
A good choice can thus help you realize the life you want.	47	95

3' | 1 | 2 | 3 | 4 |

Writing 52

Key two 3' writings.

E all letters
gwam 1' | 3'

Do you know how to use time wisely? If you do, then its	11	4	51
proper use can help you organize and run a business better.	24	8	55
If you find that your daily problems tend to keep you from	35	12	59
planning properly, then perhaps you are not using time well.	48	16	63
You may find that you spend too much time on tasks that are	60	20	67
not important. Plan your work to save valuable time.	70	24	70
A firm that does not plan is liable to run into trouble.	12	27	74
A small firm may have trouble planning. It is important	23	31	78
to know just where the firm is headed. A firm may have a	35	35	82
fear of learning things it would rather not know. To say	46	39	86
that planning is easy would be absurd. It requires lots of	58	43	90
thinking and planning to meet the expected needs of the firm.	70	47	94

1' | 1 | 2 | 3 | 4 | 5 | 6 | 7 | 8 | 9 | 10 | 11 | 12 |
3' | 1 | 2 | 3 | 4 |

Writing 53

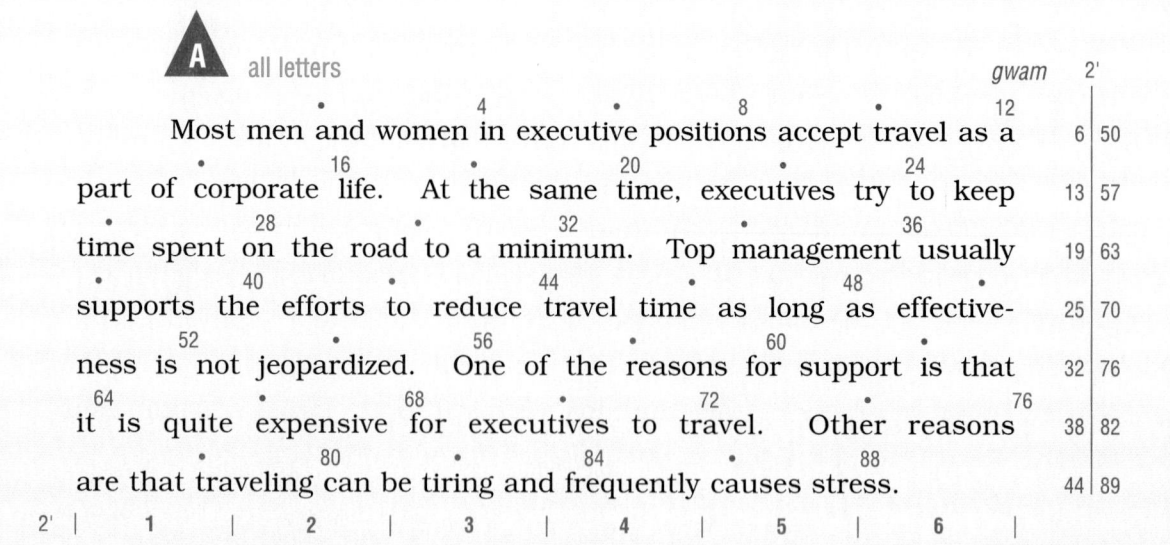

A all letters   *gwam* 2'

```
        •           4          •          8          •          12
   Most men and women in executive positions accept travel as a        6 | 50
        •          16         •         20          •          24
part of corporate life.   At the same time, executives try to keep    13 | 57
        •          28         •         32          •          36
time spent on the road to a minimum.   Top management usually         19 | 63
        •          40         •         44          •          48     •
supports the efforts to reduce travel time as long as effective-      25 | 70
        52         •         56          •          60          •
ness is not jeopardized.   One of the reasons for support is that     32 | 76
   64           •         68          •          72          •    76
it is quite expensive for executives to travel.   Other reasons       38 | 82
             •         80         •         84          •        88
are that traveling can be tiring and frequently causes stress.        44 | 89
```

2' | 1 | 2 | 3 | 4 | 5 | 6 |

Writing 54

1. Key two 1' writings on each ¶. Strive to increase keystroking speed.

2. Key one 5' writing; proofread; circle errors; determine *gwam*.

A all letters   *gwam* 1' | 5'

Working at home is not exactly a new phenomenon, but the con-   12 | 2 | 47

cept is growing quite rapidly.   For many years, people have worked   26 | 5 | 50

at home.   In most instances, they were self-employed and operated   39 | 8 | 52

a business from their homes.   Today, the people who work at home   52 | 10 | 55

fit into a variety of categories.   Some own their own businesses;   65 | 13 | 58

others bring extra work home after the workday ends.   A key change   79 | 16 | 60

is the large group of people who are employed by huge organizations   92 | 18 | 63

but who work out of home offices.   These employees are in jobs that   106 | 21 | 66

include sales, creative, technical, and a host of other categories.   120 | 24 | 69

The real change that has occurred is not so much the numbers   12 | 26 | 71

of people who are working at home and the variety of jobs, but the   26 | 29 | 74

complex tools that are now available for doing the job.   Technology   39 | 32 | 76

has truly made the difference.   In many cases, clients and customers   53 | 35 | 79

are not even aware that they are dealing with individuals working   66 | 37 | 82

at home. Computers, printers, fax machines, telephone systems,   72 | 40 | 84

and other office equipment enable the worker in the home to function   93 | 42 | 87

in the same way as workers in a typical business office.   104 | 45 | 89

1' | 1 | 2 | 3 | 4 | 5 | 6 | 7 | 8 | 9 | 10 | 11 | 12 | 13 |
5' | 1 | 2 | 3 |

Drills

Key each of the lines twice; DS between 4-line groups; key one-hand words letter-by-letter; key balanced-hand words as units.

balanced hand

1 pens turn fur slam pay rifle worn pan duck ham lap slap burn girl

2 Andy Clancy, a neighbor, may visit at the lake and at the island.

one hand

3 read ploy create kiln crate plum were pony lilly jump severe hump

4 Phillip, as you are aware, was a reader on deferred estate cases.

combination

5 did you we spent pony street busy jump held severe pant exert due

6 Were profits better when we were on Main Street than Duck Street?

| 1 | 2 . | 3 | 4 | 5 | 6 | 7 | 8 | 9 | 10 | 11 | 12 | 13 |

Writing 55

1. Key three 1' writings on each ¶.
2. Key one 5' writing or two 3' writings. Proofread; circle errors; determine *gwam*.

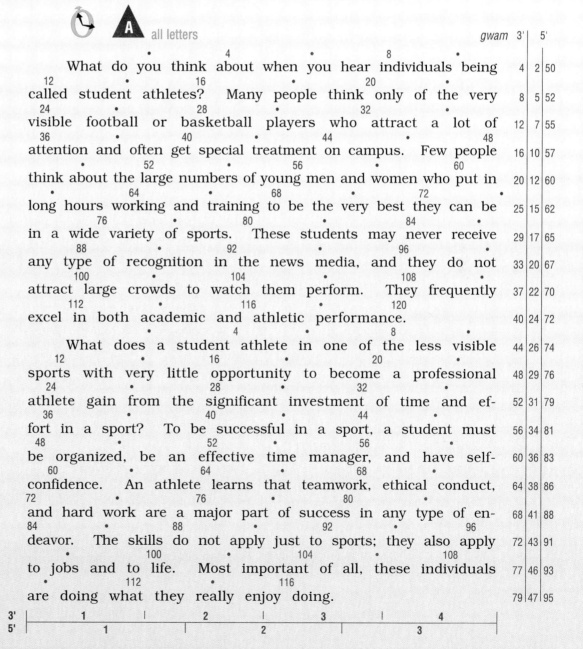

A all letters
gwam 3' | 5'

What do you think about when you hear individuals being | 4 | 2 50
called student athletes? Many people think only of the very | 8 | 5 52
visible football or basketball players who attract a lot of | 12 | 7 55
attention and often get special treatment on campus. Few people | 16 | 10 57
think about the large numbers of young men and women who put in | 20 | 12 60
long hours working and training to be the very best they can be | 25 | 15 62
in a wide variety of sports. These students may never receive | 29 | 17 65
any type of recognition in the news media, and they do not | 33 | 20 67
attract large crowds to watch them perform. They frequently | 37 | 22 70
excel in both academic and athletic performance. | 40 | 24 72

What does a student athlete in one of the less visible | 44 | 26 74
sports with very little opportunity to become a professional | 48 | 29 76
athlete gain from the significant investment of time and ef- | 52 | 31 79
fort in a sport? To be successful in a sport, a student must | 56 | 34 81
be organized, be an effective time manager, and have self- | 60 | 36 83
confidence. An athlete learns that teamwork, ethical conduct, | 64 | 38 86
and hard work are a major part of success in any type of en- | 68 | 41 88
deavor. The skills do not apply just to sports; they also apply | 72 | 43 91
to jobs and to life. Most important of all, these individuals | 77 | 46 93
are doing what they really enjoy doing. | 79 | 47 95

3' | 1 | 2 | 3 | 4
5' | 1 | 2 | 3

APPENDIX E

NUMERIC KEYPAD

Introduction

Most computer keyboards contain a numeric keypad separate from the alphanumeric keys. When you are keying a large amount of numeric input, such as spreadsheets or data entry, you will find keying numbers with the keypad much more efficient than using the numbers above the alphabetic keys.

The numeric keypad is generally located to the right of the alphanumeric keys. It is often referred to as the ten-key keypad because the numbers are arranged in the same format as a standard calculator. The skills you learn in this unit can be transferred to any electronic calculator.

College Keyboarding Numeric Keypad Software

Keypad instruction is available on *College Keyboarding Numeric Keypad* software. If you are using a 3 1/2" disk, the keypad software is on the same disk as *College Keyboarding Alpha-numeric.*

Loading the Keypad Software

1. If you are running the software from the program disk, key **keypad** at the A> prompt. If you are running the program from the hard drive, change to the directory where the program is stored and key **keypad** at the C> prompt.

2. Select the keypad that most clearly resembles the one on your computer.

Main Menu

You can select any part of *College Keyboarding Numeric Keypad* software from the Main menu by using the pull-down menus at the top—File, Lessons, Data Sets, and Open Screen. Select an option by using the left and right arrow keys and striking ENTER.

File. The File option lets you manage the information keyed. Use the arrow keys and ENTER to select; strike ESC to return to the Main menu.

Lessons. The Lessons option presents the figures 1–9, zero, decimal point, and the keypad ENTER key in four lessons. Activities include the following: Warmup, Learn New Keys, Improve Keystroking, Build Skill, and Lesson Report, which shows the exercises you completed and the scores achieved.

Data Sets. These on-screen exercises are designed to improve speed, accuracy, and facility of keypad operation. They emphasize various rows and types of data.

Open Screen. The Open Screen is designed for reinforcing the numeric keypad using the drill material on the next five pages. Exercises must be keyed from the text.

In the Open Screen, as well as in the tutorial, the computer will align the numbers at the display and display the total after the last number in a set has been entered.

Using the Open Screen

1. Key the drills on pages A21–A24 in Open Screen, keeping your eyes on the copy.
2. Strike the keypad ENTER key after each number.
3. To obtain a total, strike ENTER twice after the last number in a group.
4. Key each problem until the same answer is obtained twice; by doing this, you can be reasonably sure that you have the correct answer.

Follow the directions on p. A20.

Practice 1. Reach down with the first finger to strike the **1** key.

Practice 2. Reach down with the second finger to strike the **2** key.

Practice 3. Reach down with the third finger to strike the **3** key.

Drill 1

a	b	c	d	e	f
11	22	33	14	15	16
41	52	63	36	34	35
24	26	25	22	42	62
27	18	39	30	20	10
30	30	10	19	61	43
32	31	21	53	83	71

Technique tip

Keep fingers curved and upright over home keys. Keep right thumb tucked under palm.

Drill 2

a	b	c	d	e	f
414	141	525	252	636	363
141	111	252	222	363	333
111	414	222	525	333	636

Drill 3

a	b	c	d	e	f
111	141	222	252	366	336
152	342	624	141	243	121
330	502	331	302	110	432
913	823	721	633	523	511
702	612	513	712	802	823
213	293	821	813	422	722

Drill 4

24	36	15	12	32	34
115	334	226	254	346	246
20	140	300	240	105	304
187	278	347	159	357	158
852	741	963	654	321	987
303	505	819	37	92	10

1 | 2 | 3 | 4

Drill 5

28	91	37	22	13	23
524	631	423	821	922	733
15	221	209	371	300	25
823	421	24	31	19	107
652	813	211	354	231	187
50	31	352	16	210	30

Key the drills at the right following the directions p. A20.

Practice 7. Reach up with the right first finger to strike the **7** key; return to the home keys. Keep the fingers in home position.

Practice 8. Reach up with the right second finger to strike the **8** key; return to the home keys. Keep the second finger in home position. You may raise the first finger slightly, but keep it close to the 4 key.

Practice 9. Reach up with the right third finger to strike the **9** key; return to the home keys. Keep the first finger in home position and the second finger close to the 5 key.

Technique tip
Keep fingers curved and upright over home keys.

Drill 1

a	b	c	d	e	f
74	85	96	70	80	90
47	58	96	87	78	98
90	70	80	90	90	70
89	98	78	89	77	87
86	67	57	48	68	57
59	47	48	67	58	69

Drill 2

470	580	690	770	707	407
999	969	888	858	474	777
777	474	888	585	999	696

Drill 3

858	969	747	770	880	990
757	858	959	857	747	678
579	849	879	697	854	796
857	967	864	749	864	795
609	507	607	889	990	448
597	847	449	457	684	599

Drill 4

85	74	96	98	78	88
957	478	857	994	677	579
657	947	479	76	94	795
887	965	789	577	649	849
90	80	70	806	709	407
407	567	494	97	80	70

Drill 5

50	790	807	90	75	968
408	97	66	480	857	57
87	479	567	947	808	970
690	85	798	587	907	89
94	754	879	67	594	847
489	880	97	907	69	579

Curve the fingers on the right hand and place them over the home keys as follows:
- first finger on 4
- second finger on 5
- third finger on 6
- fourth finger on Enter
- thumb on the 0

Drill 1

a	b	c	d	e	f
46	55	56	46	55	56
45	64	45	45	64	45
66	56	64	66	56	64
56	44	65	56	44	65
54	65	45	54	65	45
65	54	44	65	54	44

Drill 2

a	b	c	d	e	f
466	445	546	654	465	665
564	654	465	545	446	645
456	464	546	545	564	456
556	544	644	466	644	646
644	455	464	654	464	554
454	546	565	554	456	656

Drill 3

a	b	c	d	e	f
400	404	505	606	500	600
404	505	606	500	600	400
500	600	400	404	505	606
650	506	404	550	440	550
506	460	605	460	604	640
406	500	640	504	460	560

Drill 4

Practice zero (0) key. Keep the thumb tucked under the palm. Strike the zero key with the right thumb, using the same down-and-in motion used on the space bar.

a	b	c	d	e	f
504	640	550	440	660	406
560	450	650	450	505	550
640	504	440	640	450	660
400	600	500	500	600	400
650	505	404	606	540	560
504	404	640	404	406	606

Drill 5

a	b	c	d	e	f
460	445	546	654	465	605
564	654	460	465	545	446
605	504	546	640	604	564
540	466	664	554	405	656

KEYPAD DRILLS DECIMALS

Follow the directions on p. A20.

Decimal points are often included in numerical data. The decimal (.) key is usually located at the bottom right of the keypad. Use the third finger to reach down to strike the decimal key.

Technique tip

Strike each key with a quick, sharp stroke. Release the key quickly. Keep the fingers curved and upright, the wrist low and relaxed.

Drill 1

a	b	c	d
.28	.19	.37	.42
.51	.67	.81	.27
.64	.50	.60	.50

Drill 2

a	b	c	d
7.10	8.91	5.64	3.12
5.32	4.27	9.21	6.47
8.94	3.06	7.38	5.89

Drill 3

a	b	c	d
3.62	36.94	86.73	.60
8.06	10.31	537.34	5.21
321.04	10.55	687.52	164.84
.75	.26	10.85	627.98
687.46	357.95	159.46	85.21
20.46	220.48	6.10	3.04

Drill 4

a	b	c	d
761.64	2.82	627.25	196.25
285.46	34.60	.29	89.24
33.99	739.45	290.23	563.21
60.41	52.79	105.87	951.32
108.97	211.00	46.24	82.47
3.54	5.79	5.41	1.32

Drill 5

a	b	c	d
.05	1.19	77.54	112.96
112.54	561.34	114.85	.24
35.67	22.01	67.90	41.08
579.21	105.24	731.98	258.96
.34	1.68	.24	.87
21.87	54.89	2.34	5.89

REFERENCE GUIDE

Abbreviations

1. If the reader may not be familiar with an abbreviation, spell it out the first time it is used and place the abbreviation in parentheses.

   computer aided design (CAD)
   Certified Public Accountant (CPA)

2. One space follows a period used after an abbreviation and no space follows a period within an abbreviation.

   Mr. Jones   p.m.

3. Spell out street names; exceptions are designators such as NW.

   Mill Avenue   Bay Street   123 Rolling Hills SE

4. Use two-letter state abbreviations only with ZIP Codes.

   Cincinnati, OH 45241-3421

5. Do not abbreviate the name of a city, state, or country except when space is a problem. ("Saint" is usually abbreviated as St. in the United States.)

   Fort Worth   Mount Ranier   Wisconsin
   St. Louis   Port Arthur   United Kingdom

6. Abbreviate names of government and private agencies, organizations, radio and television stations.

   SBA   ABC   IBM

7. Company names often contain abbreviations such as Bros., Co., Corp., Inc., Ltd., and &. Check the letterhead for proper style.

8. Abbreviate titles used with full names or last names only.

   Mr.   Messrs. (plural of Mr.)   Mrs.   Mmes.

9. Abbreviate titles, academic degrees, and professional titles following names.

   Steven Frey, Esq.
   Charles Forde, Ph.D.
   George Hays, Jr.

10. Business expressions, days and months, and measurements may be abbreviated in technical documents, lists, business forms, in some routine documents, or when space is a problem. Check a dictionary if in doubt about whether the abbreviation is correct.

acct.	accounting	Mon.	Monday
amt.	amount	Jan.	January
FYI	for your information	in. or in	inches

Capitalization

Capitalize:

1. First word of a sentence and of a direct quotation.

   She put the car in storage.
   He said, "Here is my book."

2. First word after a colon if it begins a complete sentence.

   Warning: The floors are slippery when wet.

3. Names of specific persons or places and their derivatives; do not capitalize commonly accepted derivatives.

   The New River passes by Price State University.
   The French fashions were displayed; french toast was served on fine china.

4. Distinctive title or personal title that precedes a name and a title in an address or signature line. Do not capitalize titles following names, unless in an address or signature line.

   Dr. Sun called Senator Dobbs.
   Ms. Jane Holmes, Advertising Director
   Kay is a vice president.

5. Specific course titles or courses derived from a proper noun; do not capitalize general courses.

   American History   Keyboarding 1   word processing

6. First and main words in headings or titles in books, songs, etc.; do not capitalize articles, conjunctions, and prepositions of fewer than four letters.

   I saw the photo in *Computers in the News*.
   The topic "Interview for the Position" was omitted.

7. Weekdays, months, and holidays.

   Let's meet each Monday in May except for Memorial Day.

8. Trademarks and brand names.

   I use Essex oil in my Everlasts lawn mower.

9. Specific parts of the country; do not capitalize compass points that are not part of the name.

   Midwest   South   north of town

10. Specific departments or groups within the writer's organization.

   The Board of Directors discussed the restructuring of our Sales Department.

11. Nouns before a figure except for some common nouns.

   Unit 1, Section 2   page 2, verse 7, line 2

Number expression

General guidelines:

1. Use words for numbers one through ten unless the numbers are in a category with related larger numbers that are expressed as figures.

   He bought 75 acres of land.
   She wrote 12 stories and 13 plays in the last 2 years.
   Mail two copies of the report.

2. Use words for approximate numbers or large round numbers that can be expressed as one or two words. Use numbers for round numbers in millions or higher with their word modifier.

   About fifty representatives attended the conference.
   We sent out about three hundred invitations.
   She contributed $3 million.

3. Use words for numbers that begin a sentence.

   Six players were cut from the 37-member team.

4. Use figures for the larger of two adjacent numbers.

   We shipped six 24-ton engines.

Times and dates:

5. Use words for numbers that precede o'clock (stated or implied).

   We shall meet from two until five o'clock.

6. Use figures for times with a.m. or p.m. and days when they follow the month.

   Her appointment is for 2:15 p.m. on July 26, 1998.
   The Convention will begin October 26.

7. Use ordinals for the day when it precedes the month.

   The 10th of October is my anniversary.
   The tenth of October is my anniversary. (formal)

Money, percentages, and fractions:

8. Use figures for money amounts and percentages. Spell out cents and percent except in statistical copy.

   The 16 percent discount saved me $145; Bill, 95 cents.

9. Use a combination of words and figures for very large amounts of money.

   The acquisition will cost $3 million.

10. Use words for fractions unless the fractions appear in combination with whole numbers.

    She read just one-half of her lesson.
    5 1/2   18 3/4

Addresses:

11. Use words for street names first through Tenth and figures or ordinals for streets above Tenth. Use figures for house numbers other than number One.

    My friend lives at One Lytle Place.
    Monica lives at 1590 Echo Lane.
    Meet me at Second Avenue and 53rd Street.

Punctuation

Use an apostrophe:

1. To show possession: Add an apostrophe and s to a singular noun.

   dog's   fox's arm   Doug's den   Jess's book

   Exception: If adding an additional s to a noun already ending in s makes the word difficult to pronounce, add only an apostrophe.

   series' outline   Los Angeles' freeways

2. To show possession: Add an apostrophe and s to a plural noun that does not end in s.

   men's shoes   women's dresses   children's coats

   Add only an apostrophe after a plural noun ending in s and after a proper noun of more than one syllable ending in s or z.

   trains' schedules   Hernandez' trip   Delores' report

3. To show possession: Add 's after the last noun in a series to indicate joint or common possession of two or more persons; however, show separate possession of two or more persons by adding 's to each noun.

   Sylvia and Jason's trip
   Myra's and Hank's class schedules

4. To form the plural of numbers (written as figures or words) and letters. Do not use an apostrophe in market quotations.

   5's   five's   F's   AmeriTech 4s

5. To show omission of letters or figures; as a symbol for feet and minutes. Use quotation marks for inches and seconds.

   Rob't   it's fine   Class of '95
   a 5' timing   15'6" x 10'8"   an 8' x 10' rug

Use a colon:

To indicate that a listing or statement follows.

He bought these items: a pen, six pencils, a notebook.
He said the magic words: Class is dismissed at 2:30.

Use a comma:

1. After introductory words, phrases, or dependent clauses.

   Yes, final grades have been posted.
   If I study tonight, I can go to the game.

2. Between words or groups of words that make up a series.

   Fuji, Don, Cyd, and Rod will go to Green Bay soon.
   I swam, played ball, and ran a race while at camp.

3. To set off explanatory and interrupting words, phrases, and clauses that are not necessary to the meaning of the sentence.

   I believe, however, he knows.
   Max, their expert, set up a booth next to mine.
   The outcome, he knew, was never in doubt.
   His plan, which depends on deception, will never work.
   Any students, who are late, will not be seated.
   Exception: Do not set off clauses (restrictive) that are necessary to the meaning of the sentence.
   Any students who are late will not be seated.

4. To set off words in direct address.

I know, Joy, that you prefer classical music.

5. To set off the date from the year and the city from the state.

On June 5, 1992, Sam finally graduated.

Sam arrived in Honolulu, Hawaii, on June 9.

6. To separate two or more parallel adjectives (adjectives that could be separated by the word *and* instead of a comma). Do not use commas to separate adjectives so closely related that they appear to form a single element with the noun they modify.

The quiet, efficient worker finished on time.

He lives in a small white house under a green oak tree.

7. To separate whole numbers into groups of three digits each. However, numbers that identify rather than enumerate are usually keyed without commas.

My books, all 1,640 of them, are in Room 8401.

8. To set off contrasting phrases and clauses.

Her methods, not her objectives, caused us concern.

Use a dash:

1. To show an abrupt change of thought.

Invoice #20--it was dated 3/4--billed $17.

2. To show the source of a direct quotation and certain special purposes.

A dash separates; a hyphen joins. --Anonymous

Yes--well, maybe--I'll try to finish on time.

Use an exclamation point:

After emotional words, phrases, or exclamatory sentences.

Look out!   Hurrah!   Don't drink the water!

Use a hyphen:

1. To join a compound adjective that immediately precedes the word modified.

first-class ticket on-time arrival heart-stopping movie

2. To join compound numbers between 21 and 99 and fractions used as modifiers.

She read just one-half of about forty-five memos.

Use parentheses:

1. To enclose explanatory, parenthetical, or nonessential material.

Our trees (maples) were red and gold (autumn colors).

2. To enclose letters or figures in a listing or figures that follow spelled-out amounts.

Enter (a) name, (b) address, and (c) I.D. number.

Your initial payment is fifty dollars ($50).

Use a period:

1. After a complete declaratory sentence or a courteous request (the reader is expected to act rather than answer).

We like snow. We are ski enthusiasts.

Will you please send the shipment by express.

2. After an abbreviation of a word.

Mr. Juan de Leon's birthday is Jan. 5.

3. With an abbreviation made up of more than one word; in this case, space only once after the final period.

Ellis Kato, M.D., was granted a Ph.D. today.

4. To form an ellipsis that represents an omission of words from quoted data. (Commonly 3 periods are used, but 4 are used when an ellipsis ends a sentence. Space once between ellipsis periods.)

Says Audrey, "The three diodes . . . are not functional."

The lawyer who was dressed in black denied any direct responsibility. . . .

Use quotation marks: (after a comma or period; before a semicolon or colon; after a question mark if the quotation itself is a question)

1. To enclose direct quotations.

"I am not," she said, "going."

2. To enclose titles of written works, but not book titles.

"Aida" " The Raven" "Hurricane Strikes Gulf Coast"

3. To enclose out-of-the-ordinary words or phrases.

The "bleed" line ran off the side of the page.

Use a semicolon: (one space follows)

1. To separate two or more independent clauses in a compound sentence when the conjunction is omitted.

Alan asked if Nick Curl was a guest; Sue left.

2. To separate independent clauses joined by a conjunctive adverb (however, therefore, etc.).

Our costs have increased; however, our prices have not.

3. To separate a series of items that themselves contain commas.

Provide lines for the employee's title; department; telephone number; and, of course, name.

Use an underline:

1. With titles of complete literary works.

PC World   Daily News   The Sun Also Rises

2. To emphasize special words or phrases.

Do you know the meaning of prestidigitation?

Proofreading procedures

Error-free documents send the message that you are detail-oriented and a person capable of doing business. Apply these procedures after you key a document.

1. Use a spelling checker if you are using a word processing program. If not, check spelling manually.
2. Proofread the document either on screen or in hard copy to be sure that it makes sense. Check for these types of errors:
   - Words, headings, and/or amounts omitted.
   - Extra words or lines not deleted during the editing stage.
   - Incorrect sequence of numbers in a list.
   - Incorrect figures, names, or addresses.
   - Inconsistent document formatting style.
3. If using a word processing program, make corrections and reprint. If using a typewriter, make manual corrections (see correcting methods below).

Proofreaders' marks

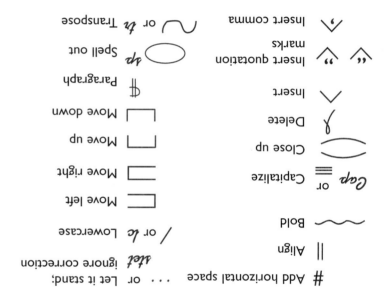

Correcting Methods

Computers

Correct errors using the backspace key or the delete key. Use the backspace key to remove characters to the left (behind) the cursor. Use the delete key to erase characters in front of the cursor.

Correcting key ("lift off"):

1. Move print point to incorrect character. (On current line, use backspace key or space bar; on previous lines, use the "previous line" function—see manufacturer's booklet.)
2. Strike the correcting key. (To erase more than one character, strike the repeat key or strike the correcting key again.)
3. Key the correct character(s).
4. Move print point to the position it was in before correction. (Relocate key is available on most electronic models.)

This procedure is for automatic correction. Manual correction with the correcting key may be required depending upon location of error. Some electric typewriters have "lift off" keys to which this basic procedure applies.

Correcting methods ("white out"):

1. Select fluid the same color as the paper.
2. Move the paper up or down to make the error accessible.
3. Brush on the fluid sparingly, lightly covering the error—no other characters.
4. Turn paper to position it was before correction; key the correct character(s).

Word division

With the use of proportional fonts found in current word processing packages, word division is less of an issue. Occasionally, however, you will need to make decisions on dividing words. The following list contains generally accepted guidelines for dividing words.

1. Divide words between syllables only; therefore, do not divide one-syllable words.
2. Short words: Avoid dividing short words (five letters or fewer).

   area   since   bonus   ideal

3. Double consonants: Divide words with double consonants between the double letters unless the root word ends with the double letters. In this case, divide after the second consonant.

   mis-sion   trim-ming   dress-ing   call-ing

4. One-letter syllables: Do not divide after a one-letter syllable at the beginning of a word or before a one- or two-letter syllable at the end of a word; divide after a one-letter syllable within a word.

   enough   abroad   starter   friendly
   ani-mal   sepa-rate   regu-late

5. Two single-letter syllables: Divide between two single-letter syllables within a word.

   gradu-ation   evalu-ation

6. Hyphenated words: Compound words with a hyphen may be divided only after the hyphen.

   top-secret   soft-spoken   self-respect

7. Figures: Avoid dividing figures presented as a unit.

   #870331   190,886   1/22/98

8. Proper nouns: Avoid dividing proper nouns. If necessary, include as much of the proper noun as possible before dividing it.

   Thomas R./Lewiston   not Thomas R. Lewis/ton
   November 15,/2000   not November/15, 2000

Addressing procedures

When preparing an envelope, follow the spacing guidelines below:

Small envelope. On a No. 6 3/4 envelope, place the address near the center—about 2 inches from the top and left edges. Place a return address in the upper left corner (line 2, 3 spaces from left edge).

Large envelope. On a No. 10 envelope, place the address near the center—about line 14 and .5" left of center. A return address, if not preprinted, should be keyed in the upper left corner (see small envelope).

An address must contain at least three lines; addresses of more than six lines should be avoided. The last line of an address must contain three items of information ONLY: (1) the city, (2) the state, and (3) the ZIP Code, preferably a 9-digit code.

Place mailing notations that affect postage (e.g., REGISTERED, CERTIFIED) below the stamp position (line 8); place other special notations (e.g., CONFIDENTIAL, PERSONAL) a DS below the return address.

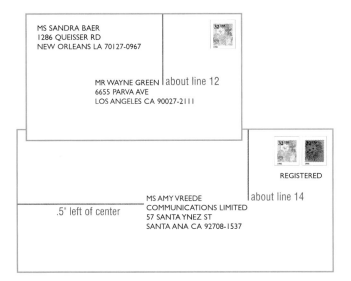

Folding and inserting procedures

Step 1	Step 2	Step 3

Large envelopes (No. 10, 9, 7 3/4)

Step 1: With document face up, fold slightly less than 1/3 of sheet up toward top.

Step 2: Fold down top of sheet to within 1/2" of bottom fold.

Step 3: Insert document into envelope with last crease toward bottom of envelope.

Small envelopes (No. 6 3/4, 6 1/4)

Step 1	Step 2	Step 3

  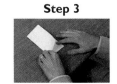

Step 1: With document face up, fold bottom up to 1/2" from top.

Step 2: Fold right third to left.

Step 3: Fold left third to 1/2" from last crease and insert last creased edge first.

Window envelopes (full sheet)

Step 1	Step 2	Step 3

Step 1: With sheet face down, top toward you, fold upper third down.

Step 2: Fold lower third up so address is showing.

Step 3: Insert document into envelope with last crease toward bottom of envelope.

Two-letter state abbreviations

Alabama, AL	Guam, GU	Massachusetts, MA	New York, NY	Tennessee, TN
Alaska, AK	Hawaii, HI	Michigan, MI	North Carolina, NC	Texas, TX
Arizona, AZ	Idaho, ID	Minnesota, MN	North Dakota, ND	Utah, UT
Arkansas, AR	Illinois, IL	Mississippi, MS	Ohio, OH	Vermont, VT
California, CA	Indiana, IN	Missouri, MO	Oklahoma, OK	Virgin Islands, VI
Colorado, CO	Iowa, IA	Montana, MT	Oregon, OR	Virginia, VA
Connecticut, CT	Kansas, KS	Nebraska, NE	Pennsylvania, PA	Washington, WA
Delaware, DE	Kentucky, KY	Nevada, NV	Puerto Rico, PR	West Virginia, WV
District of Columbia, DC	Louisiana, LA	New Hampshire, NH	Rhode Island, RI	Wisconsin, WI
Florida, FL	Maine, ME	New Jersey, NJ	South Carolina, SC	Wyoming, WY
Georgia, GA	Maryland, MD	New Mexico, NM	South Dakota, SD	

Letter parts

Letterhead. Company name and address. May include other data.

Date. Date letter is mailed. Usually in month, day, year order. Military style is an option (day/month/year: 17/1/98).

Letter address. Address of the person who will receive the letter. Include personal title (Mr., Ms., Dr.), name, professional title, company, and address.

Salutation. Greeting. Corresponds to the first line of the letter address. Usually includes name and courtesy title; use Ladies and Gentlemen if letter is addressed to a company name.

Body. Message. SS; DS between paragraphs.

Complimentary close. Farewell, such as Sincerely.

Writer. Name and professional title. Women may include a personal title; use Ms. if unknown.

Initials. Identifies person who keyed the document (for example, tr). May include identification of writer (ARB:tr).

Enclosure. Copy is enclosed with the document. May specify contents.

Copy notation. Indicates that a copy of the letter is being sent to person named.

Block letter (open punctuation)

IMAGE MAKERS
5131 Moss Springs Rd. • Columbia, SC 29209-4768 • (803) 555-0127

Dateline — January 24, 19--
QS

Letter address — Mr. Steven P. Nations, Manager
Human Resources Department
Klienwood Manufacturing Company
1486 Bistineau Street
Ruston, LA 71270-3695
DS

Salutation — Dear Mr. Nations
DS

Body — The details for the training program for all Klienwood associates who prepare documents have been finalized. An agenda of the program, a content outline, and the new Klienwood Style Manual are enclosed. The agenda indicates the trainer for each session.
DS

The word processing, spreadsheet, and graphics software training modules are scheduled first. All training sessions are scheduled in three-hour blocks and are offered twice on the same day.
DS

The session on image management that you requested for all managers and support staff is scheduled as the final session. The survey results show that many of your managers prepare some of their documents themselves. Therefore, the consistent image you desire can be achieved only if all individuals who prepare image documents follow the standard formats.
DS

Please call me if you have any questions about the program. Our trainers are anxious to conduct the program for you.
DS

Compli-
mentary — Sincerely
close   QS

Writer's — Cherie E. LaBorde
title   President
DS

Initials — xx
DS

Enclosure — Enclosures

Modified block letter (mixed punctuation)

IMAGE MAKERS
5131 Moss Springs Rd. • Columbia, SC 29209-4768 • (803) 555-0127

October 27, 19--
QS

Ms. Vera M. Hayes, President
Vera's Word Processing Services
4927 Stuart Avenue
Baton Rouge, LA 70808-3519
DS

Dear Ms. Hayes:
DS

The format of this letter is called modified block. Modified block format differs from block format in that the date, complimentary close, and the signature lines are positioned at the center point.
DS

Paragraphs may be blocked, as this letter illustrates, or they may be indented five spaces from the left margin. We suggest you block paragraphs when you use modified block style so that an additional tab setting is not needed. However, some people who use modified block format prefer indented paragraphs.
DS

Although modified block format is very popular, we recommend that you use it only for those customers who request this letter style. Otherwise, we urge you to use block format, which is more efficient, as your standard style.
DS

Both formats are illustrated in the enclosed Image Makers Format Guide. Please note that the block format is labeled "computer compatible."
DS

Sincerely,
QS

Patrick R. Ray
Communication Consultant
DS

xx
DS

Enclosure
DS

c Scot Carl, Account Manager

Envelope

IMAGE MAKERS
5131 Moss Springs Rd. • Columbia, SC 29209-4768

MR STEVEN P NATIONS MANAGER
HUMAN RESOURCES DEPARTMENT
KLIENWOOD MANUFACTURING COMPANY
1486 BISTINEAU STREET
RUSTON LA 71270-3695

Letter placement table

Letter length	Variable side margins	Standard side margins	Dateline
Short	2"	1"	line 18 (3")
Average	1.5"	1"	line 16 (2.67")
Long	1"	1"	line 14 (2.3")

- For increased efficiency, use standard placement.
- Adjust dateline up if letter contains a table or special features.
- Place dateline a DS below a deep letterhead.
- Position dateline on line 12 when a window envelope is used.

Personal business letter

Katrina W. Cassidy
763 East Hillside Drive
Bloomington, IN 47401-3692
(812) 555-6862

Current date ◄————

> The return address may be keyed immediately above the date, or you may create a personal letterhead as shown here.

Mr. Paige Bass, Editor
Financial News
2413 West Maple Avenue
Flint, MI 48507-2754

Dear Mr. Bass

Your advertisement in the Desktop Report indicates you have a production management position available for someone with graphic design experience and knowledge. I have both knowledge and experience in graphic design; therefore, please consider me for the position.

Desktop publishing training and experience as assistant editor and producer of the Central Alumni News enabled me to develop the skills you desire. The enclosed resume presents additional information showing you why I am qualified for the position.

May I come in and tell you about the project for which I won a design award? Please let me know the time and date that would be most convenient.

Sincerely

Katrina W. Cassidy

Enclosure

Resume

1" top margins

KATRINA W. CASSIDY

Temporary Address (May 30, 1994)
763 East Hillside Drive
Bloomington, IN 47401-3692

Permanent Address
3467 Senate Lane
Kokomo, IN 46902-1835

Career Objective

A graphic design position with an opportunity to advance to a management position.

Qualifications and Special Skills

Desktop Publishing Skills. Key at 70 words per minute. In-depth knowledge and experience using several leading desktop publishing, word processing, and graphics software packages.

Computer Skills. Basic knowledge of major computer operating systems and database and spreadsheet software.

Communication/Interpersonal Skills. Superior interpersonal, speaking, writing, editing, and design layout skills.

Education

Central University, Bloomington, Indiana, Candidate for Bachelor of Business Administration Degree, May, 1994. Majored in administrative management (3.2 grade point average). Serve as president of Professional Women on Campus.

Kokomo Junior College, Kokomo, Indiana, Associate Degree,1992. Majored in administrative systems (3.6 grade point average). Served as editor of the Kokomo Reporter.

Southside High School, Kokomo, Indiana, diploma, 1990. Graduated in top 10 percent of class; served as junior class vice president and senior class president.

Experience

Central University Alumni Office, Bloomington, Indiana. Assistant editor and producer of the Central Alumni News, 1993 to present time. Worked 25 hours per week. Responsible for editing six features and for the layout and production. Met every publishing deadline and won a design award. Production manager of the Central Alumni News, 1992-93. Worked 25 hours per week. Managed layout and production and supervised all desktop publishing activities.

References

Request portfolio from Central University Placement Office.

Standard memo

T.K. Design Studios
Interoffice Communications

tab (1" from left margin

TO: Maude M. Tassin   1.5" or line 10
DS
FROM: Patrick R. Ray

DATE: November 5, 19--

SUBJECT: Memorandum Forms for Vera's Word Processing Services

Please design three memorandum forms for Vera's Word Processing Services. Ms. Hayes operates word processing services in New Orleans and Lafayette, as well as in Baton Rouge. Copies of the letterheads used in each office are on file in the Design Department. DS

Ms. Hayes has requested that the forms for all three offices meet the following specifications: DS

1. Each memo form should contain the address and telephone number of one of the three offices, and the standard printed headings should appear on all forms. DS

2. All of the memo forms should be a full sheet.

3. The last character of the headings should be aligned vertically five picas from the left edge. Thus, the word processing specialists at Vera's can use the one-inch default margins on their systems both to insert the heading information two spaces after the printed headings and to block the message flush left.

I hope you will be able to have the approval drafts ready for Ms. Hayes within a week. We made a commitment to have final forms ready in two weeks. Please let me know if this schedule presents a problem for you. DS

xx

Simplified memo format

T.K. Design Studios
300 Fourth Street
New Orleans, LA 89210-2010 • (800) 555-6522

November 5, 19--   QS   1.5" or line 10

Maude Tassin DS

Memorandum Forms for Department

Please design three memorandum forms for Vera's Word Processing Services. Ms. Hayes operates word processing services in New Orleans and LaFayette, as well as in Baton Rouge. Copies of the letterheads used in each office are on file in the Design Department. QS

Patrick R. Ray

xx

Memo on a preprinted form with distribution list

T.K. Design Studios
Interoffice Communications

To: Distribution List   1.5" or line 10
DS
From: Jane Leventis

Date: Current

Subject: Multiple Recipients of Memo
DS
One way to handle a memo received by multiple individuals is to use a distribution list. This memo illustrates the use of a distribution list.

lap
DS
Distribution List:
    Charlie Phelan
    Annette Marks
    Rod Yazel

Standard unbound report and outline format

Margins. *Top* 1.5" for first page and reference page; 1" for succeeding pages. *Side* 1" or default; *bottom* 1".

Spacing. *Educational reports:* DS, paragraphs indented .5". *Business reports:* SS, paragraphs blocked with a DS between ¶s.

Page numbers. Second and subsequent pages are numbered at top right of the page. DS follows the page number.

Main headings. Centered; ALL CAPS.

Side headings. Underlined; main words capitalized; DS above and below.

Paragraph headings. Underlined; capitalize first word, followed by a period.

Note: Larger fonts may also be used for headings.

Report documentation

Internal citations. Provides source of information within report. Includes the author's surname, publication date, and page number (Bruce, 1994, 129).

Endnotes. Superior figure keyed at point of reference within report. All sources placed on a separate page at the end of the report in numerical order. Endnotes precede the bibliography or references.

Bibliography or references. List all references, whether quoted or not, in alphabetical order by authors' names. References may be formatted on the last page of the report if they all fit on the page; if not, list on a separate, numbered page.

First page of unbound report

1.5" or line 10

BASIC STEPS IN REPORT WRITING
DS

The effective writer makes certain that reports that leave her or his desk are technically correct in style, usable in content, and attractive in format.
DS

Side heading — The First Step
DS
Information is gathered about the subject; the effective writer takes time to outline the data to be used in the report. This approach allows the writer to establish the organization of the report. When a topic outline is used, order of presentation, important points, and even various headings can be determined and followed easily when writing begins.

1" side margins — The Correct Style
The purpose of the report often determines its style. Most academic reports (term papers, for example) are double-spaced with indented paragraphs. Most business reports, however, are single-spaced; and paragraphs are blocked. When a style is not stipulated, general usage may be followed.

The Finished Product
The most capable writer will refrain from making a report deliberately impressive, especially if doing so makes it less expressive. The writer does, however, follow the outline carefully as a first draft is written. Obvious errors are ignored momentarily. Refinement comes later, after all the preliminary work is done. The finished document will then be read and reread to ensure it is clear, concise, correct, and complete.

Second page of unbound report

2
DS
and thus oxygen becomes a crucial part of any aquatic ecosystem. Dissolved oxygen is derived from the atmosphere as well as from the photosynthetic processes of aquatic plants. Oxygen, in turn, is consumed through the life activities of most aquatic animals and plants (Bruce, 1994, 129). When dissolved oxygen reaches very low levels in the aquatic environment, unfavorable conditions for fish and other aquatic life can develop.

Conclusion
The absence of dissolved oxygen may give rise to unpleasant odors produced through anaerobic (no oxygen) decomposition. On the other hand, an adequate supply of oxygen helps maintain a healthy environment for fish and other aquatic life and may help prevent the development of unacceptable conditions that are caused by the decomposition of municipal and industrial waste (Ryn, 1993, 29).
DS

REFERENCES
DS

Book — Beard, Fred F. The Fulford County Dilemma. Niagara Falls: Dawn General Press, 1992.
DS
Periodical — Bruce, Lois L. "Hazardous Waste Management: A History." State of Idaho Bulletin No. 7312. Boise: State of Idaho Press, 1994.

Ryn, Jewel Scott. "But Please Don't Drink the Water." Journal of Environmental Science, Winter 1993.

Title page

FORMATTING GUIDES FOR REPORTS

2"

Prepared for
(Your instructor's name)
Keyboarding Instructor
School Name

2"

Prepared by
(Your name)
Keyboarding Student
School Name

2"

Current date

Table Format

Main heading: Centered; all caps; bold is optional.

Secondary heading: Centered; main words capitalized; bold is optional.

Columns: Vertical lists of information. Generally SS long table (20 lines or more); DS short tables. Tables within a document use the same spacing as the document.

Rows: Horizontal lines of information.

Cell: Intersection of a column and a row.

Columnar headings: Blocked or centered over columns and underlined. DS above and below. Bold is optional.

Intercolumnar space: Space between columns varies depending on the width and number of columns:

Narrow	2 columns (3 if narrow)	10 spaces
Average	3 columns (4 if narrow)	6-8 spaces
Wide	4 or more columns	4-6 spaces

Vertical placement: 1.5" or 2" top margin or centered vertically on the page. Tables within documents are separated with a DS below last line of text.

Guides to Tabs

Left tab: Aligns copy at the left.

Decimal tab: Aligns text at the decimal.

Right tab: Aligns copy at the right edge of a column. A decimal tab will also align copy at the right.

Decimal	Left	Right
1,200.50	Chambers	Helen
47.30	Montgomery	Rob

EXCELLENCE IN CUSTOMER SERVICE DS

Videotape Version DS

Title of Module ← row →	Videotape Time	Cost
		DS
Image Building	24 minutes	$ 79
Quality Service	45 minutes	99
Problem Solving	40 minutes	89

column   cell

Table: Blocked column headings

PURCHASE AGREEMENT DS

Item No.	Quantity	Price SS
		DS
R38475-L	12	$84.50
C92579-T	5	9.75
X47824-L	20	98.99 SS

Ruled table: Centered column headings

Guidelines for Formatting Tables

Use the centering feature to center columns between margins. Word processing software may utilize the table feature.

1. *Electronic typewriters:* Move margins to left and right edges of scale; clear tabs. *Word processing:* Use default margins or equal margins.

2. Center the key line (longest item in each column and inter-column space); note position of each column.

3. Set the left margin at Column 1 and tabs for the remaining columns according to the printout/display.

4. Delete the key line; center heading; key table.

Guides to Vertical Centering

Text that is centered vertically has equal or near equal top and bottom margins. Use the **center page** feature to center text if you are using word processing software. To center text vertically, follow these steps:

1. Count lines to be centered, including blank lines.
2. Subtract lines to be centered from lines available on page (66).
3. Divide remaining lines by 2 for the top margin. Begin on the next line.

$$\text{Top margin} = \frac{\text{Lines available} - \text{Lines used}}{2}$$

1.5" or line 10   **REPORT WRITING SERIES** DS

Guide 6 QS

This sixth guide in the series of ten guides is designed to improve and standardize the reporting process in all divisions of Marcus Computer Services, Inc. Guide 6 has the dual objectives of enhancing readability and emphasizing key ideas effectively. Effective formatting is central to both of these objectives.

Readability DS

Vocabulary, sentence and paragraph length and structure, and formatting affect the readability of a document. Particular attention should be paid to these factors in preparing reports.

Vocabulary. Word length affects the difficulty level of copy; however, familiarity of words may be more important than the length of words. Multisyllable, technical, and unfamiliar words should be minimized in reports to enhance readability.

Sentence and paragraph length and structure. Variety may be essential, but direct order and reasonably short sentences and paragraphs enhance readability. The following guides are helpful in judging average sentence and paragraph length: DS

Units of Measure	Sentences	Paragraphs
		DS
Words (average)	18	75
Lines (average)	2	8
		DS

Formatting. Effective use of white space affects readability. Appropriate line length, space between paragraphs, and vertical placement set material apart and make it easier to read.

Emphasis Techniques

Extra space and underlining were traditional emphasis techniques. Current technology makes bold and large-sized fonts (when they are available) more effective emphasis techniques. Both bold and underlining can be used when large-sized fonts are not available. Marcus standard style has been changed from using a triple space before headings for emphasis to using bold, which is a more effective emphasis technique. It is also easier to format.

Report with table